SCHOOLCRAFT COLLEGE LIBRARY
W9-BNF-508
3 3013 00122953 7
WITHDRAWN

BLIND SPOTS

Madeleine L. Van Hecke, PhD

BLIND SPOTS

Why Smart People Do Dumb Things

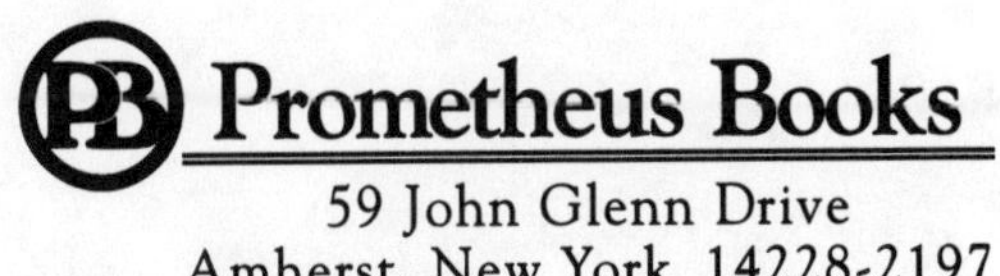

Prometheus Books
59 John Glenn Drive
Amherst, New York 14228-2197

BF
431
.V28
2007

Published 2007 by Prometheus Books

Blind Spots: Why Smart People Do Dumb Things. Copyright © 2007 by Madeleine L. Van Hecke. All rights reserved. No part of this publication may be reproduced, stored in a retrieval system, or transmitted in any form or by any means, digital, electronic, mechanical, photocopying, recording, or otherwise, or conveyed via the Internet or a Web site without prior written permission of the publisher, except in the case of brief quotations embodied in critical articles and reviews.

Inquiries should be addressed to
Prometheus Books
59 John Glenn Drive
Amherst, New York 14228–2197
VOICE: 716–691–0133, ext. 207
FAX: 716–564–2711
WWW.PROMETHEUSBOOKS.COM

11 10 09 08 07 5 4 3 2 1

Library of Congress Cataloging-in-Publication Data

Van Hecke, Madeleine L.
Blind spots : why smart people do dumb things / Madeleine L. Van Hecke.
p. cm.
Includes bibliographical references and index.
ISBN 978–1–59102–509–2 (alk. paper)
1. Intellect. 2. Stupidity. 3. Errors. I. Title.

BF431.V28 2007
153—dc22

2007001603

Printed in the United States of America on acid-free paper

This book is dedicated to my family:

My husband, Greg, the love of my life and dearest friend

My children, Kalyn and David,
whom I love with great tenderness and pride

And their spouses, who have become a treasured part of our family:

David's wife, Judith

Kalyn's husband, Salvador

And last but not least
Our awesome granddaughter, Claudia!

Open-mindedness . . . may be defined as freedom from prejudice, partisanship, and such other habits as close the mind and make it unwilling to consider new problems and entertain new ideas. (But) it is very different from empty-mindedness. While it is hospitality to new themes, facts, ideas, questions, it is not the kind of hospitality that would be indicated by hanging a sign "Come right in, there is nobody at home." It includes an active desire to listen to more sides than one; to give heed to facts from whatever source they come; to give full attention to alternative possibilities; to recognize the possibility of error even in the beliefs that are dearest to us.

John Dewey
How We Think, 1933

CONTENTS

Acknowledgments 9

Preface 13

1. Why *Do* Smart People Do Dumb Things? 15

2. Fools Rush In 35
Blind Spot #1: Not Stopping to Think

3. Often Wrong, but Never in Doubt? 51
Blind Spot #2: What You Don't Know Can *Hurt You*

4. If It Were Any Closer, It Would Bite You! 73
Blind Spot #3: Not Noticing

5. Your Own Worst Enemy 89
Blind Spot #4: Not Seeing Yourself

6. Don't Give a Cat Calendar to a Dog Lover! 111
Blind Spot #5: My-Side Bias

7. Thinking Inside the Box 133
Blind Spot #6: Trapped by Categories

8. Thinking by the Seat of Your Pants 151
Blind Spot #7: Jumping to Conclusions

9. Why It's So Hard to *Find* the Proof in the Pudding 177
Blind Spot #8: Fuzzy Evidence

10. The Usual Suspects: Why We Miss the Real Culprit 199
Blind Spot #9: Missing Hidden Causes

11. "He Can't See the Forest for the Trees" 217
Blind Spot #10: Missing the Big Picture

Afterword: Blind Spots and Hope 239

Bibliography 243

Index 249

ACKNOWLEDGMENTS

First and foremost, I want to thank my husband, Greg Risberg, who gulped only once when I said I wanted to resign my tenured teaching position in order to have more time to write. His love and support made this book possible.

If I were to create a true list of all those who enriched me, it would have to include all the names in the bibliography at the end of this book, as well as many thinkers and writers whose works I did not cite directly in this work. There are also those who taught me more directly: my past teachers, my colleagues in teaching and research, and my own students. My colleagues at North Central College, in every department from English through political science, philosophy, accounting, and biology—not to mention my home of psychology!—gave me a truly liberal education through our multifaceted discussions. Among all these, I am especially grateful to Fred Lawson and Tad Lehe for the long philosophical discussions that we had and to Priscilla Grundy for her encouragement of my writing forays. Among the countless students who stimulated my thinking, special thanks to Lisa Callahan, who shares my fascination with critical thinking. The members of the Perry Network, many of whom I was able to interview as part of my editorship of the *Perry Network Newsletter*, were models of how reflective people think. I am especially indebted to two scholars, the late William Perry for his work on intellectual development and Jim Kenney for his lectures at *Common Ground.* Both have taken me down roads I would not otherwise have explored.

Many people have been a source of both challenge and support as I wrote this book. My thanks to the members of my writing group for their feedback, which turned my book upside down and showed me ways to right it: this book was greatly enhanced by their criticism. The women who were part of the Creativity Circle to which I belonged were more important to my continuing this work than they could possibly realize. My thanks to each of them: Shawn Fyksen, Ricky Petersen, Linda Sen, and especially to creative catalyst Patsy Davis, whose spark started the group. I owe special thanks to Ranjini Iyer, my writing partner who became a friend, for the countless hours she spent reading my works-in-progress and for her unwavering humor and insight. Special thanks also to Ricky Petersen for her invaluable editorial assistance, to Shawn Fyksen for her artistic design that opens each chapter of this book, and to graphic artist Jerry Frissell, who prepared the remaining graphics. Thanks to creativity consultant Eric Maisel, who truly helped me birth this book with his coaching and encouragement. Very heartfelt thanks also to Marge Minervini, who has been a steadfast spiritual guide for me over the years.

This book would not be in your hands were it not for Steven L. Mitchell, editor in chief at Prometheus Books, who acted as its advocate. I am so grateful to the staff at Prometheus Books: Joe Gramlich, whose editorial suggestions were both thought-provoking and on target and matched by his humor to boot; to Jackie Cooke for a cover design so beautiful that it made me hope people *would* judge this book by its cover; to Jill Maxick, Marcia Rogers, and Mark Hall for their steadfast and creative marketing efforts; and to all the unsung, behind-the-scenes heroes who changed a dog-eared manuscript into a published book.

Books cannot be any wiser than the people who write them. I want to thank all the family members and friends who, in ways too numerous to describe, helped me grow as a person and so as a writer. Many of these persons, listed below, also took the time to read earlier versions of *Blind Spots* and to give me their comments. I was continually touched by the energy and care that family, friends, colleagues, and former students took in responding to my work. My apologies to anyone whom I have inadvertently left out; many thanks to you and to all the following: Katherine Ace, Cathy Blanford, Lisa Callahan, Letitia Carter, Pam Costello, Patsy Davis, Alice Dechene, Cindy Dove, Jacquie Frissell, Shawn Fyksen, Beverly Grall, Priscilla Grundy, Ravi Iyer, Jim Kenney, Brad Kolar, Sheridan Lam, Rebecca Lambrecht, Fred Lawson, Virginia McCullough, Judith McDonough, Tom McFaul, Connie Oreskovich, Liza Prince, Joy Rosenberg, Linda Sen, Paula Shur, Marjorie Shamberg, Bonnie Summers, Soon Har Tan, George Van Hecke, Tom Van Hecke, Judith Warren, Jamie Weitzel, David Wulatin, Kalyn Wulatin, Evelyn Zerfoss, and Bianca Zola.

PREFACE

A grandma was helping her three-year-old grandson, Benjamin, who had been struggling to zip up his jacket. "The secret is to make sure that you push this part far down before you zip," she said, as she demonstrated the maneuver. Looking puzzled and a little troubled, Benjamin asked, "Why is it a secret?"

We've all had the experience of suddenly realizing how differently someone else is interpreting the world. I have been fascinated by how people think, particularly how we can understand the world so differently from one another that other points of view strike us as inexplicable and therefore "stupid." Psychology has a long history of being fascinated with "intelligence" but has only recently turned its attention to "stupidity." As Robert Sternberg noted, we spend millions on tests attempting to measure how bright people are and to predict who has the intelligence to succeed, but we pay little attention to what makes even the brightest people sometimes squander their gifts in "amazing, breathtaking acts of stupidity."[1]

In *Blind Spots*, I have tried to write a book that would intrigue the person who, like myself, genuinely wonders how smart people can do dumb things! But I also wanted to go beyond theoretical answers and to offer practical suggestions to people who want to overcome their own blind spots and help others do the same. In addition, in contrast to authors of most other self-improvement books, I chose to emphasize the major repercussions that our blind spots have in the public sphere. They influence how we understand—and misunderstand—one another, and so they affect our ability to resolve the pressing political and social issues of our time. My hope is that *Blind Spots* might help people improve not only their personal lives but also the communities in which they live.

I welcome reader comments at www.overcomeblindspots.com.

NOTE

1. Robert Sternberg, ed., *Why Smart People Can Be So Stupid* (New Haven, CT: Yale University Press, 2002).

Chapter 1

WHY *DO* SMART PEOPLE DO DUMB THINGS?

When our son-in-law, Salvador, visited the United States for the first time, we drove around my hometown to show him a little of Middle America. Nearing my bank, I remembered that I needed some cash and entered the lane for the ATM machine. While we waited for the transaction to be processed, I gestured toward the monitor and said to Salvador, "We've become more sensitive to the needs of handicapped people in the United States. See the instructions here in Braille?" I waited a moment while his wife, Kalyn, translated what I had said, feeling a bit smug. I was proud of the sensitivity our bank demonstrated with this feature. Salvador murmured something in Spanish, then he and Kalyn burst out laughing. Miffed, I waited to hear what was so funny. Then Kalyn translated, "Salvador just wondered how many blind drivers you have here in Elmhurst."

The Braille instructions that I had pointed out with such pride just moments earlier now appeared totally idiotic. Even as I grasped for straws, offering the idea that a sighted driver *could be* driving a blind individual to the bank, deep down I knew that it made little sense to have Braille instructions on equipment at a drive-through facility. I felt stupid for not having seen how foolish those instructions were in this setting and for touting them as evidence of our cultural superiority. Salvador's point was glaringly obvious. How could I have missed it?

"STUPIDITY"—MISSING THE OBVIOUS

The idea that something is, or should be, "obvious" is at the heart of our judgment when we feel people are acting or thinking stupidly. Most of us aren't hard on ourselves for not grasping Einstein's theory of relativity or John Nash's notions about economics. We understand that the ideas these specialists propose are obscure, especially to the untutored person who lacks their professional background. On the other hand, we don't ordinarily deride others who have a condition that impairs their intelligence. We realize that ideas that we easily grasp may not be at all apparent to people who suffer brain damage from a stroke or who are born with conditions such as Down syndrome. But when people who are of at least average intelligence miss something that seems completely obvious to us, we roll our eyes.

In fact, most people can hardly wait to tell stories of dumb behavior. Stories of "stupid" deeds have, as a student of mine once commented, "high comedic value." Many cartoons and jokes capitalize on this value: "How many ____ does it take to change a lightbulb?" The Darwin Awards, stories of people whose blunders literally led to their deaths, thus "improving the gene pool," are featured in books[1] as well as on a Web site.[2] Winners include the man who tried to open a hand grenade with a chain saw in order to get explosives to make firecrackers for the New Year holiday.

We have competitions to gather such stories, like the "*Dilbert* Quotes" contest in which one winning memo was: "As of tomorrow, employees will only be able to access the building using individual security cards. Pictures will be taken next Wednesday and employees will receive their cards in two weeks." We shake our heads in disbelief and wonder, "What was that person thinking?!"

A DIFFERENT TONE OF VOICE

But notice the tone of voice we use when we ask that question. It's not a curious tone. We're not asking, with genuine interest, "What was that person thinking?" Our tone is scornful. It's the same tone that we've all heard directed at ourselves by our brothers and sisters, partners and friends, teachers and bosses, spouses and colleagues, parents and adult children. "And you believed that!" they jeered. Or demanded, "What were you thinking?" or "Why did you do *that*?"

What if the person criticizing us had asked these questions in a different tone of voice? What if the same questions were posed with bona fide interest and genuine curiosity? What if people honestly raised the questions: How *could* someone believe that? Why *might* they do that? What *could* they have been thinking? It is the rare person who asks, with true curiosity, what might have caused a blunder. It is the rare person who sees inexplicable "dumbness" as a puzzle to be solved.

STUPIDITY: A PUZZLE TO BE SOLVED

But it turns out that it *is* a puzzle. Psychologists who study how people think report that adults—apparently intelligent, competent adults—fail to think clearly and logically when tested on a wide variety of reasoning problems.[3] Syllogisms are one type of logic problem used in this sort of research. Syllogisms test people's reasoning by beginning with information like, "John always has basketball practice on Wednesday. Today is Wednesday," followed by a question such as, "Does John have practice today?" This example illustrates a particular type of syllogism, one that is easy to solve. In fact, the answer to the question seems obvious: "Yes, John must have practice today."

But syllogisms take different forms, and numerous studies have demonstrated that educated adults consistently have a hard time solving certain kinds of syllogisms. This is true even when the situation the adults are being asked to think about and the questions they must answer appear on the surface to be quite simple, as the study described next shows.

Here's what the researcher in this study did. Holding a box in his lap, the researcher would tell the person being tested, "If there's a cat in this box, there's also an apple in the box." Next, he would peek inside the box and declare, "There is a cat!" He would then ask the person, "Is there an *orange* in the box?" Initially, half of the adults answered no. Yet there is no reason why an orange couldn't be in the box, based on the information provided. After being presented with more examples of the same sort of problem, it dawned on these adults that the right answer to the question is that, based solely on what they'd been told, it isn't possible to tell whether or not the box holds an orange. Yet it took them some time to catch on. The researcher had to present similar problems five times before all the adults "got it."[4]

On the other hand, research on children's thinking shows that preschoolers have a surprisingly strong capacity for competent reasoning. When they are given simple syllogisms, four-year-old children commonly reach the same logical deductions as adults do. For example, in one study, preschoolers were told stories like the following about make-believe animals: "Merds laugh when they're happy. Animals that laugh don't like mushrooms." They were then asked, "Do merds like mushrooms?"[5] Not only could the preschoolers answer correctly, but also the reasons they gave when asked, "How do you know that?" were similar to those offered by adults.

In everyday experiences outside psychologists' laboratories, young children can startle us with their cleverness. I recall an incident in which an aunt was playfully nibbling on her three-year-old niece's toes. "I'm going to eat you up!" the aunt teased. "No, no, you aren't!" replied the little girl, "Because I'm going to eat you up FIRST!" "I don't think so," countered the aunt, "I'm bigger than you. I'll eat YOU up first." "No!" declared this little one, a gleam in her eye. "Because I'm going to eat your mouth first."

The contrast between the impressive capacity of children and the limitations of adults makes the puzzle of why adults sometimes think so poorly even more baffling. If you were to place the research that reveals the ineptitude of adults side by side with the contrasting research that demonstrates the competency of children, what might you conclude? One psychologist noted tongue-in-cheek that, taken together, these studies suggest "the highly counterintuitive conclusion that the pinnacle of rationality is reached by age five and goes rapidly downhill after that."[6] Of course, no one believes this! Even the proudest parents acknowledge that their gifted offspring are not at the height of intellectual achievement. We all expect children, no matter how bright, to develop their capacity to reason as they grow older, and we all expect adults to have problem-solving and reasoning abilities that exceed those of even the most precocious four-year-old. But if we had such promise as preschoolers, how is it that we sometimes appear so foolish as adults?

BLIND SPOTS

My answer to that question is that we all have blind spots, blind spots that are built into the ways that we naturally think, just as blind spots are part and parcel of a car's mirrors. Our mental blind spots can account for much of what people ordinarily label as "stupidity." When *we* feel dim-witted, whatever it is that we should have known, or should have realized, or should have thought about, seems so obvious in retrospect. How could we have missed it? When *others* seem dense to us, whatever we grasp seems so clear that we cannot fathom how they could have missed it. That's why I think that the analogy of the blind spot in our car's mirrors is perfect for capturing our experience of mental blind spots. Think about how large an automobile is. A car is a *BIG* object. It's as "obvious" as anything gets. No one standing on the street corner could miss observing a car pulling up next to our own car. But *we* can miss it if it's in our blind spot.

Our Minds Working against Us

The first purpose of this book is to alert people to the blind spots that we all share. Our minds work for us in wonderful ways—80 or 90 percent of the time. But the rest of the time, functioning in the very same ways, our minds work against us. Consider, for example, how passages like the one below are used to test people. The typical instructions given are that you should read the passage and count how many times the word "the" appears in it.

How to Avoid the Ten Mistakes
People Make When Doing the Laundry

> The first thing that you need to do is to sort the laundry. Put the darker-colored clothes in one pile and the whites or the lighter-colored clothes in another. The next thing you should do is to search ALL the pockets and empty them completely. The bits of tissue that you miss in this process can end up sticking all over the the clothes and it's very time-consuming and tedious to remove them at the point that you take the clothes out of the washer. The next challenge has to do with setting the dials correctly on your machines, and incidentals such as making sure you remove the clothes from the dryer soon after the cycle stops so you can fold or hang them before wrinkles set in.

How many occurrences of "the" did you find? It's common for people to miscount the number of times "the" occurs. There are actually twenty occurrences if you include the title of the article and eighteen if you count only those in the paragraph. It's easy to miss some of them. Yet often the comments that follow these little tests are curiously triumphant about our errors. They have a "Ha! Gotcha!" quality to them, as if the exercise has revealed that we aren't as smart as we thought we were and the tester is delighting in that fact. Yet this exercise doesn't even test our reading ability, much less our general intelligence. Someone who can't read English at all, someone with absolutely no comprehension of the passage, would be capable of counting how often the word "the" appears. The exercise is more a test of attention to detail and the ability to ignore irrelevant information in order to focus on locating a single word. Our natural inclination is to pay attention to the meaning of what we are reading and to ignore details that aren't essential to understanding that meaning. This tendency serves us well as readers. Because of it, we are capable of rather extraordinary feats, as the next passage illustrates.

> I cdnuolt blveiee taht I cluod aulacity uesdnatnrd waht I was rdgnieg. The phaonmneal pweor of the hmuan mnid. Aoccdrnig to a rscheearch at Cmabrigde Uinevtisy, it deosn't mttaer in waht oredr the ltteers in a wrod are, the olny iprmoatnt tihng is taht the frist and lsat ltteer be in the rghit pclae. The rset can be a taotl mses and you can sitll raed it wouthit a porbelm. Tihs is bcuseae the huamn mnid deos not raed ervey lteter by istlef, but the wrod as a wlohe. Amzanig, huh?

Our ability to understand this paragraph illustrates a great asset. We are able to glean the meaning of the paragraph as a whole without painstakingly attending to every letter of every word. It turns out that the paragraph overstates the case. According to Matt Davis of the Cognition and Brain Sciences Unit in Cambridge, United Kingdom, the research described was not done at Cambridge, and how easily we can read such scrambled words varies depending on factors such as the sorts of words that are scrambled.[7] Nonetheless, this passage raced across the Internet because it does indeed demonstrate our surprising capacity for processing complex information. The downside of that ability is that glossing over those very same details leads us to fail as proofreaders. Our tendency to ignore the details is a liability in proofreading. But in the task of comprehending what we are reading, it is an enormous asset.

Other ways that our minds work have this same quality of being both an asset and a liability. For example, one tendency that permeates our thinking is the inclination that human beings have to search for, and find, patterns. Ages ago, people looked at the stars in the skies and discerned patterns such as the Big Dipper. They noticed seasons of the year, a pattern of time. Scientist-monk Gregor Mendel noticed patterns in the pea plants he had sown, which led him to propose the existence of dominant and recessive genes, which eventually established him as the founder of modern genetics.

But this invaluable tendency to see patterns also works against us. It leads us to classify objects and events, and then forget that there is more to them than the handy labels we have attached to them. It leads us to misinterpret the world when our pattern-seeking minds cleverly but erroneously discern patterns that aren't really there, such as when we mistakenly read some suspicious meaning into a series of chance remarks made by a colleague. Moreover, we are prone to take patterns we have already discovered, such as a particular theory or worldview, and use them like lenses through which we view everything in the world. Restricting ourselves to that particular configuration, we risk missing the kaleidoscope of possibilities—unusual theories, alternative worldviews—that we might otherwise glimpse.

Our greatest intellectual strengths represent liabilities when they lead us to miss something that we might otherwise have noticed. They create blind spots. If we become aware of our blind spots, we can do something about them. Our car's side-view mirrors have little warnings printed on them that say: *Objects in this mirror are closer than they appear*. Once we know about this built-in limitation, we can compensate for it.

This is also true of the blind spots that are part of the way we naturally think. We can't totally eradicate them, since they are built into the system. But once we become aware of them, we can try to minimize the influence of their distortion. The first purpose of this book is to make people aware of how often we judge others as dumb when their apparent "stupidities" are really due to the blind spots that plague us all. The second purpose of this book is to help you learn strategies to counteract your blind spots. To do this, each chapter includes a set of tactics, practical ways to counterbalance the various blind spots that we all have.

THREE COMMON BLIND SPOTS

What are these blind spots that afflict us? Here are three of the ten blind spots that I'll be talking about in this book.

What You Don't Know *Can* Hurt You!

I once called a gourmet catering establishment and talked to staff member about a party I was planning. After discussing a few possible entrées, the woman announced brightly, "You know, we can also provide Chateaubriand. How about Chateaubriand?" "Oh," I answered immediately. "No, thanks. We're going to take care of the wine ourselves." I could tell by the dead silence that followed that I had made a big mistake. But I had no idea what it was. Only when I reported this conversation to a friend did I learn that Chateaubriand is not a wine but beef tenderloin prepared in a particular way.

I felt stupid. People often feel dumb when they are ignorant of information that others expect them to know. But is ignorance really a sign of stupidity? Was my ignorance of Chateaubriand a valid test of my intelligence? Or was my ignorance simply an indication of what information and experiences I had and had not been exposed to? The truth was that nothing in my background had prepared me for conversations with gourmet caterers. I hadn't even known that such people existed until ten minutes before I dialed that number. Our lack of experience and exposure can account for much of what others label "stupidity."

My ignorance played a part in my feeling stupid. But a blind spot also played a part. My blind spot was not that I didn't know what Chateaubriand was but that I didn't know that I didn't know. I mean, doesn't "Chateaubriand" *sound* like the name of a wine? Wine from the castle vineyards of the Briand family, perhaps? If I had known that I didn't know what Chateaubriand was, I would have responded differently to that gourmet caterer.

Missing the "Big Picture"

There is a *Dilbert* cartoon in which Dilbert's boss complains that he can't move the cursor on his computer screen where it needs to go because "my mouse is already at the edge of the mouse pad." The computer expert suggests that the only solution is to get a bigger mouse pad. Dilbert's boss agrees, and in the next segment we see workers providing him with a huge desk in order to accommodate an enormous mouse pad and suggesting that he may ultimately need a bigger office to have the necessary room for increasingly large pads. The cartoon is funny because it shows that the boss doesn't really understand the relationship between the mouse on the pad and the cursor on the computer screen. He doesn't "get" how all of this is connected.

Not understanding the connections between these elements, Dilbert's boss misses "the big picture." He can't see the forest for the trees. When people fail to grasp the big picture, they can appear as dumb as Dilbert's boss. But is their difficulty in seeing connections evidence that they are stupid? Or do people miss the forest for the trees simply because of the blind spot that naturally occurs when we are "too close" to something: too focused on a single piece, a solitary approach, or a limited time span?

If Only She Could See Herself!

A friend of mine complained that her boss was always criticizing his managers for putting down staff members instead of using more positive encouragement. She reported that her boss would go into tirades, ranting: "Don't you realize that you are demoralizing everyone when all you do is harangue them for their mistakes? What's the matter with you anyway!" How ironic. This boss was treating his own staff in exactly the same way that he deplored. He could clearly see what they were doing wrong, but he couldn't see the same behavior in himself.

Most people recognize that we all suffer, at times, from the blind spot of not seeing ourselves. "If only she could see herself!" people lament as they watch a friend alienate the very colleague whom she most wanted to win over or undermine the child whose confidence she hoped to boost. If she does eventually realize how she's been acting, she may well smack her forehead and exclaim, "How could I have done that!" She feels dumb for being oblivious to what was happening.

These examples illustrate three of the ten blind spots that are discussed in this book. Missing the forest for the trees describes a different sort of failing from not being able to see ourselves or not being able to detect what we don't know. The tactics offered for dealing with our various blind spots also differ from one chapter to next, depending on which one is involved.

"STUPID"—BAD WORD *BUT* GOOD CLUE

When she was seven, our granddaughter, Claudia, told me that there were certain "bad words" that children were not allowed to say in school. "Hmm," I said. "Like what?" She hesitated, then whispered: "the S word." It turned out that the "S" stood for "stupid." In Claudia's classroom, this is a bad word because it is unkind to call other children stupid.

Despite Claudia's cautionary remark, I continue to use bad words like "stupid," "idiot," and "dumb" in this book because these words are so widespread in everyday conversation that most of us, most of the time, barely notice them. If you pay attention for one week to how often such words crop up in casual conversation, on radio or TV talk shows or in letters to the editor, I think you may be surprised by their frequency. I've been told by some that this language jarred them. I use these words intentionally, hoping that the jolt they create will make us more sensitive to how often people fall back on such words to "explain" what makes no sense to them. "Why would anyone do that?" they demand. Or, "How can anyone believe that?" and "How can people think that way?" Close on the heels of these questions people conclude, "What an idiot!"

Another reason that I use words like "dumb" and "stupid" is that they can be valuable clues to help us discover blind spots in ourselves and in others. Each chapter in this book begins with a story about an apparent stupidity. I then take a closer look to see what blind spot might be hidden within it. Think of what might happen if, every time we heard someone being labeled dumb or stupid, those words made us pause. What if, instead of dismissing others as idiots, we tried to understand what might have made them think or behave in apparently unreasonable ways? What if, instead of labeling ourselves as dumb, we tried to understand what had led us to make decisions that, in retrospect, appear dim-witted?

Instead of scolding ourselves or others for being "stupid," we'd be more likely to react to missteps by saying: "Hmm. I wonder, how did that happen?" That question has marked the beginning of the most startling discoveries and innovations. Because Alexander Fleming wondered how the mold near a dish of bacteria could have killed the bacteria, he discovered penicillin. Because Swiss engineer George de Mestral wondered what made burrs stick to his pants, he invented Velcro. Our own insights into what we have missed may not lead to major discoveries like these, but the impact that they have on our personal lives can be significant.

STUPIDITY IN THE PUBLIC ARENA

Insulting the intelligence of others has become a staple commodity on numerous talk shows. As the cartoon on the next page reminds us, in the political arena it's especially tempting to label as idiots all whose opinions differ from our own.

It's tempting, but it doesn't get us very far. Calling others idiots doesn't help us understand views or actions that seem inexplicable to us. It definitely doesn't sway others. When we insult the intelligence of those who disagree with us, we alienate the very people whose views we hope to influence. In their 2004 postelection analysis of what went wrong for the Democratic Party, some political commentators argued that treating those who disagreed with them as stupid contributed to the Democrats' disappointing showing. As columnist John Kass of the *Chicago Tribune* put it, voters who invoke moral values as the driving force behind their election choices "are tired of being told they're not smart enough to understand the nuances. They're tired of being snickered at. . . . They're tired of being treated as if they were irrational peasants who think the earth is flat. . . . And on Tuesday, they simply said, 'No more.'"[8]

Of course, the tendency to mock one's opponents and belittle their intelligence isn't restricted to only one side of the political aisle. The same "moral values" voters who feel mocked by the term "Blue State, East Coast intellectuals" deride their critics in return. As Thomas Frank writes in his book *What's the Matter with Kansas?* many residents of the "Red States" scoff at those they perceive as "latte-drinking, sushi-eating, Volvo-driving, *New York Times*–reading" elitists who are ignoramuses in their own way: ignorant of "the real America," clueless as to what makes the heart of the Heartland beat.[9] Some Midwest conservatives view liberals as snobbish ivory-tower thinkers who are more concerned about saving the spotted owl than about how the residents of the Heartland will feed their families.

Liberals and conservatives alike are stunned by what they see as the irrational stances taken by their opponents. *Chicago Tribune* public editor Don Wycliff, who reviewed hundreds of letters to the editor during the campaign, quotes a typical comment made in response to another reader's opinion: "Are you a complete idiot or just uninformed?"[10] Our blind spots impact other people and reverberate far beyond our personal lives. They affect the ways in which we understand, and misunderstand, one another.

Our knee-jerk dismissal of people whose views seem "stupid" to us prevents us from having the very conversations that we most need to hold. It's hard to imagine how we can begin to heal the divisiveness that troubles our country in the aftermath of the 2004 election if we perpetuate the attitude of the *London Daily Mirror*, which derided those who had voted for George W. Bush with its postelection headline, "How Can 59,054,087 People Be So Dumb?"[11] How can we possibly forge a working partnership or regain our sense of community with our fellow citizens if we continue to write off the views of millions as inexplicable and therefore idiotic? In addition to helping readers overcome their own blind spots, I also hope that this book will make readers more aware of the repercussions of our blind spots and those of other people.

It's very hard for most of us to admit that our judgment of others as idiots is as much a comment on our own blind spots as it is on the flaws we detect in other people. Those flaws may be devastatingly real, but if we truly cannot understand why or how others think or act in the way they do, then we, too, must have a blind spot: something is preventing us, at least at the moment, from grasping the perspective that differs from our own.

OKAY, YOU'RE NOT STUPID—YOU'RE IN THE WRONG

When the puzzling behavior of others annoys or angers us, we don't always react by deciding that they are stupid. Author and business trainer Barbara Pachter quotes a letter to Ann Landers in which a reader, whom I'll call Jasmine, describes an experience she had in an elevator.[12] Another passenger in the crowded elevator continually moved her head

Reprinted with permission
from Betsy Streeter

from side to side, causing her hair to hit Jasmine in the face. Exasperated, Jasmine finally threatened: "The next time your hair hits me in the face, you will not need a haircut for a very long time."

Jasmine acted as if the other woman had been intentionally smacking Jasmine's face with her hair. But how likely is that? What would motivate a perfect stranger to deliberately annoy another person in this way? Although it's possible that the passenger was aware of what she was doing, it's not very likely. We *know* this, if we give the matter a little thought. Yet people often have an automatic reaction just like Jasmine's: they decide that there are only two alternatives. Either the person annoying them doesn't realize what she's doing, which makes her stupid, or she does know what she is doing, which makes her a jerk, inconsiderate, and "in the wrong." The possibility that the person might simply have a blind spot offers an alternative to these two harsh judgments.

Similarly, in the public arena, many of us are quick to decide that if those who disagree with us are not stupid, then they must be corrupt. Conservatives decide that liberals don't care about moral values; liberals decide that conservatives don't care about social justice. In making such judgments, we condemn whole groups of people as ethically flawed—groups that bear labels such as Democrats, Republicans, the Religious Right, the Liberal Left, Realists, and Idealists. We attribute the worst possible motives to our opponents and place the most negative interpretations upon their actions. Thinking in this way widens the gap between political camps: accusations of moral bankruptcy are at least as great an obstacle to healing America as charges of stupidity are.

BUT SOMETIMES PEOPLE *ARE* JERKS!

Sometimes when I'm talking about these matters in the classes that I teach, one of my students will object. "But Madeleine," she might say. "I think you are too optimistic about people. You act as if people only act insensitively or incompetently by accident, because of their blind spots. I don't think that's true at all. Sometimes people *do* behave badly. Sometimes people are irresponsible, selfish, greedy. I don't think that you can explain away every 'bad' thing someone does by saying that they just had a blind spot."

I agree. I don't believe that moral shortcomings are "nothing but" blind spots. Surely history attests only too clearly to the capacity of both groups and individuals to engage in morally reprehensible actions prompted by unworthy motives. Becoming more aware of our own blind spots, or those of others, won't solve the problem of evil in the world. The question of how to deal with people who are motivated by pure malice is a different issue and outside the scope of this book.

Nevertheless, I have two reasons for urging that we slow our judgments to a crawl when we are tempted to explain other people's behavior by deciding that they are morally defective. First, behavior that appears to be a simple matter of greed, selfishness, or laziness frequently reveals itself to be more complicated when we scrutinize it closely. Second, treating others as if they were irredeemably flawed makes it very difficult for them to change for the better.

Here is a simple example. Some people are very unobservant visually. They can unlock the car that their spouse just washed for them or encounter a colleague in maternity clothes or sit in a room whose walls are covered with their friend's most recent photography—and fail to notice any of these changes. They can leave the kitchen where they have just done the dishes, oblivious to the crumbs on the counter or the dirty pots and pans standing on the stove. Their lack of awareness could be due, at least in part, to a blind spot, the blind spot of "not noticing." But it is likely to be interpreted as a character flaw. Others will label the person who fails to notice the pregnant colleague or the friend's photographs as self-absorbed. Spouses will decide that anyone who doesn't notice their newly washed car must be unappreciative, and those who wash the dishes but ignore the pots and pans will be labeled lazy or inconsiderate.

"Hold on," you may be thinking. "You can't let these people off the hook that easily, excusing them because they have a 'blind spot'!" But does acknowledging that a blind spot might play a role in behavior necessarily give people an easy out? I think that the opposite is true. Only when we detect that we have a blind spot can we decide to do something about it. Once I realize that my friend feels hurt when I fail to notice her new photographs, I can make a concentrated effort to remember to scan her walls when I visit. Instead of shrugging my shoulders and saying, "Sorry I didn't notice that . . . but I have a blind spot in that area," my recognition of my blind spots enables me to compensate for them.

BLENDING CHALLENGE AND SUPPORT

In our day-to-day lives, people of goodwill inadvertently bungle situations because of their blind spots far more often than they commit acts of malice. If we think twice before condemning others, we have a chance of helping them recognize what's gone wrong. To help us see that our own blind spots are causing harm, we need what educational leader Arthur Chickering described decades ago as a sensitive blend of challenge and support. If we repeatedly excuse a friend because "she just can't see what she's doing," we are overbalanced on the side of support, failing to challenge her to notice what she has missed. On the other hand, if we dismiss that friend as irredeemably selfish or insensitive, we are overbalanced on the side of challenge, not providing the support she may need to come to grips with her own limitations.

I heard a story about a gay woman, a corporate executive who was attending a meeting with members of the upper echelons of her company. Of the nine people in the boardroom, she was the only female. Two of the men were African American, while the rest were Caucasian. There was a break in the meeting, during which the two black men left the room. Moments after their departure, one of the remaining white men, "Dave," gestured at the others to lean toward him. Then he murmured, "Now that *they've* gone, let me tell you a joke." It was clear that his joke was going to deride African Americans in some way. The gay woman was faced with the dilemma of how to react.

Gathering her courage, she interrupted Dave: "You know, I need to stop you here, because I think I can see where this joke is going. It will end with you insulting black people. And I can imagine where other jokes might go after that. Maybe next you'll be telling anti-Semitic jokes. Sooner or later, you'll get to jokes demeaning gay people, and since that's the minority that I happen to belong to, I think it would be better if I just stopped you now and left the room before that happens." The woman then walked out—and hard on her heels, the white men followed, leaving Dave alone at the table, protesting, "Hey, c'mon, I didn't mean anything by it. It's just a joke. You know I'm not a bad guy."

I am impressed by the courage that this woman showed. How tempting it must have been for her to remain silent. *Her* membership in a minority group wasn't obvious. She could so easily have kept it hidden. Instead, she offered a clear challenge to her joke-telling colleague, and the others joined her in that challenge when they, too, left the room. Perhaps Dave needed this strong of a jolt to see that what he was doing was truly wrong, not just temporarily unfashionable because of some diversity-training whim that the company had adopted.

Wiping Out Bad Deeds with Good Ones

Yet I had misgivings upon hearing this story. Philosopher Martha Nussbaum argues that there is a big difference between shame and moral guilt, because moral guilt can be atoned for, while shaming makes us feel utterly soiled and offers no way to redeem ourselves. Imagine a child who tears a toy from the hands of her baby brother. If her parent's response is, "What a terrible thing to do! You selfish brat! Shame on you!" that child will experience humiliation. The parent can instead trigger a better alternative—moral guilt—by admonishing, "Don't take that toy from him! You have to share. Now it's his turn. Look how he's crying. Now tell him you're sorry, and give that toy back. Give him a hug."

For adults, making amends won't always be so simple or so easily accomplished. But the point is that when a child experiences moral guilt rather than shame, she learns that she can use a "reparation" strategy: she "can wipe out bad deeds with good ones."[13] In order to change, in order to become better people, children need a loved person who, instead of making impossible demands for perfection, "holds the child in her imperfection, telling her that the world contains possibilities of forgiveness and mercy, and that she is loved as a person of interest and worth in her own right."[14]

As adults—adults who have blind spots, who make mistakes, who harm others, who fail to think—we, too, need persons who can accept us with all our imperfections and still assure us of the possibility of forgiveness, even as they point out the moral demands that our actions impose on us. We will be more likely to correct our moral compasses if we are both challenged and supported. And so I wish that one of Dave's colleagues had taken Dave aside and said, "I know you're not a bad guy, Dave—I watched you stand up for Theresa in your department when everyone else was ready to let her be the scapegoat; I've seen you coach little league; I know you serve as a deacon in your church. In lots of ways, you really are a good guy. But you've got to see that what you keep trying to believe is harmless isn't. Your jokes demean people."

A response like this offers Dave support, along with a glimpse into how he might atone for what he has done, how he might, in Nussbaum's words, "wipe out bad deeds with good ones." Just as I hope that the ideas in this book will help readers recognize and counteract their own blind spots, so I also hope that the blind-spot concept can help us find ways to both challenge and support others when their blind spots cause damage.

IN A NUTSHELL

The story of Salvador commenting on the Braille instructions at the ATM drive-through illustrates how dumb we can feel when we miss something that seems obvious in retrospect. This book weaves together ideas from the fields of education, creativity research, cognitive psychology, critical thinking, child development, and philosophy to explain and support my contention that blind spots are responsible for much of what people commonly label "stupidity." Like the blind spot built into our car's side-view mirror, these mental blind spots can cause us to miss what is obvious. The first purpose of this book, then, is to describe ten blind spots that plague us and to offer strategies to help us offset them.

Second, this book is intended to increase awareness of how often we scorn those who differ from us, judging their ideas and actions to be either stupid or ethically flawed. In this book, I propose an alternative explanation: the possibility that blind spots, rather than intellectual or moral deficits, might explain what seems inexplicable and that our own blind spots may prevent us from understanding perspectives that seem peculiar to us. My hope is that the blind-spot perspective will change the tone of the discussions we have about what divides us, including our discussions of the issues that divide us politically. I also hope that the concept of blind spots helps us challenge others in a more supportive way when their blind spots do harm.

SNEAK PREVIEW

When I have lectured about these ideas, a skeptical student will occasionally hang around at the end of class. "C'mon, Madeleine," he might object. "You don't really believe that every stupid thing someone does can be explained away as a 'blind spot,' do you?" This question is often followed by a story in which someone's actions are totally illogical. For example, how do we explain the bank robber who writes his hold-up note on a deposit slip torn out of his own bankbook, complete with his address? This kind of "stupidity" is the focus of the next chapter.

NOTES

1. Wendy Northcutt, *The Darwin Awards* (New York: Dutton, 2000).

2. http://www.darwinawards.com

3. J. Evans, *The Psychology of Deductive Reasoning* (London: Routledge & Kegan Paul, 1982).

4. B. Rumain, J. Connell, and M. D. Braine, "Conversational Comprehension Processes Are Responsible for Reasoning Fallacies in Children as Well as Adults: If Is Not the Biconditional," *Developmental Psychology* 19 (1983): 471–81.

5. J. Hawkins, R. D. Pea, J. Glick, and S. Scribner, "Merds That Laugh Don't Like Mushrooms: Evidence for Deductive Reasoning by Preschoolers," *Developmental Psychology* 20 (1984): 584–94.

6. David Moshman, "The Development of Metalogical Understanding," in *Reasoning, Necessity, and Logic: Developmental Perspectives*, ed. Willis F. Overton, 205–25 (Hillsdale, NJ: Erlbaum Associates, 1990), p. 207.

7. Matt Davis, "Aoccdrnig to a rscheearch at Cmabrige," http://www.mrc-cbu.cam.ac.uk/~mattd/Cmabrigde/index.html (accessed May 5, 2006).

8. John Kass, "Moral of This Election: Don't Dismiss Values," *Chicago Tribune*, November 7, 2004.

9. From a 2004 TV commercial reviling onetime Democratic presidential candidate Howard Dean, sponsored by the conservative Club for Growth, cited in Thomas Frank, *What's the Matter with Kansas?* (New York: Metropolitan Books, 2004), p. 17.

10. Don Wycliff, "2004 Campaign May Qualify as the Most Divisive," *Chicago Tribune*, October 28, 2004, final edition.

11. *Daily Mirror*, front-page headline, November 4, 2004.

12. Barbara Pachter, *The Power of Positive Confrontation* (New York: Marlowe, 2000), p. 10.

13. Martha Nussbaum, *Upheavals of Thought: The Intelligence of Emotions* (Cambridge: Cambridge University Press, 2001), p. 215.

14. Ibid., p. 217.

Chapter 2

FOOLS RUSH IN

BLIND SPOT #1: NOT STOPPING TO THINK

A computer expert who offered technical support over the telephone described how she was guiding a virgin computer user, step by step, through the process of installing a program. The expert had gotten to the point where the new user needed to open the door on his disk drive in order to insert a disk. After she gave the instruction, "Now open the door," there was a brief silence. Then she could hear her student shuffle across the room and open his office door. "How," she demanded, "could that person possibly think that it mattered whether or not his *office door* was open or closed? You don't have to be a rocket scientist to realize that this doesn't make sense—you just have to have a brain!"

Why did that person act so illogically? That's an intriguing question if we ask it in a different tone of voice. If we don't assume that the person is stupid, then that question takes us back to the main theme in this book: how is it that intelligent adults do dumb things?

"NOT THINKING" LEADS TO FOOLISH MISTAKES

What would have happened if I had tapped the virgin computer user on the shoulder as he shuffled across the room and asked him, "Why would you need to open your door in order to install a program?" It's likely that in an instant he would have realized that what he was doing didn't make sense. He might have said, "I just wasn't thinking." I believe that explanation is more on target than people realize. "Not thinking" leads people to appear foolish.

Once I was having coffee with several adults who were taking my course in critical thinking. Commenting on the class, one young man said, "I am totally different at work now. I make different kinds of decisions than I would have before. I say different sorts of things at meetings, and I can tell that the other people are listening in a way that they didn't before. The other day I talked to my boss about an idea that I had, and even though it's not certain that they'll use it, I could tell that he was impressed." What had he learned in class to cause such a transformation? "Well," he confided, "I taped a sign on the wall above my desk, so I see it all the time and I repeat it to myself often during the day. It reminds me of what I need to do." We were really curious now. What magical message was on this sign?

It turned out that his sign said, "Think First." "Think first!" I thought. That's it? That changed his life? It would take me years to appreciate just how important developing the apparently obvious habit of thinking first might be—and to realize how difficult it is for many of us to do just that. As long as we think that something should be "easy," we are likely to belittle ourselves and others when we fail to think. But is our failure to stop and think a sign that we lack intelligence, or is it another blind spot?

"NOT THINKING" AS A BLIND SPOT: MISSING "OPPORTUNITIES" TO THINK

Harvard psychologist David Perkins[1] believes that recognizing "now would be a good time to stop and think"—recognizing what he calls "thinking opportunities"—is not as easy as it sounds. In one of Perkins's studies, law students wrote essays about cases involving controversial issues, such as "Would a bottle deposit law in the state of Massachusetts reduce litter?"[2] The students needed to carefully consider both sides of an issue in order to write an effective analysis. Many failed to do so. Despite their education that emphasized the need to always consider both sides of a case in a legal defense, the students didn't consider both sides in writing their essays. For example, a student who favored a bottle deposit law might do an excellent job in providing justification for his own position, but he would fail to even mention the concerns or arguments of someone opposed to the law.

The fascinating sidebar to Perkins's study was the relationship between the law students' IQ scores and the likelihood that they would consider both sides of the issue. The correlation was zero. This means that the most intelligent students were no more likely than the least intelligent to address both sides of the controversy. Perkins concluded that noticing thinking opportunities was critical to intelligent behavior—yet it was independent of the students' IQ scores and their reasoning abilities. Perkins's proposal that "sensitivity" to thinking opportunities not only is crucial for intelligent behavior but also may be less developed than people's ability to reason intelligently was directly borne out in a study by Lisa Callahan. Her research with employees of a large Fortune 100 company indicated that people's lack of sensitivity to times when it might be important to think "may be a greater barrier to intelligent behavior than either lack of motivation or limited ability."[3]

Each time someone says, "I didn't think about it at the time, but I realize now that . . . ," that person is recognizing a time in the past when she failed to recognize that it would have been valuable to take more time to think.

I realize now that:

- I could have just stayed an extra day and avoided the travel hassle brought on by the snowstorm.
- I should have addressed the underlying resentment about having to attend the meeting before I tried to tackle the agenda.
- The signs that our industry was changing had been there for a long time, but I just hadn't paid attention to them.
- If I had just combined the two processes, they would have worked beautifully together.
- All my life I've been trying to prove myself to someone who never doubted me in the first place.

CAUSES: WHY DO WE FAIL TO STOP AND THINK?

It turns out that our minds have some characteristics that make it difficult for us to realize that we need to stop and think. One is an all-too-familiar problem: our thinking processes are disrupted when we are under emotional stress, so we sometimes fail to think when we're under a deadline or in a crisis situation. But people also often fail to think in noncrisis situations. How does this happen? There are two situations in which people are at high risk for "not thinking." The first is when they are learning something new, a situation in which information overload is a real danger. The second occurs when people are lulled by their everyday routines.

Information Overload

Our minds can process only so much information at one time. Cognitive psychologists have a phrase for the processing capacity of a typical person: "7, plus or minus 2," meaning that on average we can hold only between 5 and 9 bits of information in our consciousness at one time. In any particular circumstance, we can focus only on a limited number of aspects of the situation. Unless we make a conscious effort to consider various elements, we will miss some of them.

Whether we are seven years old and learning how to "carry" when we subtract large numbers, or thirty-seven years old and learning how to construct a spreadsheet, it's easy to become overwhelmed. Often the best we can do as learners is to try to follow the prescribed steps. We can't, at the same time, think analytically about those steps, what they mean, or how they are all related. Initially, we aren't usually trying to understand what is happening in any depth. This, of course, leads us to go through the steps in a rote fashion, and that leads to mistakes like the one the computer novice made when he opened his office door. We fail to think because we are snowed under by the sheer amount of new information that we are trying to take in.

Lulled by Everyday Life

We also fail to think when we are caught up in our everyday lives. Immersed in our normal day-to-day activities, we don't stop to think about what we are doing. An old Chinese proverb says, "The fish is the last to know that it is in water." Being immersed, caught up in the flow of daily life, we barely notice what we are immersed in, and we rarely stop to think about it.

When she was three years old, I watched our granddaughter, Claudia, playing with paints. She was immersed in this activity until she dropped three globs of yellow paint onto some red paint and stirred. "Oh!" she exclaimed, startled by the brilliant orange that appeared. Momentarily surprised by her result, Claudia was taken aback.

I think of this quite literally as a physical motion, being taken aback. That startled movement away from what we've been doing, what we've been viewing, what we've been thinking about, or how we've been living allows us to look at it again in a more conscious way. In order for us to stop and think about the ongoing activities that engage us, we must "step back" from them and view them as objects of our scrutiny.

My friend Evelyn described how her daughter Katherine, a professional artist, periodically steps back from the painting she is working on and sits in a chair some distance away, reflecting on her work. During these minutes, Katherine may wonder, "For this theme, do I want the figure on the right to appear more fragile? If so, what would be the most effective way to create that impression?" Or, "I want to introduce an incongruous element here that is chilling yet subtle—what would work in this scene?"

Like Katherine, we need to find a place to sit, literally or metaphorically, some distance back from what we were previously immersed in, and reflect on it. Psychologist Robert Kegan has written extensively about the price we pay when we are unable to do this.[4] Whatever we remain embedded in, such as our needs or our viewpoints, will limit us. When we see the world only through the lens of our own needs, we will be trapped and blind to the perspectives of other people. Only when we are able to take these lenses themselves as the object of our thoughts can we escape being subject to them.

For example, when I'm looking at the world only through the lenses of my own needs, I may think, "I work best when I can work independently. Why can't my supervisor see that when she micromanages my work, it just irritates me and slows me down?" Once I understand that I'm looking at the world solely through my own needs—"*I* need to work independently"—then I can see other perspectives. In particular, I can consider my supervisor's needs: perhaps she needs more reassurance that I'll be able to meet the deadline or that I understand the new system. Now I can place these two sets of needs side by side and work on a solution to the dilemma. I can ask, "How can we do both? How can I work more independently *and* still reassure my supervisor that I'm making good progress toward meeting the deadline?" Once I've been able to look at the lenses through which I've been seeing the world, I can evaluate my worldview. I can assess its usefulness, question its validity, recognize its strengths and limitations, modify it in light of new information, and compare it with other views.

TACTICS: HOW CAN WE STOP AND THINK WHEN WE NEED TO?

Thinking in a Crisis

Most people appreciate the fact that emotional stress and pressure to act quickly interfere with our ability to think clearly. How can we be more effective in these emergencies?

Tactic #1: Use Our Crisis Feelings as a Cue to Trigger "Time-Out!"

In crises, the very emotions that disrupt our ability to think carefully about what is happening could become the cues that help us to remember to stop and think. What if the sense of feeling panicky, time pressured, or frustrated became a trigger for us, a signal that whistled "time-out!" in our minds?

Some people react to emergencies by becoming very still. A voice in their heads whispers: "Okay, let's think for a second." As a result, they are less likely to act impulsively. They take a few moments to recall what they learned in their CPR class, to consider what would be the quickest way to get additional help, or to ask themselves questions like "What are the risks in taking the action that I'm considering?" or "What should I do first?"

Those of us who don't react automatically in this calm way may need practice to replace our knee-jerk, crisis reaction with a more reflective response. Initially, the best we can do may be to look back and with hindsight realize what we should have done. But as time goes on, we can practice noticing that we are feeling panicky, under pressure, or angry. We can remind ourselves that those feelings mean it is particularly important for us to stop and think before we act. If we practice noticing those feelings and using them as a reminder to stop and think in urgent but not life-threatening situations, we increase the chances that we'll react in this more thoughtful way if a life-and-death situation should present itself.

When I received a dire e-mail from a friend warning that she might have inadvertently infected my computer with a virus, I panicked. I felt great pressure to remove the virus from my computer, to follow the instructions that my friend had included, and to inform the hundred-plus people in my address book that their computers, too, might have become infected. Soon after I had e-mailed warnings to these hundred people, I began getting return messages from some of them telling me that this virus was a hoax and that the method I had used to remove the so-called virus from my computer had actually deleted a program that my computer needed. Not only had I wasted hours of time, but also some of the people in my address book had, like me, taken immediate action and so spread the hoax. The number of hours wasted by people trying to fix something that wasn't broken becomes incalculable in a virus hoax situation. I felt very stupid.

Why hadn't it occurred to me to make sure that the virus I was being warned about was a real danger and not a hoax? Part of the problem was my lack of experience; this incident was the first time I had ever received such a message. Another part was my lack of knowledge. I didn't know that there were Web sites that would tell me whether a particular virus was a legitimate threat or a prank. But even with my inexperience, I might have acted differently—had I stopped to think.

I learned from the virus hoax incident that I could use "feeling panicky" as a cue to remind myself to stop and think. I could use feeling time pressured as a trigger to ask myself, "How much time do you really have here?" Certainly I could have taken an extra ten or fifteen minutes to think more carefully about what to do that day instead of immediately taking action. In many cases, we will realize we have several hours, or even days, before we need to make a final decision about what to do. Often, we can buy the time we need, and that's Tactic #2.

Tactic #2: Buy More Time in Pressured Situations

My friend Myra found herself agreeing to do all sorts of things that she didn't really want to do: take on an additional project at work, bake cookies for an event at her daughter's school, attend a lecture in which she had no interest. When Myra reflected on the circumstances that led to these decisions, she had two important insights. The first was that she could easily recognize this kind of situation, because it always included three components: (1) someone asking her to do something, (2) her heart sinking in dismay, and (3) her mind scavenging for some respectable excuse to decline the request. She could use these cues to signal the thought, "I need time to think before I decide about this." The second insight that Myra had was that she could almost always buy more time. With a little practice, Myra refined ways in which she could do this diplomatically. For instance, she could say to her boss: "That sounds like a very interesting project. Let me think about that to see if I can work out a way to be involved without having my current projects run into trouble." She could tell her friend extending the invitation to hear a boring lecture: "I'm not sure I have the time. Can I let you know tomorrow?"

After thinking more carefully about the requests that others make of her, Myra may sometimes still agree to things that she's not entirely enthusiastic about, but she's made room for other possibilities. She's created time for herself to consider what she really wants to do and to generate alternatives. Myra might, for example, negotiate with her boss to reduce some of her other responsibilities in order to take on the extra work. She might realize that her friend isn't impelled by a burning desire to hear this particular lecture but by her loneliness. This opens the way for Myra to suggest a different activity to share with the friend, one that they both would enjoy. Using our feelings of panic or pressure as a trigger that we need to stop and think would reduce the number of our hasty decisions.

STOPPING TO THINK IN EVERYDAY SITUATIONS: TACTICS FOR EVERYDAY LIFE

In many instances when we fail to think, we aren't in a crisis. In fact, ironically, the opposite is true. We fail to think when we are in the midst of familiar routines. How can we notice "opportunities for thinking" when there's no crisis—no pressure, no fast-beating heart—to prompt us to take a time-out?

Tactic #3: Building Time-Outs into Our Routines

One professional, Amol, described how his team had been meeting for several weeks. Each Friday, they ordered pizza, turned off their cell phones, and spent a long lunch hour discussing a problem that had plagued the company for months. Despite their best efforts, this roomful of bright, dedicated people seemed to be getting nowhere. "In the midst of yet another intense discussion," Amol said, "I found myself feeling really tired. Tired of all the effort, drained by all the strong emotions being expressed. Then it was as if I somehow detached myself from the group. I felt like I was watching a movie, something unrelated to me. And I saw clearly, for the first time, that we were spinning our wheels. So when the discussion reached what seemed to be yet another dead end, I asked a question."

The question that Amol asked was a simple one: "What is it that we are really trying to do here, anyway?" Many of his co-workers were puzzled by the question; some were annoyed. But Amol persisted, asking each person to write a statement describing what he or she thought the group was trying to accomplish. "To our astonishment, it turned out that we all had different ideas about what we were trying to achieve. What was so surprising about this wasn't so much that we all had different ideas, but that we didn't *know* that we all had different ideas."

Amol's experience of feeling removed from what was going on happened by chance. But you can deliberately step back from your ongoing activities and take some time to think about them. You can intentionally ask yourself questions about these experiences. Here are the kinds of questions that might be useful to pose at the end of a work session or meeting, after a family gathering or a formal presentation, or at the end of each day:

- "How did that go?"
- "What did I learn from that?"
- "What might have made this a better experience?"
- "Is this achieving what we had hoped for?"
- "What could we do differently next time?"

- "What surprised me about that?"
- "If we weren't already involved in this, would we begin it now?"
- "If I hadn't publicly committed myself to this, would I continue it now?"

What might happen if we stepped out of our experiences, even as they occurred, in order to consider them? Imagine that you've taken the children on what was supposed to be a fun trip to the zoo. The baby is whimpering, and your five-year-old son is leaping in front of his younger sister to block her view of the monkeys. What if, instead of being reactive to these individual problems, you intentionally stepped back to reflect on the situation first? Maybe you'd realize that everyone is getting tired and thirsty and crabby—including yourself! Maybe you'd realize that it's become colder than you expected, and it's no longer fun to stand outside in the biting wind. Maybe it will hit you that you've been acting as if the goal of the outing was to "cover every inch of the zoo," rather than to "have fun and see some interesting animals," so that you've been herding the children away from exhibits just as their attention has been captured by them.

Since there are no conspicuous cues in our daily routines to alert us that "this is a time when it would be good to stop and think," we need to develop a habit of reflecting on our ongoing activities. To keep from missing subtle opportunities for thinking—opportunities that don't announce themselves by pushing our panic buttons or whispering "problem" in our ear—we probably need to program review sessions into our daily routines. In the whirlwind lives that many of us lead, we need to build in "reflection time" in the same way that some people build in time to exercise or time to spend with family or friends. Like companies that automatically review sales at regular intervals, or have managers attend annual retreats or training sessions, we can plan "time-outs" to think about what is happening in our lives. Instead of being the fish who is the last to know that it is in water, we can be the fish who periodically jumps out of the water in order to see and reflect on what we've been swimming in.

One manager told me that he decided to replace his afternoon coffee break with a twenty-minute "thinking" walk. He began visiting an empty warehouse on the grounds of his manufacturing plant every day around three o'clock, just walking up and down the deserted aisles. He used the time to think about anything that had intrigued him, puzzled him, or upset him that day. He was surprised how often this activity led him to see a different perspective or to clarify a problematic situation. "Thursday," he announced with a grin, "I thought of a way to solve a recurrent problem. It will save me hours and hours of work."

WIDENING THE CIRCLE: THE CHALLENGE TO LEADERS

Why don't more people spend more of their day as this manager did, simply thinking? It's easy to be misjudged when we take time to deliberate. I recall hearing someone years ago criticize his boss for "doing a Ted Koppel." "What does that mean?" I asked. "Oh, you know," the person responded, "how Ted Koppel says, 'Well, there's this . . . but then on the other hand, there's also that. . . .' Well, that's how our boss is, never being clear—always going back and forth instead of just making a decision!"

To the speaker, ABC News veteran Ted Koppel's style, which could be viewed as reflective or evenhanded, was instead viewed as indecisive. It was associated with being wishy-washy, sitting on the fence rather than taking action. It was, in other words, a character flaw or at least a liability. The person who was criticizing his boss for "doing a Ted Koppel" apparently felt that leaders must be both decisive and action oriented in order to sustain the respect of their followers.

Impatience with people who "think too much" is widespread. Many people want their leaders, in business and in politics, to be decisive—or at least to appear decisive. They don't want leaders who sound like weather forecasters predicting a 50-50 percent chance for rain. Most people aren't swayed by a politician who says, "Though further research is necessary, the evidence thus far suggests that this program has about a 75 percent chance of stimulating the economy, creating as many as 250,000 new jobs, though the number could be as few as 50,000." In listening to discussions of political issues, many of us are like the television viewers who become impatient when the weather forecaster tries to explain the complex meteorological data that are the basis for his final judgment that there's a certain chance for rain. We want our politicians and our weather forecasters to get to the bottom line and just tell us what to expect. Do we need to carry an umbrella tomorrow or not? Will the proposed program work or not? Leaders who fail to do this risk losing support.

In the business world, where the ability to take action and be decisive is valued, leaders who take more time to reflect may be judged negatively. I recall an administrative assistant who poked fun at her new boss. "Half the time, he just sits in his office thinking!" she scoffed. If the boss is criticized in this way, what chance do lower-level employees have? They might well be accused of wasting time or doing "nothing" if they take time to think. It takes courage to be reflective in these settings.

GLITCH: ANALYZING LIFE INSTEAD OF LIVING IT?

It's not only action-oriented people who aren't enthusiastic about "stepping back" from their experiences in order to reflect on them. Some people dislike the idea of reflection because they don't want to distance themselves from what they are encountering. "I don't want to analyze my experiences to death," they say. "I want to *live* life—not constantly dissect it!"

I think they are right to be cautious. There is some danger that we might substitute *thinking about* our experiences for living them fully. Becoming a detached observer changes the quality of the events in our lives. If a father is constantly monitoring how he is interacting with his child, there is a sense in which he is not really simply *with* his child, building sand castles at the beach or tossing a football in the backyard. He's at a distance instead, like the vacationer who never really sees the whales in front of him because he is too busy filming them.

Some people fear that if they analyze their experiences too much, they will forfeit a more holistic or emotional or aesthetic appreciation of life's events. The fear of diminishing their emotional or aesthetic experience of music, for example, is what makes some people wary of learning to identify the various instruments that come into play during a symphony. The same fear makes others reluctant to study how a poem is put together or what causes rainbows to appear.

On the other hand, people who are experts in their own fields argue that "knowing more" can enhance, rather than diminish, our experience. For example, in his book *Unweaving the Rainbow*, Richard Dawkins describes how rainbows work.[5] Each drop of water acts as a prism. Breaking up light just as a prism does, a band of thousands of raindrops gives us blue light, while another band gives us yellow or red light. Yet all of these drops are falling or blowing about so that the drops that gave us red light a moment ago are now giving us yellow. Despite the constant and rapid changes that occur as the raindrops fall, what we see appears to be stationary, an unmoving rainbow. For Dawkins, understanding the intricacies of how this happens deepens rather than diminishes his sense of wonder.

As Dawkins asserts, "knowing more" can sometimes make our experiences more meaningful, more moving. Yet it also seems true that we can analyze our way out of the aesthetic or emotional or spiritual dimensions of an experience. Ethnologist Lewis Thomas describes an ecstatic experience he once had at the Tucson Zoo, watching a family of otters and a family of beavers through a glass wall as they swam below the water:

> I was transfixed . . . there was only one sensation: pure elation mixed with amazement at such perfection . . . I wanted no part of the science of beavers and otters, I wanted never to know how they performed their marvels. . . . All I [wanted] was the full hairy complexity . . . of whole, intact, beavers and otters in motion. . . . It lasted, I regret to say, only a few minutes and then I was back in the twentieth century. . . . I became a behavioral scientist . . . an ethnologist . . . and . . . lost all the wonder and the sense of being overwhelmed. I was flattened.[6]

Who would choose to become more reflective if the result was to be flattened? Who would want to live in a dull, single-dimensional world and lose the aesthetic or emotional or spiritual facets of life? Trying to reflect on every experience could diminish our living, reducing all our experiences to "learning opportunities" in the same way that carrying a camera could potentially reduce all the photographer's experiences to photo opportunities. They are that, but they are much more.

For me, the image of Katherine in the midst of her painting is a helpful reminder of the solution to this dilemma. Reflection is only one part of the rhythm; the other part is immersion in the experience itself. I can almost hear the slap of Katherine's slippers as she treads across her studio floor, going back and forth quite naturally between being absorbed in her painting to stepping back and reflecting on it. It's this pattern that I believe could enrich our lives if we were able to make it a more intentional habit: the pattern of "living life"—being immersed in our physical and social activities, being immersed in the ideas and information that we encounter—but periodically stepping back to reflect on what we are encountering.

IN A NUTSHELL

The opening story of the computer novice who misunderstood his instructor's directive to "open the door" illustrates how our failure to stop and think can lead people to blunder. It turns out that it's much harder than it appears to realize that "now would be a good time to stop and think." The natural ways in which we react to crises and to familiar circumstances make it easy for us to miss noticing that "I need to stop and think now." We need to practice recognizing the cues that could alert us to take a time-out to think in pressured situations. We need to interrupt our humdrum activities with regularly scheduled reflection time.

SNEAK PREVIEW

One of the most common situations that lead us to judge others as stupid is when the other person is ignorant of something that we believe "everyone knows." This is what happened to the doomed hero in our next opening story, someone you might remember because his blunder was witnessed by millions. The victim of this blind spot was a contestant on the TV quiz show *Who Wants to Be a Millionaire?*—and his nemesis was a nursery rhyme.

NOTES

1. D. N. Perkins and S. Tishman, "Dispositional Aspects of Intelligence" (unpublished paper, 1998), 1–45. See also D. N. Perkins, E. Jay, and S. Tishman, "Beyond Abilities: A Dispositional Theory of Thinking," *Merrill-Palmer Quarterly* 39, no. 1 (1993): 1–21.

2. D. N. Perkins, R. Allen, and J. Hafner, "Difficulties in Everyday Reasoning," in *Thinking: The Frontier Expands*, ed. W. Maxwell, 177–89 (Hillsdale, NJ: Erlbaum Associates, 1983).

3. Lisa Callahan, "The Role of Sensitivity and Ability in the Intellectual Performance of Business Professionals" (master's thesis, North Central College, 2004), p. 2.

4. Robert Kegan develops the whole notion of needing to step back from what we are embedded if we are to reach higher "levels of consciousness" in two different works: *The Evolving Self: Problem and Process in Human Development* (Cambridge, MA: Harvard University Press, 1982), and *In over Our Heads: The Mental Demands of Modern Life* (Cambridge, MA: Harvard University Press, 1996).

5. Richard Dawkins, *Unweaving the Rainbow* (Boston: Houghton Mifflin, 1998).

6. L. Thomas, *The Medusa and the Snail* (Harmondsworth, Middlesex: Penguin, 1981), p. 17.

Chapter 3

OFTEN WRONG, BUT NEVER IN DOUBT?

BLIND SPOT #2: WHAT YOU DON'T KNOW *CAN* HURT YOU

One contestant on *Who Wants to Be a Millionaire?* was asked, as his first question, "What did little Jack Horner pull out of a pie?" Since Jack Horner is a character in one of the more well-known Mother Goose rhymes, there were probably thousands of children watching the show that night who knew the answer. But looking over the four choices, the contestant astonished viewers by picking blackbird rather than plum.

This incident is a great example of how quickly we label someone as stupid when that person doesn't know something that we believe everyone should know. "How could he be so stupid!" viewers exclaimed. "How could he not have known that?" But was this contestant's ignorance a sign that he was stupid?

It's clear that no one is born knowing what Jack Horner pulled out of a pie. It's also clear that it's not possible to logically reason out the answer to this question. The contestant had to know specific information, and he himself had remarked that he was afraid of getting a nursery rhyme question because he hadn't been exposed to these rhymes as a child. That comment triggered a second criticism of this contestant. "He just said that he didn't know the Mother Goose rhymes. So why didn't he use one of the lifelines to help him out here?" viewers asked. The answer to that question is simple: the contestant failed to get help because he didn't know that he didn't know the answer.

HOW CAN WE KNOW WHAT WE DON'T KNOW?

How can people know what they don't know? To do this, you have to be able to notice an absence of something. This apparently is not a straightforward thing for us to do; it doesn't happen as easily as noticing the presence of something does.

If the young man on the quiz show hadn't mistakenly believed that he knew the right answer, he would have used one of his lifelines to get help with the nursery rhyme question. Our belief that we know the answer blinds us to our ignorance. As a result, we ignore the signs that we might be mistaken. Then we are embarrassed by the gaps in our knowledge.

CAUSES

Our difficulty in knowing what those gaps are is part of the human condition, built into the way our minds work. Our natural tendency is to assume that the answers we have are the right ones, not to habitually question what we think we know. This probably serves us well most of the time. It keeps us from reinventing the wheel. But it also has a drawback: sometimes our failure to question what we think we know blinds us to other possibilities.

June Goodfield's story of medical researcher D. Carleton Gajdusek illustrates how certainty that we have the right answers can blind us to the truth, while questioning what we believe to be true can lead to Nobel Prize–winning discoveries.[1] In 1953 Dr. Gajdusek investigated a strange disease afflicting the Fore people of Papua New Guinea. The Fore people called the disease "kuru," meaning "trembling with fear and cold" because shivering and tremors were early symptoms. Dr. Gajdusek suspected encephalitis; the neurological symptoms of the disease suggested some form of brain infection. But he could find no evidence of the characteristic signs of infection: no fevers, no change in the white blood cell count of victims, no infectious agents showing up in blood, urine, feces, or lumbar spinal fluids. Animals injected with tissue samples from ill individuals remained healthy for weeks, and no changes were observed in the brains of these animals when they were sacrificed a month or two later.

Given these results, it was reasonable for Dr. Gajdusek to reject the idea that an infectious agent such as bacteria or a virus was causing kuru. It was reasonable—but it was wrong. Dr. Gajdusek was wrong because the prevailing knowledge of the day was wrong. During the 1950s, when Dr. Gajdusek was working on this problem, scientists expected to see brain changes within a few weeks of becoming infected because they "knew" that infectious agents were fast acting. Ultimately, Gajdusek realized that this was not true for all infectious agents. As research done on AIDS has so dramatically illustrated, some viral agents can incubate for years, even decades, before wreaking their havoc on the body. Dr. Gajdusek ultimately identified such an agent as the cause of kuru, an agent that turned out to be implicated in other disorders such as mad cow disease, and was awarded the Nobel Prize.[2]

Like Dr. Gajdusek, we all accept many of the prevailing ideas of our time and our culture. We couldn't possibly call each of these into question and investigate its validity before we would accept it. And once we believe that we know the right answer to a question, we don't naturally pursue other possibilities. Creativity expert Roger von Oech describes an exercise in which there are many possible answers, which are all equally correct.[3] In using this exercise, von Oech is trying to point out that most of us, most of the time, stop at "the first right answer" because we believe that it is The Answer.

Stopping at the first right answer is often a reasonable action to take. In our everyday lives, when we are trying to solve problems, to make headway with a project, or to move on to the next issue we have to deal with, questioning what we already know to be true or searching for additional right answers seems like a luxury that we can't afford. But we may pay a high price for failing to detect these other possibilities.

TACTICS I: WAYS TO DISCOVER WHAT YOU DON'T KNOW

How can we notice crucial gaps in what we know?

Tactic #1: Create a Question Map

One useful approach is to create a question map. This simple method involves writing a topic in a center circle and then generating questions about that topic. See the example about cell phones in fig. 3.1 and fig. 3.2 based loosely on Bean and Ramage's text.[4]

You can create a question map alone, but it's especially powerful when you do it with others. This activity not only reveals the gaps in our knowledge, but also helps us rekindle the natural curiosity that we have about different subjects. One question leads to another, and generating those questions is like blowing on the embers of our natural inquisitiveness.

Tactic #2: Create "Know" and "Need-to-Know" Lists

Another method that is valuable in discovering what we don't know about a particular topic is to generate two sets of lists, one labeled "What We Know" and the other "What We Need to Know." This strategy is a standard part of a teaching approach called problem-based learning.

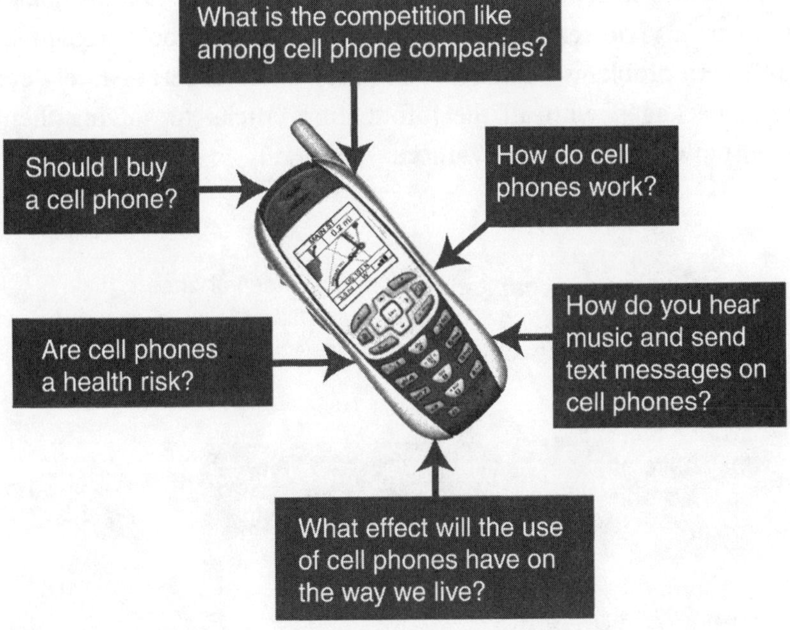

Fig. 3.1: Cell Phone Question Map

Imagine, for example, that you were Dr. Gajdusek, trying to figure out what might be causing this terrible disease called kuru. Dr. Gajdusek might have filled in the information shown in fig. 3.3 on his lists. The need-to-know list illustrates some of the important questions that Dr. Gajdusek and other researchers initially wondered about. Lists like these help us identify what we don't know. They reveal some of the gaps in our knowledge.

Once I attended a presentation by a mathematician who began by having us work out a math problem. Then he asked us, "What was the first step that you took?" Several people commented that after making sure they understood what the problem was really about, their first step was to figure out if they'd been given adequate information to solve it. I was startled to hear this. It had never occurred to me that this nice mathematician would ask us to try to solve a problem without providing us with all the information necessary to solve it. Certainly no math book I had ever had in school would play such a dirty trick. But his demonstration was a vivid reminder that, in contrast to textbook problems, "real life" math problems—like real-life problems in general—rarely come to us prepackaged with all the information crucial to solving them. We almost always need to know more.

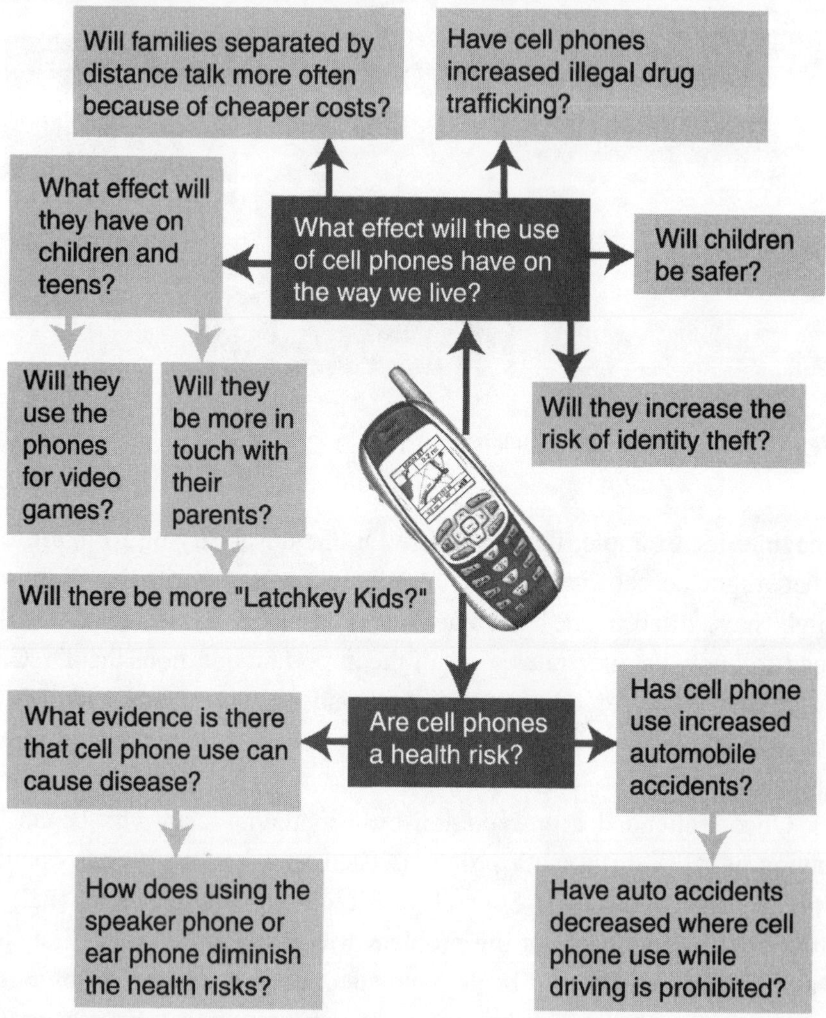

Fig. 3.2: Cell Phone Question Map

WHAT WE KNOW	WHAT WE NEED TO KNOW
Members of the Fore tribe are getting sick with kuru, but members of other tribes in the area are not.	If kuru is not caused by an infectious agent, what IS causing it?
Women of the Fore tribe get kuru, but men do not. However, among children, both boys and girls get kuru.	When did the Fore people start getting sick with kuru? What happened or changed in their lives at that time?
The symptoms of kuru suggest a brain infection.	Is there a family history of kuru that would suggest a genetic basis for the disease?
Animals injected with tissue from people who had kuru don't get sick, even after three weeks. So, kuru cannot be caused by an infectious agent like a virus or bacteria. Also, when autopsies are performed on the animals four weeks later, their brains show no signs of encephalitis.	What are the Fore women and children doing or experiencing that the men of the Fore tribe are not — and that the people in other tribes of the region are not?

Fig. 3.3

Sometimes when someone complains about what a boss, co-worker, family member, or friend is doing, I'll ask, "Why are they doing that?" It's surprising how often the answer is "I have no idea!" Clearly, to even begin to address the problem, we need to know why it's happening. Yet because of our blind spot—our failure to notice that we have a gap in our knowledge that is important to fill—it's not clear to us at all. Techniques like generating know and need-to-know lists can help offset the blind spots that prevent us from seeing what information we need to gather.

Tactic #3: Question the "What We Know" List

When I've watched people creating these lists, what has intrigued me is how often they switch items from one side to the other. They take a second look at a fact that they initially listed in the What We Know column, and realize that they aren't as sure of the information as they initially thought or that their knowledge is not as complete as it needs to be. One useful strategy is to relabel our What We Know lists after we make them and instead call them What We Think We Know. Then we need to ask ourselves if it's possible that some of the facts we are so sure of might be off the mark, even a little bit. Try returning to your What We Know list and ask yourself some questions about the items there, such as, How do I know this? How sure am I that this is true? Is it possible that this fact might be mistaken or only partially correct?

TACTICS II: WAYS TO COPE WITH IGNORANCE

These strategies can help you reduce the number of times that your ignorance causes you to slip up. But there will always be times when we don't know something, since no one can know everything. Yet despite their acceptance of this reality, people continually act amazed by other people's ignorance, as if the gaps in their knowledge were inexplicable. Most of us learn, at quite a young age, that we'll be judged dumb if we're ignorant of information that others expect us to know. We catch the raised eyebrows; the quick, knowing looks exchanged over our heads; the half smiles. So we try to conceal our ignorance. We learn to bluff it. We pretend to grasp what everyone else is talking about when really we are clueless. We feign knowledge about some current event that everyone seems familiar with; we laugh at jokes that we don't get. We do this because we've learned that those who are in the know treat those who don't get it disdainfully.

For this reason, you need an extra set of tools to cope with this blind spot. In addition to tactics that help you identify what you don't know, you need self-defense measures to deal with the reactions of others when your ignorance surfaces.

SELF-DEFENSE: MEASURES THAT BACKFIRE VERSUS TOOLS THAT WORK

To defend themselves, some people treat bodies of knowledge that they aren't familiar with, or interested in, with contempt. Faced with evidence of their own ignorance in a particular area, they sneer that what they're ignorant of isn't worth learning anyway. So the person who can answer all the Greek mythology questions on *Jeopardy!* but is stymied by a pop-culture question comments that he wouldn't want to stuff his mind with such worthless trivia. The pop-culture virtuoso can't believe that people so unaware of the world around them could consider themselves well informed.

These reactions to feeling stupid when we're ignorant of information are understandable. Faced with the possibility of being mocked by others, most people need to protect their image of themselves as intelligent. But to belittle the knowledge of others in an attempt to prop up our faith in our own intelligence isn't particularly constructive. What else can we do?

Self-Defense Tool #1: Acknowledging the Role of Experience

The first tool that you need is the conviction that very little is obvious. When other people think that what they know or realize is obvious, they usually have a blind spot themselves: they fail to see how their own experiences taught them what they now think you should know because "it's self-evident."

Imagine that a psychologist gives you the following test.

- The psychologist counts out ten pennies and places them on the table in front of you. "How many pennies are here?" she asks. After you confirm that there are ten, she stacks those pennies up, one on top of another. "Now how many are there?" Surprised, you say, "Ten!" She then arranges the same pennies in a circle on the table, and asks you again how many pennies there are.
- The psychologist asks you to lend her your keys. While you're

> watching, she places your keys under a napkin on the table. Then she asks you if you can find your keys.

To adults, the answers are so obvious that the questions themselves seem stupid. Unless some sort of deception, such as a magic trick, is involved, the right answers seem self-evident and logically necessary. Where else could the keys be but under the napkin? How could the number of pennies have possibly changed?

It turns out that these facts are not obvious but are learned, though at so young an age we don't remember learning them. The test question about the keys, for example, is the classic test of *object permanence*, designed by that great-granddaddy of research into children's thinking, Jean Piaget. In this test, researchers present a baby with an attractive toy but then, at some point, cover that toy with a cloth—in full view of the watching infant. Prior to seven or eight months of age, infants behave as if the toy is "all gone"—poof!—disappeared out of existence. They act as if objects have no permanent, continuing reality. One of the great intellectual accomplishments of infancy is learning this fact about reality: things exist even when I don't directly perceive or experience them. Similarly, we aren't born understanding that ten pennies will continue to add up to ten no matter how they are arranged. But because we no longer remember the time before we understood this fact, it now seems obvious to us.

My husband, Greg, told me about an eight-year-old boy who had a terrific way of reacting to derision. Greg was working as an interior home painter at the time. As he was priming an upstairs bedroom, the young boy watched him curiously for a while then asked if he could help. Greg gave him a roller and a few tips. The youngster had been priming the wall for about five minutes when his older brother leaned on the doorjamb to observe. After a moment, the older boy said, "That looks terrible. You're doing a terrible job." With barely a perceptible pause in his work, the eight-year-old responded, "Well, of course, I'm just learning. This is the first time I've ever done this." And he went on working.

If only we could adopt this boy's matter-of-fact acceptance of the reality that knowledge and expertise require experience and exposure! If only more of us could truly accept that ignorance is part of the human condition, a sign of our humanity rather than a sign of our stupidity. Wouldn't that acceptance make us more tolerant, more forgiving of ignorance when we encounter it in others and in ourselves?

Self-Defense Tool #2: Understanding How Quickly "Stupid" Turns to "Bad"

Once I trailed behind a family walking up a road at a summer camp. It was clear that the father was supposed to be watching the two-year-old while the mother attended to the fussy baby in the stroller. When a car unexpectedly turned the curve on the usually deserted road, the father realized he needed to rein in his toddler and keep hold of his hand. There was a moment when I froze, along with the family, as the auto loomed toward the child in the middle of the road. And then the danger passed. The driver spotted the child and slowed down, and the father snatched his son into his arms. I'll never forget the mother's reaction. Perhaps because she had been terrified, she lashed out at her husband. "What's the matter with you? You were supposed to be watching him! He could have been killed!" Her incredulous tone showed clearly that she could see no reasonable explanation for this man's failure to keep hold of his son's hand during their walk. Her tone was scathing. How could he have been so stupid?

Was this father stupid—or merely inexperienced? To someone who has had practice in caring for small children, it's obvious that you can't trust two-year-olds to navigate roads safely on their own. But how do we learn this? Caregivers gain all kinds of experience that they may not be aware of, such as learning to what extent they can trust different children at different ages to handle different situations, like the car-in-the-road situation. To the mother, it seems obvious that the father needed to be more watchful.

But it wasn't at all obvious to the father, and not knowing this doesn't mean that he is a stupid person—just as not knowing that her car may grind to a sudden halt if she fails to get the oil changed doesn't make his wife a stupid person. I can imagine a different near tragedy in which the same family is endangered when the car abruptly loses steam on the expressway because the wife failed to take care of the oil or even to notice the light on the dashboard that indicated a potential problem. With their roles of "expert" and "novice" reversed, it's easy for me to imagine her husband being angry at her for neglecting the car and finding her stupidity unbelievable, just as she did his.

Most of us are pretty intolerant of other people's ignorance when their lack of knowledge causes us anxiety or inconvenience. We lash out at them for being stupid. If they try to defend themselves by arguing, "Well, I didn't know that little red light on the dashboard was important," or "I thought the kid was okay walking by himself," we counter with an angry, "Well, you *should* have known!" We end up blaming them for their ignorance, arguing that they are in the wrong because a responsible person (a responsible parent, a responsible driver) would have made it their business to know.

Self-Defense Tool #3: Standing Up for Yourself

We need to stand up for ourselves when others treat us as though we were stupid. As adults, many people continue to experience the kind of ridicule that was a routine part of their lives as children. They may have an impatient boss who berates them for every mistake, a teacher who writes sarcastic comments on their term papers, or a spouse whose grimace conveys the "you idiot!" message more powerfully than words ever could. It's very hard to sustain a sense of ourselves as intelligent human beings when people react to us in these demeaning ways.

In response, some people mute themselves. In discussions, they are silent or put forth their views apologetically, prefacing them with comments like: "I don't really know anything about this, but . . ." In their interviews with women, the authors of *Women's Ways of Knowing* identified some women whom they described as "silent" and "having no voice." These women had no confidence in their ability to say anything intelligent. One said, "I had trouble talking. If I tried to explain something and someone told me it was wrong, I'd burst into tears over it. I'd just fall apart."[5] How can we react to the harsh judgments of others so that we don't stifle ourselves or, at the other extreme, belittle others in order to protect our identity as intelligent human beings?

QUESTIONS TO HELP YOU DEFEND YOURSELF

A friend of mine, Connie, has two handy questions ready for anyone who treats her as stupid when she is simply ignorant of information. The questions are: (1) How would I know that? and (2) How did you learn that? For example, after being unable to figure out how to fill out a form, Connie is on the phone with a company representative. The representative sputters, "Well, you have to check off the second box in that case!" Connie asks, "And how would I know that?" It often becomes apparent in the ensuing discussion that the form itself is unclear or presupposes knowledge that can't be taken for granted. When Connie's daughter says, "Well, *Mo*-om, you can't put dishes with silver on them in the microwave!" Connie simply asks, "How did *you* learn that?" She is countering the attitude of these people that what she doesn't know is obvious, and therefore she is stupid if she is ignorant of it, by pushing them to see that they weren't born with that information. They learned it.

People need to directly call others on their belittling behavior. "Don't talk to me as if I'm a stupid person," I once overheard a husband say to his wife. "I'm not a stupid person. I just don't happen to know how this washing machine works." In order to react more assertively when others put you down, you might need practice. The first step might be to simply notice when others are treating you as if you were stupid. In the beginning, you may only be aware of feeling hurt, angry, or confused. But in thinking back on the incident, you realize that the person was using sarcasm or ridicule.

As time goes on, you'll start to notice what's happening sooner and be able to respond right away. You might begin by saying, "You don't have to be so sarcastic." Or you might assert, "You make it sound like no one but an idiot would agree with me, but that's not true." Even when your options seem very limited, you can often push back a bit at the person belittling you. In a work situation, you might merely say, "I know it seems to you that you've had to tell me that three times. But I'm trying to absorb a lot of new information here, whereas this stuff is as familiar to you as the back of your hand. It's going to take me a little time." The truth is that when more-experienced people belittle others, those experts have a blind spot themselves. They are unable to see the challenges of the job from the viewpoint of an inexperienced person.

WIDENING THE CIRCLE: CHOOSING IGNORANCE, CELEBRATING DIVERSITY

In every culture, certain fields of knowledge are considered more valuable, and certain forms of intelligence command greater respect. As a result, those who excel in the areas valued by their culture are likely to have faith in themselves as intelligent people, while those who struggle in those areas come to question their intellectual self-worth.

The tactics described earlier—the question maps, the Know and Need-to-Know lists—are designed to help people discover their areas of ignorance so that they can compensate for them, at least to some extent, when they wish to do so. But there is a different choice that we sometimes make when confronted with the gaps in our knowledge. We choose ignorance. We may decide that we are simply not interested in football or poetry or history or the stock market, then we do our best to avoid having to learn about these areas. Our decision to remain ignorant will, of course, be lamented by people who are passionate about football, who love poetry, who are intrigued by history, or who are absorbed by the stock market. When we resist our teachers, bosses, partners, or friends as they urge us to appreciate what they love, our resistance may create tension.

But what would it be like in a society where a variety of interests are genuinely valued? People seem to differ, often from a very young age, in what they are naturally drawn to. One person is fascinated by politics but bored by how a car engine works; another is captivated by geometric patterns but disinterested in poetry; yet another is absorbed in a literary novel but indifferent to the constellations in the sky. What would happen if our society truly valued all the different fields of knowledge and areas of skill?

Howard Gardner's Theory of Multiple Intelligences

Psychologist Howard Gardner has identified various abilities that he believes reflect different types of intelligences. In his initial research, Gardner described seven different intelligences, including the verbal intelligence of authors, the musical intelligence of composers, the physical intelligence of athletes and dancers, and the intrapersonal intelligence of the person who is sensitive to her inner life, emotions, motives, and personal values. More recently, Gardner has introduced two other intelligences into the mix.[6]

Some "intelligences" that Gardner describes aren't what we typically call intelligence. Our society tends to reserve the term "intelligence" for academic capacities, such as verbal or mathematical ability. We don't ordinarily describe musical ability as musical intelligence. We don't typically refer to social skills as interpersonal intelligence or to someone's self-knowledge as intrapersonal intelligence. And we're even less likely to refer to physical intelligence. We'd rather talk about the physical talent or the exceptional motor skills of an accomplished athlete or dancer than about their bodily intelligence. Why use the term "intelligences" rather than saying "abilities" or "talents"?

Part of the answer is simply that the abilities in these less academic areas are crucial to intelligent behavior in our everyday lives. Take, for example, what Gardner calls *intrapersonal intelligence*. Intrapersonal intelligence involves the ability to be aware of our own inner lives, particularly our emotions, and to use this heightened self-knowledge to guide what we do. People who possess a high degree of intrapersonal intelligence are sensitive to nuances in their emotional reactions. They may notice a fleeting, vague uneasiness that most of us wouldn't catch, and they'd be more likely to revisit that feeling in their minds and try to understand it.

Some psychologists, such as author Daniel Goleman, refer to this capacity as *emotional intelligence*, and they discuss the critical role this plays in our lives.[7] As one example, Goleman cites the instance of a straight-A high school student who stabbed his physics teacher after the teacher gave him a B on a quiz. When we don't know what we feel,

Goleman argues—when we have little insight into our reasons for our own behavior—we may do irrational things even though we are highly intelligent in other, more academic, areas.

But in addition to the fact that these different capacities contribute to intelligent behavior in everyday life, there is a second reason why Gardner wants to call these abilities "intelligences": we don't value these talents equally. If people valued the nonacademic intelligences to the same degree that they valued academic learning, then they might naturally call all these capacities "intelligences." Or they might call *all* of them "talents" or "skills," commenting that someone has a flair for physics or a talent for logic as easily as we now say that someone is musically talented or good with people or skilled as an athlete. By insisting on applying the label "intelligences" to all these abilities, Howard Gardner urges us to broaden our definition so that we recognize the intelligence of people even when their gifts are not academic. He wants us to value the rich diversity of people's abilities rather than identify the ones more crucial to academic success as the signs of "real" intelligence and relegate what remains as talents or skills.

Labels Create Children Who Feel "Stupid"

Because our society equates intelligence with school learning, children who have difficulty developing the academically prized capacities are at high risk for feeling "stupid." Children with reading disabilities, for example, find it difficult to think of themselves as smart. They discount evidence of their intelligence, such as well-developed social skills, clever problem solving in building a soapbox car, or even above-average scores on IQ tests. The mother of one such child told me about an incident that happened when her son Matt was playing at a neighbor's home. The neighbor later commented, in a surprised voice, "Matt's really witty! I mean, I knew he was in the special reading group . . ." Her voice trailed off as she realized what she was saying, and Matt's mother, like every parent whose child struggles with academic learning, had to contend with yet another person who felt that such children cannot be intelligent.

Think of how different the experience of children who labor over math or reading is from children with minimal musical or artistic or athletic ability. We don't react to children who lack an ear for music as if they were in any way limited intellectually. Their self-images as intelligent individuals are unmarred by knowledge of these deficits. Like adults who cheerfully acknowledge "I'm tone deaf" or "I can't draw," these children know that no one will, on that basis, decide that they are dumb. In contrast, people are quick to assume that a child who has been placed in a remedial reading group must not be very smart.

Years ago when my work involved doing therapy with children, I asked a ten-year-old to draw a picture of his family, with everyone "doing something." He worked industriously on a big manila paper with crayons and colored pencils. When he had finished, he had drawn an elaborate home, cross-sectioned so that you could see the people in the various rooms. He came from a large family. One sister was depicted in the kitchen cooking dinner with his mom, another sister lying on her bed reading, a brother and sister watching TV in the living room, two other brothers and his dad playing basketball in the driveway. "But what about you?" I asked. "Where are you in the picture?" "Oh!" he said, shrugging and turning the paper over. "I couldn't fit myself in, so I drew me on the other side." There, crouched in the corner of the empty page, was the figure of a boy.

You don't have to have a psychology degree to realize that this child did not see himself as part of his family. It's clear that he didn't feel that he "fit in" or "belonged" in the same way that the other family members did. Think of all the children who aren't drawn to the same activities or interests as the rest of their family members. There are innumerable examples: the highly active, athletic child in a sedentary family that enjoys reading quietly; the quiet child who sits mute during raucous and freewheeling family discussions of politics and current events; the inveterate reader who hides in a corner with a book while her siblings badger her to play soccer. The point is that it's easy for children to feel that there's something wrong with them if they aren't interested in the activities and areas of knowledge valued in their particular family. They decide either that they are dumb for not grasping the knowledge or mastering the skills that seem to come so easily to their siblings or that they are in the wrong—that they are not trying hard enough or that they do not care enough. How different their experiences would be if we went way beyond simply accepting our differences and instead genuinely valued them.

Imagine growing up in a family—or living in a world—in which everyone accepted matter-of-factly that we all have different gifts, that we are fascinated by different bodies of knowledge and drawn to developing different skills. How altered our experience would be if our differences were not viewed as signs that we must be either flawed or stupid.

GLITCHES: "BUT I DON'T BELIEVE ALL KNOWLEDGE IS EQUAL!"

"Well, just a minute," you may be thinking. "This sounds nice, but there's a problem here." Perhaps you have some of the following thoughts:

- I *do* think some knowledge is more important than other knowledge.
- I don't think that athletic ability is the same as math ability.
- I value philosophy more than I value learning to cook.
- I think everyone *should* learn about history, current events, and politics so that they can be responsible citizens, and I think they're wrong if they don't bother to do so.

When I ask people who make these sorts of comments to expand on them, the gist of their objection is something like this: "It sounds great to say that we should celebrate the diversity of talents and interests that people have, but an attitude that is too accepting is dangerous. It makes it seem as if all abilities are equally valuable, all areas of knowledge are equally worthwhile, and I don't think that's true. If people believed that, then why would we require kids to learn certain subjects in school and not others? What would be the reason for encouraging our children to play the cello, or soccer, or to learn a second language? If there are things that we believe people should learn about, then it seems that this 'celebrating diversity' attitude endangers that. It gives people an excuse to not learn what we think they should, to say, 'I'm just not interested in that.'"

Recognizing that people have different interests doesn't mean that we can never demand that others overcome their ignorance in certain areas. The various fields of knowledge that exist, and the intelligences that people have, serve different purposes. We can recognize that certain information or skills are important because they further those purposes. On that basis, we can argue for teaching certain subjects in school or for devoting public funds to certain projects. We expose our children to certain experiences based on our own values, personal interests, and preferences. We can, for example, insist that our child learn some basic math in order to get along in the world as it is today, even if she is disinterested in math and weak in mathematical intelligence.

What is different about this attitude from the one many people assume is that it doesn't involve the judgment that there is something wrong with the child because she doesn't care for math. We don't act as if her disinterest means she is fundamentally flawed. We don't decide that she's dumb if it's hard for her to master mathematics. Instead, we simply acknowledge that this child is more drawn to different areas, that she is weaker than the average child in mathematical intelligence, and that she is stronger in other, nonmathematical, intelligences. We can acknowledge and accept her difference, without thinking that accepting it means that we can't require that she develop her mathematical intelligence. This gets us over the hurdle that makes many people reluctant to acknowledge that a specific body of knowledge or a particular intelligence is simply different rather than innately superior or inferior. It opens the doorway to truly celebrating, and not merely tolerating, diversity.

Some people are fascinated by the television program *This Old House* and what it teaches about home renovation. Others can play golf or the French horn for hours. Still others are captivated by the intricacies of how fax machines work, by the movements of stars in the skies, by the details of how French Canadians settled in Chicago or of how the red cliffs of Sedona were formed, by quilting patterns, or by the characters in Jane Austen's novels. If we really believed that our society would be diminished if any of these sorts of people were to disappear, we would find ourselves celebrating diversity and not merely tolerating it. If we truly valued the different intelligences that these areas of interest involve, we'd be more likely to see ourselves and others as intelligent.

IN A NUTSHELL

The opening story of the contestant on *Who Wants to Be a Millionaire?* shows how readily we label people as stupid simply because they don't know some information that we believe everyone should know. This lack of knowledge is not a blind spot. The blind spot related to our ignorance is that we often don't know what we don't know. The gaps in our knowledge are hard to detect. We can compensate for this blind spot to some extent by using methods like question maps and What We Know and What We Need to Know lists. But since no one can possibly know everything, we also need strategies for dealing with people when they act as if our ignorance means that we must be either stupid or flawed. If we accepted that people are drawn to different areas, and if we genuinely valued all the intelligences that mastering those areas involves, we might be more accepting of ignorance in ourselves and in others and more able to celebrate the diversity of intelligences that people display.

SNEAK PREVIEW

When the Arts & Entertainment channel aired a biography program spotlighting singer and composer Peter Frampton, the program included a snippet of an interview in which Frampton's parents described a remarkable incident. When Peter was a child, the family was listening to a live radio program. A few minutes into the musical piece, five-year-old Peter reportedly remarked, "There's something wrong with the piano." His parents, hearing nothing awry, were perplexed. Moments later, Peter repeated, more adamantly, "There is something *wrong* with that piano!" He protested once again toward the end of the piece. Frampton's parents were astonished when the announcer subsequently commented, "We apologize to our more discerning listeners, who no doubt noticed a problem with the piano." The broadcaster then explained that a sheet of music had slipped into the piano, affecting the tone of a few of the keys played in the piece.

Most of us would not have noticed what Peter noticed. He was especially sensitive to sound, particularly musical sound. Other people are more sensitive to texture or color or temperature. But the reverse is also true: some of us are relatively *insensitive* to the sounds or to the sights around us. Moreover, all of us miss noticing what has become familiar to us. As the story that opens our next chapter illustrates, not noticing can easily look like stupidity.

NOTES

1. June Goodfield, *The Quest for the Killers* (Boston: Birkhauser Press, 1985).
2. For an updated account of research on kuru and related diseases, including mad cow disease, see Robert Klitzman, *The Trembling Mountain: A Personal Account of Kuru, Cannibals, and Mad Cow Disease* (New York: Plenum, 1998).
3. Roger von Oech, *A Whack on the Side of the Head*, rev. ed. (New York: Warner, 1990).
4. J. C. Bean and J. D. Ramage, *Form and Surprise in Composition* (New York: Macmillan, 1986), p. 155.
5. Mary Field Belenky et al., *Women's Ways of Knowing* (New York: Basic Books, 1986), p. 24.
6. Howard Gardner, *Intelligence Reframed: Multiple Intelligences for the 21st Century* (New York: Basic Books, 1999).
7. Daniel Goleman, *Emotional Intelligence* (New York: Bantam Books, 1995).

Chapter 4

IF IT WERE ANY CLOSER, IT WOULD BITE YOU!

BLIND SPOT #3: NOT NOTICING

Several months ago, I was arranging to pick up a friend at the airport. At the tail end of our telephone conversation, she asked, "Oh, and what color is your car?" I hesitated, then murmured, "Just a second." Figuring that I wasn't sure which car I would be taking, she expected to hear me checking that out with my husband. But that wasn't the question she overheard next. Instead, she was amazed to hear me call out, "Honey, what color is my car?"

Now, most people notice and remember the color of their cars without any particular effort. So the reaction of many people to this anecdote is to think, "How could she be so stupid?" How could anyone—except perhaps a color-blind person—have trouble remembering what color her car is? It's an obvious feature, something I see every day.

Why We Fail to Notice: Filtering Our World

Or do I? Why do people miss noticing things that are obvious? Why is it that we can walk to a store three blocks from our home, repeating a route we've taken time and again, yet notice a particular house for the first time? How is it that we can drive home from work and realize as we arrive at our front door that the entire ride is pretty much a blank in our minds?

No one can constantly notice every aspect of the environment. If you are, for example, being interviewed for a job, you cannot simultaneously notice the words of the interviewer, the temperature in the room, the scratchy feeling of your sweater, the cool metal of your watchband, the sound of the air conditioner, the birdsong outside the window, and the phone ringing down the hall. We would be overwhelmed with stimulation if we were not able to filter out most of the sensations that are present at any given moment.

How do we do this? First, we are neurologically programmed to habituate to sensory stimulation so that we ignore the familiar but notice change. For example, when we first enter a home, we may be acutely aware of the aroma of pizza in the air. But within a few minutes, we become habituated to the smell and no longer notice it. Second, some individuals are more dominant in one sensory modality than in another. They may notice sound more than touch, for example, and so they are not bothered by a scratchy sweater. Or they may be very alert to seeing what's around them, but they pay little attention to the temperature of the room or to the sounds there. Our tendency to habituate and our inclination to notice some kinds of sensory data more than others are two main sources of the blind spot of not noticing.

"After a While, You Get Used to It"

Sensory adaptation is extremely useful. It allows us to "get used to" the train whistle during the night and learn to sleep through it. It allows the people who live near a paper mill to get used to the odor that makes visitors to their town wrinkle their noses. This kind of habituation allows us to notice what is different in case we need to react to some change—and then to ignore it so that we can turn our attention elsewhere. But it has a drawback. We can miss any change that occurs slowly because we are habituating to it without even realizing it. This means that the same sensory habituation that enables us to sleep through the train whistles can cause us to miss noticing smoke if it has been seeping very slowly into the room. Just as sensory habituation keeps us from noticing familiar sounds, sights, and smells, familiarity makes it likely that we will ignore whatever is commonplace in our environments. Instead of noticing something that should alarm us, sheer familiarity causes us to accept it as normal.

The students, faculty, and staff at Texas A&M University had long been familiar with the custom of burning an enormous bonfire each year prior to the football game with their archrival, the University of Texas. The tradition of students building a huge structure from literally thousands of tree trunks had been around for nearly a hundred years. But on November 18, 1999, the huge structure, towering fifty-nine feet high, suddenly collapsed. Twelve students who were working on the structure were killed, crushed under the tumbling mass of logs, while scores of others were injured. Subsequent investigations showed that some personnel at A&M had expressed concerns about the design of the structure and some students drinking during its construction. But the vast majority of students, university personnel, and townspeople never questioned the safety of this practice: they had gotten used to the idea of students, supervised only by older students who had built the bonfire structure in previous years, undertaking this project. The whole enterprise seemed normal to them, and so they failed to really notice the danger. In contrast, an outsider coming upon the scene might well have questioned how safe the practice was.

We can be lulled into thinking that things are normal even if only a few aspects of the situation are familiar to us. The book and movie

Catch Me If You Can[1] describe Frank Abagnale's career as a con artist: he passed more than $2.5 million in bad checks, and he successfully impersonated people with complicated jobs, such as pilots and physicians. In one of his schemes, he bought a delivery uniform and then stationed himself with a canvas bag next to a deposit box where, at the end of each day, merchants from a large mall generally dropped their cash and check receipts for the bank. He posted an official-looking sign that said *Drop Box Broken—Please Give Deposits to Bank Messenger.* People cheerfully dropped their money into the bag that he so politely held open for them. Being accustomed to depositing their receipts at that time and place and used to seeing delivery uniforms, no one looked closely at the man or at the situation. As the con man himself later said, "In what sense could a drop box, which is after all just a slot in a metal container, be 'broken'?" But at the time, people failed to question what was happening.

Our ability to adapt is an enormous asset. It has, for example, enabled human beings to survive an ice age and to thrive in varied climates throughout the world. But a liability is part and parcel of this asset: our ability to adapt allows us to get used to what is familiar to the point that we fail to perceive it at all.

Failing to Notice the World Inside: Not Noticing What's Going On in Our Own Minds

One set of experiences that is extremely familiar to us are the thoughts, emotions, and drives that make up our inner life, the world inside our own minds. This world isn't directly visible to others. Only we ourselves have direct access to it. Yet often we are oblivious to it. The interviews that author and linguist Vera John-Steiner conducted with creative individuals revealed that their thoughts were different, depending on their area of creativity.[2] Novelists and other writers, as one would expect, report hearing a stream of words as they think, while both painters and poets more often see images. Engineers, like poets, think in images, but the images in their minds are dominated by shapes in various relationships to one another rather than by the scenes in the poets' minds.

Physicists and mathematicians sometimes think in numbers, equations, and functions, as one would also expect, but many of them report that their thinking is dominated by images. When asked whether he has a mental image of something mathematical or of something physical when he thinks about black holes, for example, cosmologist Martin Reeves commented, "Whenever possible [I use] a physical image because I tend to think more easily in terms of pictures and diagrams than in terms of equations . . . [so] I think of what it would be like if you were sitting just outside a black hole, how light rays would bend, and what the forces would be . . . how it [would affect] matter orbiting near it."[3]

It is clear from interviews with these gifted individuals that our thoughts can take various forms. Yet many people have trouble answering the question, "What form do your thoughts usually take?" They have to stop and think when asked: "Do you think mainly in words? Are your thoughts filled with images? And if so, what are these images like? Shapes? Pictures of scenes that suggest a story? Diagrams?" Most people don't have quick answers because most of us have never thought much about our own thoughts. Much of the time, our thoughts, like our emotions, stream through our consciousness so quickly that we barely notice them. Rarely do we step back from the thoughts we have in order to make them the object of our scrutiny. As a result, we fail to notice both how we think and what we are thinking about.

Not Noticing What We Are Thinking About

If you've ever asked a five-year-old, "What are you thinking?" you may have had a glimpse into how unaware children are of their own thoughts. Often I have the feeling when children answer this question that they are making something up on the spot, for my benefit, rather than searching their minds for what was actually going through them. Research with children suggests that the minds of preschoolers are pretty much a blank to them. In one study, developmental psychologist John Flavell and his associates asked young children to think about the room in their house where their toothbrush was located. *Immediately* after this request, the children were asked to tell the researcher what they had been thinking about. In their answers, the five-year-olds in this study failed to mention either bathrooms or toothbrushes.[4]

Now, as adults we are better than children at being able to step back, as it were, to look at our own thoughts and to report on them. Beginning at adolescence, our capacity to have this sort of awareness seems to take a leap forward. Despite this growth in capacity, most of us, most of the time, continue to be only minimally aware of the goings-on of our own minds.

Yet the content of our thoughts has a tremendous influence on our lives. Author and philosopher Sam Keen writes:

> Imagine the different type and quality of life you would have if the questions you asked when you got up each morning were the following: Where can I get my next fix of heroin? How do I serve God? What will the neighbors think? What happened during the big bang when the world was created? Who will love me? How do I get power? How can we destroy our enemy? How can we end violence? Where will I spend eternity? How can I make enough money? Who are my friends? How can I be comfortable? Is my cancer curable? How can I become famous? How do we heal the Earth? Where can I get food for my children?[5]

Because most of us rarely eavesdrop on our own minds to find out what we're thinking, we have to make some effort to discover what we really think, believe, or feel about a situation or an idea. I'm not referring here to the effort needed to discover the kinds of deeply hidden, unconscious thoughts, feelings, and motives that Freud proposed are at the root of much of our psychological distress. I'm talking about material that is easily available to us. Our conscious thoughts, feelings, and beliefs often pass undisguised through our minds. They emerge clearly in our awareness, but only briefly. Like footprints on a shore, they are washed away by the next wave—the next thought, feeling, or external distraction.

That's why when we try to capture our own "stream of consciousness" by techniques such as writing down everything that comes into our mind, we are often surprised by what we've written. "I didn't know I felt that way," we say, or "I didn't realize that I thought that." That's why we seek out friends who can be sounding boards. In our conversations with them, we are able to discover not so much what they think, though that may be valuable, but what *we* think.

Not Noticing Our Thinking Styles and Learning Styles

Because most of us fail to notice our own thinking processes, we may favor a particular thinking style or learning style without realizing that we do so. For example, some people are top-down thinkers, preferring to master complicated ideas by grasping an overall picture, only later filling in the details. Others are more bottom-up thinkers who would rather master the simpler components and build slowly from one idea to another until they've constructed a complex edifice.[6] Many people routinely use strategies for solving problems without being aware that they are using them. In fact, one of the biggest differences between experts and novices in various fields is that the experts have more strategies, bags of tricks to bring into play, and they are more adept at recognizing opportunities for using those. Yet those same experts are often only minimally aware of the strategies that they employ so effectively. They do so intuitively.

Educators now recognize that becoming more aware of how we think can be useful when we are learning new skills, such as how to read. As a result, teachers are urged to help even first and second graders become more "metacognitive," more aware of their own thinking and of the strategies that they use when they run into trouble. "Did you see that word 'guppy'?" a teacher might ask her young charges. "Did you notice that word? What did you do when you saw it?" She hopes the children will become aware that when they see an unfamiliar word, they might react to it in different ways. They might speed ahead (away from it, trying to ignore it), or ask the teacher what the word means, or try to puzzle out the meaning based on the picture, or try to sound out the word phonetically. Once the children become aware of what they typically do, and of all the other choices available to them, teachers hope that they will begin to choose the strategies that are most helpful to them as individuals.

Adults, too, can become better problem solvers by increasing their awareness of how they think. Becoming more aware of the strategies that we use to create a successful business plan, class, or vacation enables us to consciously draw on those strategies in the future or to seek even more effective methods. Becoming more aware of the learning style that works best for each of us can enhance our learning experiences as well. For example, if you know that you learn best by visually observing other people doing the job and describing what they are doing as they go along, then you won't try to design a garden or learn a computer program solely by studying manuals. Instead, you might consider attending a workshop or hiring a tutor.

What Color Is My Car?

In addition to failing to notice what has become familiar, there is a second way that people come to ignore what's around them. Some people are so dominated by a particular sensory mode that they ignore other kinds of sensory information. I missed noticing and remembering the color of my car because I'm not a very visual person. My friend Evelyn told me about what happened one day when she was gazing at a meadow with her artist-daughter Katherine. On this spring day, the countryside was a patchwork of greens: the dark of the evergreens, the chartreuse of prairie grasses, the rich Kelly green of the oak leaves. Katherine exclaimed, "Look at all those different greens!" "And," Evelyn related, "after Katherine said that, suddenly I saw them too—so many different greens that I had never noticed before, in all the times I've stood and looked at that meadow." Hearing this story, I wondered, Is this what it's like to perceive the world the way an artist does? It struck me that Katherine takes in a different world from the one that I routinely see and that she has probably been seeing the world in terms of color, shape, and light since infancy.

As individuals, we differ in what we notice. Unless we have a hearing deficit or a visual problem, we take in most of our sensory information through sound and sight. We all share the kinesthetic sense; we are aware of our body's position in space as well as of heat, cold, pressure, and pain. Yet some of us are highly visual in our perceptions. The interviews that linguist and author Vera John-Steiner conducted suggested that artists and engineers not only think in visual images but also notice visual aspects of the world more often than others do.[7] Artists and engineers notice shapes more than the average person does, while musicians are more sensitive to sound. Standing in the same meadow with Katherine that morning, a musical person might be exquisitely receptive to the birdsong, while impervious to "all those different greens." The person more sensitive to touch might be acutely aware of the breeze on her face or the feel of the cool grass or the squishy mud under her bare feet.

When one sensory mode is more dominant for us than another, it's as if everything we experience in the world comes through a filter. One person's filter is very porous to shape and color, while touch has a harder time getting through. For another person, sound might permeate the filter easily, while visual aspects of the world have a tougher time making an impression. This means that our natural inclinations to notice some kinds of stimuli while remaining oblivious to others can create blind spots.

TACTICS: COMPENSATING FOR NOT NOTICING

If we don't realize what we are filtering out of our worlds—if we don't know that we are missing the birdsong or the gradations of all those greens—then we can't decide whether or not we want to make more effort to notice these aspects. Similarly, if we aren't aware of our own style of learning or thinking, we can't use that information to structure our learning experiences more effectively. We need to identify the blind spots that we have in order to compensate for them if we wish to do so. How can we discover them?

Tactic #1: Identify Our Sensory Handicaps

We might be able to identify our sensory handicaps by thinking about the criticisms that others habitually level against us. If we are routinely taken to task for not seeing what others thought we should have noticed, or not hearing what they'd argue everyone else in the room had heard, we might suspect that we are less visual or less auditory than most people.

We can also approach this from the opposite end and consider where our strengths are. Think about a simple activity such as filling a pitcher with water. Most people determine when the pitcher is almost full by watching it, seeing the waterline rise. But I know people who can close their eyes and know when the water is getting to the top by the sound of it. Others could tell by the increasing weight whether the pitcher was half or three-quarters full. These judgments are based partly on experience, but they also reveal an inclination to notice sounds and kinesthetic sensations such as weight more than they do the visual.

Sometimes the language we use reflects our dominant sensory modality without our even being aware of it. Linguists Richard Bandler and John Grinder[8] studied videotapes of family therapist Virginia Satir in an attempt to figure out what made her so effective. One factor that they uncovered was that Satir was uncanny in her ability to match the style of each member of the family as she spoke to them. If a family member said things like "I see what you mean," or "Do you get the picture?" Satir would also use words emphasizing visual images, such as "It looks like you believe that . . ." Another family member might say, "What I hear you saying is . . . ," or "It sounds to me as if . . . ," and Satir would respond in kind. Still another might comment, "I feel that the right thing to do . . . ," or "I was really touched when he told me that . . ." The words we use to express ourselves are clues as to what sensory systems might dominate for us.

Many of us have never paid much attention to what aspects of our environment we tend to notice. You can become more aware of what your dominant sensory modality might be. Try going for a walk, or sitting alone in a park, or doing a job that doesn't take a lot of concentration, like folding the laundry. Set a timer to go off every five minutes or so, and just observe what you have noticed each time it interrupts you. Were you mostly aware of the warmth of the laundry that you were folding? Or the sound of the cars swishing on the wet street as they passed by?

Once you discover what you tend to notice, you can play the "what's missing" game. If you realize that you aren't very visual, you can intentionally pay attention to what is going on around you visually.

Tactic #2: Find Fresh Ways to Experience the Familiar

Because it's so easy for us to get used to the familiar, we need to find fresh ways to experience what we've become accustomed to. When

artists are working on a canvas over a period of time, they can get used to what the painting looks like and find it hard to see it with a fresh eye. Some artists place their paintings in different spots so that they can come upon them unexpectedly. Turning the curve in the staircase and suddenly seeing a work in the hallway allows an artist to see it anew.

The ability to see what is familiar from a fresh angle is considered part of what it means to be creative. Some people seem to have a knack for doing this; it comes naturally to them. But it's possible for all of us to do this more often if we step back from our customary routines and look at the world around us anew. Try looking or listening more closely in a familiar situation, and then ask yourself, "What do I notice that I haven't paid much attention to before?"

Tactic #3: Talk to Strangers

One surefire way to gain a fresh perspective on the familiar is to bring in people who are unfamiliar with that situation. Once I asked a Japanese exchange student what she had noticed that was different about college courses in the United States. She hesitated, not wanting to offend me as her professor. So I encouraged her to answer by giving her an example of my own. I told her that I had heard that in some college classrooms in France, the professor would smoke while teaching. This was shocking to me but accepted as normal in that country at the time. At this my student eagerly chimed in, "Yes, I understand—that's how I reacted when I saw you drink a Coke during class. In Japan, a teacher would never eat or drink while teaching a class." It was jarring to realize that what had seemed an innocent activity to me was as shocking to her as the French professor's smoking was to me.

People from a different family, culture, religion, social class, or professional field will notice aspects of the world that we take for granted. And they can often see different possibilities or new opportunities. The new hire, the person with the least experience at the firm, might be the most insightful about some aspects of the company because he can notice what everyone else has become used to. The new in-law might be the most observant witness of the family. "Why do you cut the salad ingredients so small?" my sister-in-law Joyce questioned. The only answer anyone could come up with was "Mom always did it this way." Weeks later Joyce visited Mom, who said, "Oh, I just started doing it that way after I got false teeth. It made salad easier for me to eat." We fail to question what is familiar simply because we fail to notice it at all, and we end up continuing a custom even though the original reasoning behind the custom no longer applies.

Tactic #4: Discover Your Own Learning Style

The simplest way to discover your preferred learning style is to reflect on how you go about learning something new when you are free to approach it any way that you like. Imagine, as an example, that someone is trying to decide whether or not to use natural childbirth. She might prefer to:

- Trot off to the library to get a dozen books on the subject and study these on her own.
- Interview experts, such as gynecologists.
- Speak to people who have personally experienced what she wants to learn about, such as other mothers, even if they aren't experts.
- Seek experiences, fictional or simulated, that would help her see what it's like to be there in that situation, such as reading a novel or seeing a film.
- Enroll in a formal class or seminar on the subject.
- Experiment on her own, which in this case would mean just doing it and seeing what happens.

You can apply this same approach to other matters, from understanding the Vietnam War to learning how to build a bat house. Just ask yourself how you would prefer to learn something new if you had full freedom to arrange your own learning experiences. Another way to discover your preferred learning style is to reflect on the best and worst learning experiences you have ever had, asking yourself what made the best experience so fruitful and the worst experience so dismal.

WIDENING THE CIRCLE: SHEER FAMILIARITY AND ACCEPTING WHAT IS APPALLING

Beyond our personal lives, this blind spot influences what we notice, or fail to notice, in our own culture. For example, the sheer familiarity of traditional child-rearing practices makes us take them for granted. In US culture, even before we had baby monitors, tiny infants slept alone in rooms distant from their parents, a practice that seems inexplicable to Japanese families, whose babies cuddle nightly in bed with mom and dad.

Our natural inclination to get used to what is familiar means that appalling circumstances can come to seem normal, especially if we experienced them as children. That dad should drink a six-pack every night, that mom would hit the kids with a belt, that we wouldn't even consider pursuing a higher level of education or a professional job because of our social class, gender, or race—all these attitudes can be grounded in what we have come to consider normal. When one of my night school professors suggested that I study for a PhD in psychology, I burst out laughing. "What's so funny about that?" he asked. "I don't know," I stammered, suddenly taken aback. "It's just that . . . people like me don't get PhDs." Fortunately for me, that professor changed my mind about what the daughter of a janitor could aspire to. But often we fail to question how things are, or we cannot see possibilities for change simply because what is familiar seems normal and even inevitable to us.

By getting used to what everyone is doing, we come to accept activities that, in another light, we would view as questionable or unethical. For example, some people who would never dream of shoplifting will unhesitatingly copy computer software from a friend rather than buy it themselves. When we are in a setting where taking small bribes or filching a few pads of paper from the stockroom are common practices, the sheer familiarity makes these deeds seem normal and therefore somehow okay. When a teacher discovered that the locker of a second grader was filled with school supplies stolen from his classmates' desks, she called his parents in for a conference. The boy's father was flabbergasted by his son's actions. "I can't understand why he would do this!" he exclaimed. "He has loads of paper, pencils, office supplies—I bring them home from work all the time!"

The power of the familiar to seem normal to us is part of our useful human ability to adapt to circumstances. But sometimes we pay a high price for that adaptation: we come to barely notice what would be obvious to anyone who hadn't either grown up in our circumstances or adapted to them over time. When we get used to situations that limit ourselves or damage others, the cost of this blind spot is high.

IN A NUTSHELL

Sheer familiarity leads us to miss aspects of our surroundings that would be striking to others. We also miss noticing the busy world *inside* of us. Our passing thoughts and feelings rise in our consciousness, then disappear, barely having registered. In addition, individual differences in what we tend to notice can act as a filter, causing us to be especially sensitive to some aspects of the world but oblivious to others. The strategies discussed to counterbalance this blind spot are aimed at helping us find ways to discover what information we may be filtering out and to see in a new light what we've become accustomed to. Beyond our personal lives, our ability to get used to and therefore fail to notice what is happening around us can lead us to accept what is faulty or appalling as normal.

SNEAK PREVIEW

As this chapter emphasizes, we often fail to notice what's right in front of us. So maybe it's not surprising that we fail to see something that is always with us, but only occasionally in our field of vision—ourselves. Like the father mentioned above who could not see how he was indirectly encouraging his son's thievery, we can be oblivious to our own behavior. Why is it so difficult for us to see ourselves? That blind spot is the focus of the next chapter.

NOTES

1. Frank W. Abagnale and Stan Redding, *Catch Me If You Can: The Story of a Real Fake* (New York: Random House/Broadway Books, 2003).

2. Vera John-Steiner, *Notebooks of the Mind* (New York: Oxford University Press, 1997).

3. Lewis Wolpert and Alison Richards, *A Passion for Science* (New York: Oxford University Press, 1988), p. 27.

4. John H. Flavell, Frances L. Green, and Eleanor R. Flavell, "Young Children's Knowledge about Thinking," *Monographs of the Society for Research in Child Development* 60 (1995): 1–96.

5. Sam Keen, "What You Ask Is Who You Are," *Spirituality and Health*, Spring 2000, p. 30.

6. Gordon Pask, "Styles and Strategies of Learning," *British Journal of Educational Psychology* 46 (1976): 128–48.

7. John-Steiner, *Notebooks of the Mind.*

8. Richard Bandler and John Grinder, *The Structure of Magic* (New York: Science and Behavior Books, 1990).

Chapter 5

YOUR OWN WORST ENEMY

BLIND SPOT #4: NOT SEEING YOURSELF

In a classic study conducted at Princeton Theological Seminary decades ago, ministry students were led to believe that they needed to rush over to another building in order to deliver a sermon they had been in the midst of preparing.[1] The topic of the sermon was the parable of the Good Samaritan, the story of an unfortunate fellow who has been robbed, beaten, and left to die on the side of the road. The point of the Good Samaritan story is that the religious men of the time fail to stop and help;

only the Good Samaritan, a traveler of low social status, stops to offer assistance. In this study, each ministry student was routed to his talk past a doorway in which an accomplice of the researchers was already positioned, slumped and apparently ill. Would these well-intentioned, good-hearted ministry students act like the Good Samaritan and stop to offer help? Or would they speed past the apparently ill person in order to take care of their important business? Of those who believed they were late, only one in ten offered help.

How could these seminarians not see that the way they were acting contradicted the very message that they themselves were rushing to deliver? The parallel seems glaringly obvious to us as outside observers. Yet as the authors of this study ruefully noted, "On several occasions, a seminary student going to give his talk on the parable of the Good Samaritan literally stepped over the [ill person] as he hurried on his way!"[2]

WHAT CAUSES THE BLIND SPOT OF NOT SEEING OURSELVES?

Many of us have a quirky attitude toward this blind spot. On the one hand, we readily acknowledge that it can be hard for people to see themselves. On the other, we are nevertheless continually amazed at how blind others can be to how they are acting. And we may be even more surprised when by accident we suddenly see ourselves more clearly.

"If only he could see himself!" people remark. "Doesn't he realize what he's doing?" they wonder as they watch a man at a party flit from one group to another, groups that seem to dissolve minutes after he's joined them and has begun to hold forth with his booming proclamations. Like the ministry students, this man fails to notice what is so obvious to us, looking at the situation from the outside. He is truly like the driver who is oblivious to the car that has sidled up, smack within his car's blind spot. We, on the other hand, are like the person standing on the corner who can see the other car so clearly.

Part of what causes this blind spot of not seeing ourselves is the simple reality that we never do see ourselves directly. Unless we happen to catch a glimpse of ourselves in a mirror or we record our own behavior in some way, our physical selves are not right in front of our eyes. Sure, we catch a glimpse of an arm or a hand, but the image of our whole body and our body language, especially our own facial expressions, is simply not in our view. So perhaps it's not surprising that people often miss what is so apparent to others. People remain ignorant of idiosyncrasies that they've exhibited for years, while a stranger notices these oddities after only a few minutes' acquaintance.

In order to offset the difficulty we all have in being aware of our own behavior, there are options: athletic teams study videos of their games, artists record and review their own music, instructors videotape themselves teaching, and job applicants are advised to tape a simulated practice interview. These techniques can be extremely helpful, but it's hard to apply them in everyday life. Most of the time, we don't have videotapes to help us see how we address a colleague at work, a client, a child, a first date. As a result, we can remain ignorant of how we come across to others, how we appear to them, and how we affect them.

Another reason that others can be amazed at our lack of self-awareness is that we often hold beliefs about ourselves that we accept unquestioningly —beliefs that, to others, have little or no basis in reality. "She's one of those moderately attractive women who think they are stunning," one of my friends once described an acquaintance. We've all known people whose images of themselves seem singularly inaccurate. The strong athlete who doubts that she is much good, the independent youngster who lacks confidence, the competent manager whose self-doubts prevent him from aspiring to promotion—all these people seem to have an image of themselves that is out of kilter. Moreover, when friends use logic and counterevidence to try to convince us that the beliefs we hold about ourselves are wrong, their well-meaning efforts frequently fail. This can happen even when they are trying to convince us that we are *better* than we think we are: more attractive, more gifted, or more competent. It surely happens when others suggest that we are not quite as impressive as we believe we are.

Imagine a woman, Marcy, who sees herself as self-sacrificing, a veritable Mother Teresa who consistently puts the needs of others before her own. She is forty years old; she has spent her adult life trying to live up to this demanding self-image. Her self-esteem depends on denying that, in truth, she is human like everyone else. She has petty impulses; she often pursues selflessness not out of caring for others but as a means of gaining their approval; her continual attempts to appear generous, giving, and eternally empathic have led her to be dishonest—to present a façade that doesn't reflect what she really thinks or feels. There would be some definite benefits to Marcy if she were able to shed her belief that she is the next Mother Teresa. She'd be able to discontinue her exhausting daily efforts to prove how good she is. But there would also be a price to pay. Colleagues at work might stop viewing her as a savior. Friends might stop relying on her quite so much, triggering fears in her that they might not remain friends. Church acquaintances might stop gushing about her generosity. And she herself might look back on the previous twenty years with anguish: has all her self-sacrifice been meaningless, if it was done to preserve a false image that she wanted to show the world?

These are painful questions to face, and they give us a glimpse into why it might be so hard to achieve a more accurate image of ourselves. Not only do we have to compensate for the fact that we're rarely directly in our own line of vision, we must also find ways to somehow see our physical selves and our external behavior more objectively. In addition, we have to identify and then question the beliefs that we hold about ourselves, even when that questioning leads us to distasteful conclusions.

TACTICS: HOW CAN WE SEE OURSELVES?

Tactic #1: Take Advantage of "Accidental" Sightings

Sometimes we discover ourselves by accident, as it were, by noticing another person who unintentionally mirrors us. Parents sometimes have this experience when they overhear their children: a daughter mimics her mother's overprotective style as she warns her dolly to hold her hand tightly, or a son mimics his father's dictatorial style as he orders a younger playmate around. Our blindness to ourselves is so great that we may fail to see ourselves even when the tableaux we witness closely replicate our own behavior. But when we do see ourselves mirrored in others, the experience can be powerful.

A student of mine, whom I'll call Cathy, confided, "When I was in my twenties, I recall actually bragging to people that 'I only see things in black and white. There is no gray for me.' I considered this a very sophisticated stance and was very proud of it." What changed her, Cathy said, was her marriage. "Aha!" I thought. "Cathy married someone very different from herself, someone who could show her a different way of thinking." I was wrong. In fact, Cathy married someone who thought exactly as she had. How could that change her? As Cathy put it, "I never realized how I sounded or appeared until I listened to my husband using this same style. Hearing him made me examine my own thinking and behavior. . . . I decided to eliminate this unproductive perspective from my life. I learned to temper my previous role of omniscient, inflexible seer of the 'only real side' to any argument with listening and questioning . . . [and] found that friends, family, and business associates became far more receptive to my ideas."[3]

We don't always deepen our self-knowledge when we experience an "accidental sighting" of ourselves in others. For example, a person might have a glimpse of her tendency to offer unsolicited advice to her siblings when she sees her brother press his opinions in a similar way. But then she quickly decides that it's not really the same for her. When she does it, she is doing it out of concern, while her brother (it seems to her) is doing it because he's never learned to mind his own business or because he's just naturally bossy and overbearing.

To take advantage of accidental sightings, we have to notice that little hitch in time during which we try to readjust the scene so that what we habitually do no longer appears to be "the same" as the behavior of that other person in whom we briefly saw ourselves. We have to be able to go back to the moment before the readjustment and ask ourselves, "What would it mean to me?" What would it mean to me to discover that I am more like my brother than I had imagined? If we can identify why we resist accepting that this image, too, is part of who we are, we might be more able to incorporate this part of ourselves into a fuller, more complex picture of ourselves. Perhaps we would even be able to laugh at ourselves, at our valiant but doomed attempts to deny what another person's behavior has inadvertently revealed to us: the similarity between ourselves and the less-than-flattering image of how we sometimes behave.

Tactic #2: Get Feedback from Others

Since others often see us more clearly than we can see ourselves, they have the potential to be a valuable source of information about how we sound, behave, move, and affect other people. An obvious conclusion to draw from this is that we could compensate for this blind spot by seeking useful feedback from others. This turns out to be harder than it sounds. In his book *Fearless Creating*,[4] creativity coach Eric Maisel discusses how artists often either fail to seek feedback from others about their work—thereby depriving themselves of useful criticism—or place themselves at risk by exposing their work too early or to the wrong person at the wrong time. To increase the odds that the feedback you get from others will be useful rather than destructive, ask yourself some questions before you seek their input.

Question #1: "What Kind of Feedback Do I Need at This Time?"

Maisel advises that we ask ourselves what it is that we need at each point in our creative work. Do we want to put forth budding possibilities—an early probe, a rough sketch, a basic concept, the gist of a design—in hopes of finding some encouragement for our general direction? If so, we don't want to ask for feedback from the detail-oriented person or the cynic, the one who will glance at our few pages, or rough sketch, and see all that is incomplete and potentially problematic with it. They are too likely to stomp on tender shoots of ideas that have barely begun to take root. On the other hand, at a later point when our work is well under way, the same person might be a tremendous asset. The detail person might provide the more meticulous critique that may be exactly what we need at that time. The cynic might help us identify the gaps in our work or the areas that are most vulnerable to legitimate criticism.

While Maisel's words are directed primarily toward artists, I think they are applicable to all of us in many different spheres of our lives.

When we are trying to attain a more accurate picture of ourselves, of our interactions with others, or of our performance, we, too, need to think about what kind of feedback would be most helpful and who would be most able to provide it.

Question #2: "Who Is Both 'In My Corner' and Willing and Able to Provide Honest, Useful Feedback?"

In order to remain open to feedback from others, we need to hear from people who are supportive of us, "in our corner" in some way. We also need people to be knowledgeable, observant, frank, and willing to challenge our own conceptions of what we are like. It turns out that this combination of challenge and support is not an easy mix to find.

When we're in positions of power, people may be too intimidated to tell us what they really think. The result is that we end up with CEOs who are oblivious to the impact that their own actions have on their organizations. When we're seeking feedback from our colleagues, we may fear that competitiveness or jealousy will prevent them from giving honest or useful input, or we may sense that even to ask for their help would place us in a vulnerable position. They might disclose our weaknesses to others in order to promote themselves. When we're with friends or family members, we may find they are either overly protective or overly critical. So trying to do something about this particular blind spot requires both courage and prudence: we need good judgment to figure out who would be most able and willing to provide the sort of feedback that would be helpful, and we need courage to seek it out despite the genuine risks involved in doing so.

Once I attended a luncheon where a friend of mine, Juan, was giving a presentation. Afterward, as we strolled in the garden on the hotel grounds, Juan asked me how I felt he had done. I thought his talk was passable, but not great. Concerned about hurting his feelings, I pointed out a couple of aspects of his presentation that I thought had been well done, then I mentioned one feature that had been really dismal. But I downplayed how badly that feature needed work, merely mentioning it and making a suggestion for addressing it. Juan was silent for a few moments. He stood in the sunlight, apparently admiring the bed of roses where we had paused. Then he said, "Madeleine, I'm scheduled to give this same talk next month for a much larger group, and I want it to go better than it did today. Would you give me your honest feedback about how I could improve it?" You can imagine how differently I responded to that question.

Question #3: "What Unsolicited Feedback Have I Gotten That Is Hard to Take but Might Still Have at Least a Germ of Truth in It?"

My children gave me unsolicited feedback about myself when we were celebrating my daughter Kalyn's fourteenth birthday. The butter on the restaurant table was in a porcelain cup, whipped and imprinted with a fancy design. It didn't look much like butter to me. I thought that it could easily be mistaken for sour cream or a cheese of some sort. So I lifted it up to point it out to Kalyn and her brother, and I said (no doubt in my most teachery voice), "Kalyn, David, this is butter." They found my statement hilarious. Throughout the dinner, they continuously capitalized on my earnest and well-meaning attempt to educate them about the nuances of fine dining. When the waiter brought the rolls, Kalyn drawled, "Oh, David, what is in this pretty basket? I don't think it's bread, do you?" while eleven-year-old David responded in careful, drawn-out words: "Those are rolls, Kalyn, *ro*-olls . . . you can *eat* them." Their teasing forced me to see myself, to recognize that I was once again being the overprotective mother. Years later, they continue to use the "This Is Butter" story when I stray too far in that direction.

Sometimes the most worthwhile feedback people can get comes in forms that make it hard to take. "There goes Mom again," the children say, rolling their eyes. It's really hard to be willing to look at how someone else sees us when they are rolling their eyes. Or smirking. Or scolding. It's difficult to stay open to the possibly helpful perspectives of others when they seem bent on showing us just how flawed we are. But since unwelcome feedback is often the most valuable to us, we need to be open to it. At the same time, we shouldn't simply swallow it whole. Instead, we need to ask the next question.

Question #4: "How Valid Is This Person's Perspective?"

After hearing what others think, we still have a lot of thinking to do. Once we've seen our artwork or our hockey game or our style of conducting a meeting through someone else's eyes, we need to evaluate how valid their feedback is. We might ultimately reject the version of ourselves that others offer us, believing that they are presenting a distorted picture. We might sift through their ideas and select the two or three insights that ring true to us, discarding the rest. We might file their ideas away for future consideration. In some cases, we might need to get feedback from several different people and try to juggle their views to come up with a picture that rings true to us.

This is a tricky business. We know how blind we can be to ourselves. It's not always easy to decide which version to believe when people offer conflicting accounts. It's not easy to tell when we're leaning toward rejecting someone's feedback because it's truly off target and when we're tempted to reject it because it's unpalatable.

Tactic #3: Examine Your Beliefs about Yourself

In addition to trying to see our external selves more clearly, if we are to deepen our self-awareness and self-knowledge, we need to be able to see the beliefs we hold about what kind of individuals we are. All people hold a host of beliefs about themselves. I may see myself as talented in gardening but helpless at following a map. I may see myself as beautiful or plain, funny or serious. Sometimes our beliefs are well founded. At other times, our friends or teachers or colleagues raise their eyebrows in surprise when they learn how we view ourselves, and they beg to differ.

Among the most crucial beliefs that people hold are their convictions about their own power, their ability to influence the events in their lives. "Oh, I couldn't do that," a friend comments when we suggest a perfectly reasonable solution to her dilemma. "Other people" might be able to work less, spend less, ask more of their family members, talk directly to a neighbor about a problem. But our friend can't. Her belief that she can't is a belief that she has about herself—one that severely restricts her options.

What limits us is not that we are unaware of what we believe about ourselves. We don't usually have a blind spot about that. Most of the time we are quite clear about it. What limits us is that we cannot entertain even the possibility that our ideas of what we are like, and what would happen if we acted differently, might be in error. Our belief that we can't act differently because "that just isn't me," or because terrible things would happen if we did change, puts chains on us. We are unable to take advantage of options actually available because, to us, they are *not* available. Our automatic rejection of these options blinds us. We can't see them as possibilities for ourselves.

In his classic studies of learned helplessness, Martin Seligman conducted experiments in which dogs were subjected to mild electrical shocks through the grid floor on which they stood. A bell or buzzer would sound just before the shock occurred, but the dogs had no way of escaping from the enclosure. After the dogs had had repeated experiences of being unable to escape the shocks, Seligman placed them in a different enclosure, one that had a side so low the dogs could easily step over the barrier when the buzzer sounded and so avoid the shock. But they didn't do this. Having learned earlier that there was nothing they could do, they stood helplessly and endured the shock.[5]

These studies demonstrate all too clearly why it might be possible for one person to see all sorts of solutions to another person's dilemma, while the sufferer sees none. What can we do to see that the possibilities that others view as perfectly feasible are available to us?

Question #1: "What Am I Afraid Would Happen If I Did What I Believe Is Impossible for Me to Do?"

Our answers to this question might reveal why we need to deny that other ways of behaving might be possible for us. It sometimes helps to do an exercise in which you create a phrase describing the behavior that you shrink from, such as:

- "If I stood up to my mother . . ."
- "If I tried to be closer to my son . . ."

- "If I quit my job . . ."
- "If I were more assertive with my boss . . ."
- "If I told my colleague off to his face . . ."
- "If I admitted how unhappy I am in this marriage . . ."

Then jot down whatever words pop into your head as endings for your phrase. Often our responses reveal what therapists used to call our *catastrophic fantasies*—the terrible things that we fear would ensue if we were to act differently. If your answers uncover a fear you have, you can ask yourself Question #2.

Question #2: "Do I Have to Jump into the Deep End, or Can I Put in a Toe to Test the Waters?"

Some therapists in the 1970s urged their clients to discover whether or not their catastrophic fantasies were true by actually doing what they most feared. The assumption, of course, was that people had unrealistic fears about what would happen. Often this assumption was accurate. But every once in a while, the outcome of the test was every bit as bad as the person had feared it might be, and sometimes worse. Even when that wasn't the case, for many people it seemed so overwhelming to take such a leap, like jumping into the deep end of the pool, that they failed to take any action at all.

As an alternative to doing what you most fear, you can ask yourself what smaller test you could make to see if your belief is valid or not. If you fear that your boss would fire you if you questioned his instructions, it would be wiser—and less anxiety provoking—to figure out the tiniest test possible of your belief. You might choose an issue or a project that your boss is more open about; you might seek advice from experienced people who interact with your boss more successfully than you do. What you want to do is to find what Robert Kegan and Lisa Lahey call a "safe test," where the risk is minimal, putting in a toe to test the waters rather than jumping into the deep end of the pool.[6]

Question #3: "Is My Own Self-Image Getting in the Way?"

Sometimes our response to exercises like the ones above reveal that what is at stake for us, what we'd lose if we dared to change, is a self-image that we've grown awfully fond of. Imagine that Marcy, the woman who always put others first, had completed the question, "If I stopped trying to be Mother Teresa . . ." Marcy might discover her fear that she'd lose her saintly reputation as a caring person if she let people see the seething resentment she sometimes felt when faced with yet another request. Like Marcy, we, too, might realize that what's at stake isn't quite as worthy as we had thought. Marcy *thought* that what she was trying to protect were her values of being a kind, generous, and thoughtful person. In fact, Marcy does have those values and strives heroically to live up to them. But she oversimplified her motives. She saw only the positive, admirable motives that, while genuine, were only a part of the picture. She was blind to the less admirable motive of wanting to have everyone think highly of her, of wanting to avert their disapproval.

Once she recognized the role that these less laudable motives played, Marcy could see the possibility of being a more genuine person. She could acknowledge that she often offered to help even when her help hadn't been requested and could learn to rein in this automatic inclination. She could catch herself when she was acting much more interested in another person than she really felt and could bring her behavior into a little closer alignment with her actual feelings. She could sometimes say no to requests.

You, too, might discover that what you're really like is different from the self-image that you ordinarily spend lots of energy and effort maintaining. That self-image might bear little resemblance to Marcy's Mother Teresa. It might be the image of the totally independent person who doesn't need anyone else, or the leader who is never discouraged, always confident. Whatever it is, you can evaluate the image to see if it is realistic. Is it possible for any human being to fulfill that image—to be that sort of a person, every moment of every day? If you realize that it's not, then you can explore what sort of person you really are. You are certainly more complex than any oversimplified version of someone who must deny a lot of his or her humanity in order to live up to impossible standards. Recognizing the idealistic image that we have striven so hard to fulfill is the first step to questioning it and seeing ourselves more realistically.

Tactic #4: Examine Your "Yes, Buts"

Our "Yes, buts" can be a great clue to uncover the areas in which we feel relatively powerless. We might say: "Yes, but . . . I just can't do that," or "I'm not like that, I'm not the sort of person who can [be more assertive, ask others for help, live by myself, lower my standards, take it easier in my work life, etc.]." You can fill in the blanks. The more vehemently we refuse to consider an option that others see as perfectly feasible, the more likely we are underestimating our power in that situation.

Imagine that we can't decrease the pressures we're under at work because to "do less" would mean to lower our standards. "I can't do that," we think. "I'm a perfectionist. That's just the way I am." Yet what would we answer if someone asked, "Don't you *ever* adjust your standards—to the importance of the task, time pressures, other priorities?" When questioned closely, most people will admit that they do make such adjustments. If we can acknowledge that we do modify our standards, at least a little, in response to various circumstances, then we have a small wedge to press against our assumption that we are helpless to adapt what we are doing.

Sometimes people shore up their sense of powerlessness by claiming that they can't act differently because to do so would violate their ethics. Once I spoke with a young high school teacher who was headed for burnout by the end of his third year of teaching. It became apparent to me that he demanded so much of himself that he ended up working twelve-hour days. In an effort to help his students improve their writing, he required many more writing assignments than most of his colleagues did, and he spent nearly every weekend correcting those assignments from dawn to dusk, giving the students detailed feedback about their papers. Similarly, he took on extra work, such as being the faculty sponsor of the school newspaper, then he committed many hours to helping the students with extracurricular activities. When others suggested that he might cut down on the number of writing assignments or leave the student editors more on their own, he objected that he couldn't because he was committed to his students.

I wanted to ask him, "Can you think of ways in which you can be committed to your students that don't necessarily require devoting nearly every waking hour to them?" I would have liked to have him tell me about teachers whom he saw as committed to their students, but teachers who also somehow managed to have lives for themselves outside of school. What I'd be trying to do, of course, is to help him question his assumption that the *only way* to be a good teacher is to utterly sacrifice one's personal life. I imagine asking this young man, "Do you think that, in order to be a good teacher, someone pretty much needs to live like a monk, devoting himself entirely to his students, never marrying, never having a family, giving up his personal interests and hobbies to dedicate all his time to his students?" I suspect that he would reject these extreme statements. Because they are excessive, such demands would bring his assumptions about what it means to be a good teacher into sharp focus. This might enable him to see them clearly for the first time. As a result, he'd evaluate their validity. He'd come to grips with the question of what it really means to be committed to one's students, of just how much a teacher needs to do in order to be a good teacher. As a result, he would be able to see more options for himself.

PERSONAL RESPONSIBILITY AND HOW WE SEE OURSELVES

Most of us have experienced the frustration of trying to help a friend who counters every suggestion we make with "Yes, but." When people don't believe that they have the power to act differently, they also logically conclude that they shouldn't be blamed for not changing. How can they be held responsible when they are powerless to act any other way? A friend of mine, David, described one of the college students who worked as an aide at his daycare center. The student was wonderful with the three-year-olds in the class where she assisted, but she was unreliable. She was often late and sometimes failed to show up at all. What most irritated David were her excuses: "The thing is, I had to stay up late to study for a test. I was up until 4 a.m., and if I hadn't slept, I wouldn't have done well. And

I have to do well, or I'll lose my scholarship. So I couldn't come to work." When David suggested that the young woman needed to plan her time better so that she could study earlier for exams, she had a slew of reasons why this was not possible, given her current life and her personality.

When we contend that reasonable solutions are not possible for us, usually the only way out we see is to have the problematic situation disappear. If only . . . my stepchildren didn't live with us, my boss were less demanding, my co-workers were more willing to help, then everything would be all right. Usually we can't work these miracles, so we remain mired in helplessness. We won't discover other options unless we overcome the blind spot we have about our own power. In the meantime, we are likely to exasperate our parents, partners, friends, bosses, and spouses when we plead that we are helpless to do anything different.

WIDENING THE CIRCLE: NATIONAL BLINDERS

It's not only as individuals that we fail to see ourselves. Business organizations, religious communities, nations—whole collections of people can fail to see how their group acts or comes across to others. Surely in the bewildered question "Why do they hate us?" that echoed through the United States in the wake of the terrorist attacks on September 11, 2001, we see evidence of a blind spot that many people had about our own country. Many citizens of other nations were astonished by our question. In particular, they were amazed that we could be so unaware that, from the perspective of many other nations, the United States often conveyed an arrogance that triggered resentment.

Some time ago, I attended a seminar given by a business guru, an author who has sold literally millions of books and who commands high fees when he speaks at corporate meetings. Two attributes of this man came out clearly during his talk. First, this businessman believed in capitalism. He boasted at the outset of his presentation that he was a capitalistic pig and proud of it. Second, it was clear that he despised arrogance. He told several stories making fun of arrogant CEOs. As it turned out, I think the combination of these two traits upset this guru's world. The cause of his inner turmoil cropped up in the middle of his speech, when he drifted from his prepared remarks to speak spontaneously, providing a fascinating glimpse into the mind of a man in transition. He was just beginning to comment on how confusing and messy the times had become after the September 11, 2001, terrorist attacks, when he paused. "You know, I just attended the World Economic Forum. It was interesting, but . . . it confuses you sometimes, as you listen to those international speakers. I don't know what I think—this isn't really part of my prepared remarks, but a lot of people think we are pretty arrogant. I don't know how to think about it . . . but three-fourths of the world is starving, and [a global banking institution] springs a million dollars so that Elton John can sing at [a recent gala event]. . . . My beliefs are not shaken, but they are a little shaky." At this point, the speaker relocated to the groove of his prepared remarks and left his detour.

What an intriguing comment! "My beliefs are not shaken, but they are a little shaky." Here is the poignant dilemma of a person who is struggling so hard to hold fast to the beliefs and values that have been important to him that he asserts that they are not shaken. He expresses the contradiction, seemingly unaware of it. Isn't this how we often feel when we are in the process of being enlightened, when we are losing a blind spot? We have a sense of confusion; perhaps things aren't quite as we believed them to be. We want to protect the values we have held that seem threatened by this alternative possibility. Yet we may also have the insight and the courage to acknowledge that something has been shaken up, something that we need to think about in order to sort it all out. The speaker was distraught by his dawning realization that he himself, who so abhorred arrogance, might have shared the arrogant attitude that the international speakers at this conference so scathingly condemned.

I don't know what that guru ultimately did with his turmoil. It's awfully tempting for us, in these situations, to try to protect what has become threatened. We often find some way to suppress or ignore those dangerous new insights. Only rarely, perhaps, do we sit ourselves down to reflect on what all this might mean, and allow our insights to impact some of our most fundamental views. We might be able to do this more often if we could find some support while we were going through the pain and uncertainty of questioning what we were once so sure of. If only we could talk with someone else about what we were experiencing—someone who would commiserate with us, someone who could appreciate just how much was at stake, someone who would admire our courage for looking at the issue at all.

That support might enable us to acknowledge the ways in which we have been blind to our own arrogance, but that sort of support is hard to find. Consider how this business guru's colleagues are likely to react to him. Holding values similar to his own, they are probably going to be as threatened by this alternative view of the United States as he is, and they may well shore up his old belief system by pooh-poohing the challenges to it. They might feel defensive and dismiss charges of US arrogance by offering a counter-explanation—other nations resent us because they are jealous of us. This statement might itself strike people of other nations as egotistical, evidence of the very arrogance that we are trying to deny. But armed with this more attractive rationale, our guru could ignore his earlier misgivings.

And what is likely to happen if this guru goes to others who eagerly agree with the view that the United States has been arrogant? *They* may well fail to appreciate the struggle that he is engaged in. They may convey a superior attitude toward him for having taken so long to grasp a truth that they themselves realized long ago. When we sense that kind of condescension, it is very difficult for us to sustain a sense of our own worthiness, and we need that psychological safety zone in order to question and revise our beliefs. No wonder it's so hard for us as individuals and as nations to acknowledge our own blind spots.

GLITCHES: LATERAL MOVES AND RETREAT

Truly seeing ourselves brings us the kind of knowledge that, in Robert Kegan's words, can "transform" rather than merely "inform" us.[7] Imagine a sharp young man named Brad, a trivia buff, smart, self-confident—in fact, something of a know-it-all. When Brad watches the quiz show *Who Wants to Be a Millionaire?* he is impatient with contestants who make poor choices. "Why did she do that?" Brad scoffs when a woman ignores her gut instinct about an answer and goes with the audience's vote-in answer instead—one that turns out to be wrong. Later, when Brad becomes a contestant himself, we hear him say on national television (as so many contestants have commented in that taken-aback tone), "It's a lot different here than playing at home."

If Brad fails to see himself, his experience as a contestant may leave him relatively unchanged. He becomes informed about what it's like to answer questions when you're not safely tucked in the corner of your couch at home, but not transformed. Merely informed, Brad may later admonish others who criticize the decisions he made on the program by sneering, "You have no idea what it's like to be up in that chair." If before he was the know-it-all who shook his head in disgust at contestants who made poor decisions, now he becomes the know-it-all who knows what it's like to be a contestant and scoffs at the ideas of others who haven't had this experience. Most of us have made such lateral moves, letting our experience expand our knowledge, but in ways that leave our understanding of ourselves fundamentally unchanged.

I once heard someone lament, "If experience is the best teacher, why don't I have a PhD?" We know that experience can have a huge impact on our lives. Yet we've all seen people who appear to have grown older without growing much wiser. Wisdom comes when we allow experience to transform us rather than merely inform us. But this wisdom requires that we allow the experience to reveal something about *ourselves*, something that we had missed before.

Of course it is possible to know ourselves better, to see ourselves more clearly. But it's difficult. I think what we commonly do is make small forays into self-knowledge and then retreat as the landscape becomes too unfamiliar or disconcerting. At times, we may retreat directly back into the mind-set that had initially been challenged.

I believe this is what happened to radio talk-show host Rush Limbaugh after his five-week treatment at a drug rehabilitation center. Limbaugh, archconservative and critic of political liberals, had grasped something important during his treatment: he had realized that people can and do have feelings and motives that influence their behavior without their awareness. For example, in his first program on the air after his treatment,

Limbaugh said, "I can no longer anticipate what I think people want and try to give that to them. I can no longer live my life trying to make people happy. I can no longer turn over the power of my feelings to anybody else, which is what I have done a lot in my life."[8] Limbaugh apparently came to question the powerlessness he had previously felt when he believed that he must live his life for others. In contrast, after his treatment, he was able to see that he had other options. This, I believe, was transformative for Rush Limbaugh.

But in applying the realization that people are sometimes guided by beliefs without knowing it, Limbaugh also made a merely lateral move. He realized, Rush related to his radio audience, that it was no use trying to convince Democrats that Republicans are good guys because Democrats have hidden motives and feelings that prevent them from being able to accept this truth about Republicans. Limbaugh applied his insight—that people can have beliefs that distort their perceptions—to Democrats, but he failed to apply it to his own political beliefs. He didn't seem to grasp that his own hidden motives and feelings could have distorted his perceptions of Democrats just as the hidden motives of some Democrats might distort their perceptions of Republicans.

My point here is not that Limbaugh is utterly wrong about the Democrats. I suspect that he is right. No doubt there are some Democrats with distorted views of Republicans, blind to the possibility that a member of the Republican Party could be both intelligent and ethical. Such Democrats have their own blind spots. But Rush, too, has his. At least at the time of his first program on-air after his treatment for addiction, I suspect that Rush Limbaugh wasn't quite ready to explore further this aspect of the newly discovered landscape of his inner life. Instead he used his newfound insights in the service of his old, familiar role as a critic of liberals and Democrats.

IN A NUTSHELL

The opening story describing the ministry student who, in his rush to deliver a sermon on the Good Samaritan, literally stepped over a person in need illustrates how utterly we can fail to see ourselves. Others often have a clearer view of us than we do ourselves, so getting their perspective could help us overcome this blind spot. But getting helpful feedback turns out to be more difficult than it first appears. Many of the tactics suggested in this chapter involve ways to obtain useful feedback. Other tactics focus on challenging the perceptions we have about ourselves, especially our beliefs about the degree of power we have. The question that rang throughout the United States after the September 11, 2001, terrorist attacks, "Why do they hate us?" shows that nations, as well as individuals, can have blind spots that make it hard to see themselves clearly.

SNEAK PREVIEW

We know how hard it is to see ourselves, yet we are repeatedly surprised by evidence of this blind spot. I think we are continually amazed because the distorted beliefs, or the counterproductive actions, of others are so obvious to us. If only they could see themselves from *our* perspective! This, it turns out, is very difficult to do. Shifting perspectives doesn't come naturally to us. And this isn't true only when we are trying to see ourselves from a different perspective. It's also hard for us to look at a point on a map, an object on a table, a novel or a play, a problem at work from multiple perspectives. This difficulty in seeing alternative viewpoints creates the blind spot that we'll look at in the next chapter.

NOTES

1. John M. Darley and C. Daniel Batson, "'From Jerusalem to Jericho': A Study of Situational and Dispositional Variables in Helping Behavior," *Journal of Personality and Social Psychology* 27 (1973): 100–108.

2. Ibid., p. 107.

3. Thanks to "Cathy," a student in my critical-thinking class who wished to remain anonymous, for her reflections.

4. Eric Maisel, *Fearless Creating: A Step-by-Step Guide to Starting and Completing Your Work of Art* (New York: Putnam, 1995).

5. Martin Seligman, *Learned Optimism: How to Change Your Mind and Your Life* (New York: Simon and Schuster, 1998).

6. Robert Kegan and Lisa Lahey, *How the Way We Talk Can Change the Way We Work* (San Francisco: Jossey-Bass, 2001), p. 85.

7. Robert Kegan, *In over Our Heads: The Mental Demands of Modern Life* (Cambridge, MA: Harvard University Press, 1996), p. 163.

8. Arian Campo-Flores and Evan Thomas, "Rehabbing Rush," *Newsweek*, May 8, 2006, p. 28.

Chapter 6

DON'T GIVE A CAT CALENDAR TO A DOG LOVER!

BLIND SPOT #5: MY-SIDE BIAS

Once I attended a live broadcast of the radio show *Whad'Ya Know?* Just before airtime, the program's host, Michael Feldman, came out and asked how we would respond when he posed a question during the program. "For example," he said, "how would you answer if I asked how many of you have never attended a live radio program before?" About two-thirds of us raised our hands. Scanning the sea of hands, Michael nodded and asked, "How well is raising your hands going to work for a radio show?" As his point dawned on us, we began to laugh—but our laughter was pretty subdued because we also felt a little stupid for failing to consider that radio listeners would not see our raised hands.

LOOKING MAINLY FROM OUR OWN POINT OF VIEW

People naturally see the world from their own perspective. When our children were young, their father and I discovered that when they were in a certain section of the basement, the sounds of their playing floated up through the heating vent into our living room. One day, as I was reading on the couch near that vent, I was astonished by how clearly I could hear every word they were saying. For a few minutes, I listened intently. But then I felt sneaky, eavesdropping like this. So when they scrambled up the stairs and dashed into the living room demanding lunch, I divulged the secret: "You know, when you're playing in the corner of the basement, Daddy and I can hear every word you're saying through this vent." I thought they'd be surprised, but they weren't. They just shrugged their shoulders. "We know," they said. "We hear you and Daddy talking, too."

I was shocked. I tried to remember exactly what their father and I might have talked about in some of those "private" conversations on the couch. It hadn't occurred to me that they could overhear us just as well as we could overhear them, though this was obvious as soon as they mentioned it. How difficult it must be for us to take a perspective different from our own if something this apparent eludes us!

It's easy to see that young children have a hard time taking the perspective of other people. The tableau of a preschooler nodding her head vigorously while she's talking on the telephone to Grandma is the classic example of this tendency. "*Tell* Grandma yes," her parents admonish. "She can't see you nod your head." But my stunned realization that my children could also hear me through the vent is a vivid reminder that adults also forget to consider the perspectives of other people.

CAUSES: THE POWER OF "MY-SIDE BIAS"

I think that we have underestimated just how difficult it is for us to become aware of other points of view and how hard it is to keep them in mind after we notice them. John Flavell, a developmental psychologist who spent decades studying how children develop the ability to understand different perspectives, puts it this way: "Our own perspectives produce clear signals that are much louder to us than [the signals from other people], and they usually continue to ring in our ears while we try to [understand other views]. . . . It may take considerable skill and effort to represent another's point accurately through this kind of noise, and the possibility of . . . distortion is ever present."[1]

Even when we do notice other viewpoints, we often ignore them. As critical thinking researchers Patricia King and Karen Kitchener put it, it's as if we notice other perspectives out of the corners of our eyes and immediately set them aside—we don't really deal with them.[2] Dominated by our own standpoint, we simply fail to give alternative viewpoints more than a passing glance.

Intellectually, in the abstract, we all *know* that people can look at issues from many different standpoints. Intellectually, we even concede that at least some of the perspectives that differ from our own have something to offer—a new slant on the problem or an insightful notion. We may even, like the law students in David Perkins's study described in chapter 2, be perfectly capable of bringing these opposing perspectives to our minds. Yet we persist in focusing on our own viewpoint, a tendency that Perkins calls *my-side bias*.[3] This my-side bias acts like a default setting. It overrides our intellectual understanding that different interpretations of events and different opinions about them are highly likely so that we revert to seeing the world from our own point of view even after acknowledging opposing positions.

Sometimes, of course, we can't ignore opposing perspectives. What happens then? Well, at times—like the audience attending the radio program—we recognize our blind spot, accept it in good humor, and adjust. In the radio audience, we adjusted by clapping our hands, rather than raising them, in response to questions from the host. At other times, when we grasp a different perspective, the light dawns and we say, "Oh, I see." It may take just a little explaining from a co-worker, for example, for us to understand why a new procedure is being required. Or perhaps a friend in human resources coaches us on how to prepare for a great job interview, and we appreciate for the first time that we need to think more about the perspective of the company and the person interviewing us. In these sorts of scenarios, we become aware that we have had a blind spot, and we grasp the alternative perspective fairly easily, then we adapt to it.

All this seems reasonable. But in many situations, we don't seem to react in this reasonable way. We either persist in ignoring the very existence of the viewpoints that don't mesh with our own, or we simply reject them outright as wrong.

A father orders college catalogs for his son in hopes that the boy will choose one of the better colleges. The father sees this as an act of caring; the son condemns it as controlling. A daughter lies over the phone to her mother's boss so that he won't find out that her mom is too drunk to go to work. The daughter sees her lie as an act of loyalty; a counselor laments it is enabling her mother's drinking. As psychologist David Levy points out, the very language we choose not only reflects the different interpretations we make of other people's behavior but also implies our moral judgments.[4] Is the other person greedy or ambitious? Pushy or assertive? Rigid or steadfast? Intrusive or concerned?

Or is the same action both caring *and* controlling? Taking alternative perspectives seriously draws us into a more complicated world. It's unsettling to have to come to grips with this complexity. We'd rather convince the person whose perspective contradicts our own that they are simply wrong. The scenario of artist Katherine, mulling over her painting from her chair, comes back to my mind. But now I picture Katherine hauling her chair across the room to a different spot, trying to see her work from a different angle. This image reminds me that appreciating a different perspective requires effort. I'm comfortable in my chair, and I think I can see the world quite adequately from the view that I have, thank you very much. When others are trying to get me to see their perspective, it's as if they're waving to me from across the room, shouting, "Come on over here!" And I don't want to. I'd be much more willing for them to come to me. Then they could *tell* me about their view while I nod but continue to hold comfortably onto mine, secretly believing that our disagreements would dissolve if I could just get them to see it my way. I don't want to have to grapple with the possibility that I may be wrong or only partially right.

TACTICS: WHAT HELPS US TO TRULY SEE ANOTHER PERSON'S PERSPECTIVE?

What can we do to counterbalance this tendency? How can we detect when this blind spot is holding us captive?

Tactic #1: Listen for the "Stupid" Judgment

Here are some comments that people typically make when what others are thinking or doing makes no sense to them:

- "I'll never understand him!"
- "Why would she do that? It makes no sense at all!"
- "How can people think that way? I can't figure it out."

When we make statements like these, we are usually implying that the person we are shaking our heads about must be stupid. But if we are truly clueless about how or why anyone could think or behave in that way, then *we* must have a blind spot. We are unable to grasp some alternative point of view that would make sense of what the other person is saying or doing or thinking. So noticing that we are judging others in this way is a sign to us that this blind spot is at play.

What would it take for us to be able to truly understand that person's perspective? We need to see the world through their eyes. We need a certain insight, something different from the bald facts of the matter. To truly see the world through a different lens, to "really" know what it looks like to another person, entails more than an intellectual exercise. It requires that we use not only our analytical and logical thinking skills but also our imaginations.

"REALLY" KNOWING: THE POWER OF PERSONAL, EXPERIENTIAL KNOWLEDGE

In his 1968 novel, *Cancer Ward*, Alexander Solzhenitsyn describes what happens to a physician, Dontsova, when she discovers she has cancer:

> Dontsova had never imagined that something she knew inside and out and so thoroughly could change to the point where it became entirely new and unfamiliar. For thirty years she had been dealing with other peoples' illnesses, and for a good twenty she had sat in front of the X-ray screen. She had read the screen, read the film, read the distorted, imploring eyes of her patients.
>
> . . . She had written articles and argued with colleagues. . . . In her mind, medical theory grew increasingly coherent . . . etiology, pathogenesis, symptoms, diagnosis . . . prognosis . . . all these were real enough. The doctor might have sympathy with the patient's resistance, doubts and fears; these were understandable human weaknesses, but they didn't count for anything when it came to deciding which method should be used. There was no place left for such feelings in the squares of logic . . . then, suddenly . . . her own body had fallen . . . and was now like a helpless sack crammed with organs—organs which might at any moment be seized with pain and cry out. Within a few days everything had been turned inside out. Her body was, as before, composed of parts she knew well, but the whole was unknown and frightening.[5]

Dontsova knew about her body and about disease before she became ill. She even knew, in an intellectual way, about her patients' thoughts and feelings as they went through treatment. But until she herself was struck, she had never "really" known what it was like to hear a diagnosis of cancer.

When people talk about how personal experiences change them, they say things like, "Once I believed *x*, but now I realize . . . ," or "What I *really* learned from this was . . ." This personal knowledge has the power to dramatically alter the way we view the world. We say things like, "I'll never be quite the same again," or "I'll never look at *x* the same way that I did before." Certainly if Dontsova recovers from her cancer and returns to treating patients, she will never look on her patients' experience in quite the same way again.

In order to see the world through someone else's eyes, we need to gain this experiential knowledge without necessarily having the exact experiences ourselves. How can we do this?

Tactic #2: "Really" Listen to a Vivid Story

Sometimes we can walk in other people's shoes through conversations with them. If the person we are trying to understand can tell his story in a way that conveys his reality vividly to us, we may grasp more clearly what it is like to be him and why he feels or thinks in the way he does. But to do this, we need to practice "really listening," an art that author Tony Hillerman describes in his depiction of Jean Jacobs, one of the characters in his detective novel *Coyote Waits*:

> She was a talented listener. He had noticed it before. When you talked to this woman, she attended. She had all her antennae out, focused on the speaker. The world was shut out. Nothing mattered but the words she was hearing. Listening was ingrained in the Navajo culture. One didn't interrupt. One waited until the speaker was finished, gave him a moment or two to consider additions, or footnotes, or amendments, before one responded. But even Navajos too often listened impatiently. Not really listening, but framing their reply. Jean Jacobs really listened.[6]

When we really listen, we are trying to genuinely grasp what it would be like to be the other person. This is hard to do and is not our typical response to other people's stories. Philosopher Nel Noddings describes how a teacher is likely to think about a boy in her class who hates mathematics: "Aha, I think. Here is the problem. I must help this poor boy to love mathematics, and then he will do better at it." But what, asks Noddings, is the teacher doing when she says this? She is not trying to grasp how it would feel to be a student who hates mathematics. Instead, she imposes her reality onto the student, saying, "You will be just fine if only you learn to love mathematics."[7]

Isn't this what most of us do most of the time? To overcome this blind spot, we have to set aside our natural inclination to define problems in terms of our own experience and instead understand them in terms of the other person's perspective.

Tactic #3: Use Simulation Exercises and the Arts to Experience Unfamiliar Worlds

Sometimes we are able to grasp a different reality through the arts: we read a novel or watch a film that makes us realize for the first time what a worldview very different from our own might be like. An ophthalmologist once described to me how upset he was when a patient, who had had cataracts from birth, complained about the results of her surgery. In his mind, the operation had been a phenomenal success. There were intricacies involved in her condition that made the surgery particularly tricky, yet he had executed a near-perfect performance. He was so proud of his work that he had written several of his colleagues to tell them about it and was planning to write a journal article describing his triumph.

But instead of being grateful, his patient complained bitterly during follow-up appointments: she couldn't make sense of what she was seeing; light was too bright; it was all confusing; she had been better off with the cataracts. To the physician, this woman's reactions were inexplicable—until he attended *Molly Sweeney* by playwright Brian Friel, a play whose main character has an experience similar to that of the ophthalmologist's patient.[8] Glimpsing the reality of what the world looked like to the character in the play, he was able to grasp his patient's dilemma and have empathy for her.

Simulation exercises in which we temporarily experience what it might be like to be blind or in a wheelchair are aimed at creating just this sort of quasi-experiential knowledge. As in film, dance, literature, or painting, simulation experiences that manage to convey another person's experience to us are a powerful means of overcoming our blindness to alternative perspectives.

Tactic #4: Ask Yourself, "When Have I, Too, Felt This Way?"

When I read Franz Kafka's novella *The Metamorphosis*, I had a hard time with it.[9] The book annoyed me. I mean, the main character is a man who awakens one day to find that he has turned into a huge bug, a helpless bug at that. "This is stupid," I thought. In a chance conversation with Fran, one of the literature professors at my college, I confided my feelings about the book. "But Madeleine," Fran said, commenting on the emotions experienced by the bug, "haven't you ever felt that way?" Her question took me aback. The answer was that I had felt exactly like that, and I had a name for the experience. I called it depression. Now I could view the book as a story about depression and its accompanying feelings of frustration and helplessness, instead of seeing it as a story about a bug. In fact, now I could understand why the book annoyed me so: I had always been impatient with myself when I succumbed, even for a few days, to depression. I was impatient with others, too. When they acted like the bug in the book, I wanted them to snap out of it, which was exactly how I felt about the bug.

When we have a hard time seeing the world through the perspective of another person, it sometimes helps to ask when in our own lives we have had similar feelings. The situations may be very different on the surface, but the similar emotions might allow us to connect with the other person's experience.

Tactic #5: What Common Ground Do We Share?

Sometimes, despite genuine struggles to understand and empathize with another person's position, we remain at an impasse. Abortion is one example of an area in which it may seem that there is no way to find common ground. When one individual, for example, views a fetus as human, while another does not, how can they find any common ground from which to discuss the issue? In his book *God's Politics: Why the Right Gets It Wrong and the Left Doesn't Get It*, liberal activist and evangelical minister Jim Wallis suggests that we can still discover shared values and shared goals that can allow people to work together, even on issues as volatile as abortion. Wallis writes, "Couldn't both pro-life and pro-choice political leaders agree to common ground actions that would actually reduce the abortion rate, rather than continue to use abortion mostly as a political symbol? Instead of imposing rigid pro-choice and pro-life political litmus tests, why not work together on teen pregnancy, adoption reform, and real alternatives for women who are backed into dangerous and lonely corners?"[10] Certainly most individuals, whether pro-life or pro-choice, do not want to see teenage girls becoming mothers, or women routinely using abortion as the first line of birth control, or desperate women sent to prison. We could talk about how best to minimize outcomes that no one considers desirable and how to maximize those that nearly everyone would favor. If, for example, we lament the poverty that plagues many single mothers, we can move away from dead-end discussions about the abortion issue and focus on supporting initiatives that address the poverty itself, such as programs to make childcare affordable for mothers who need to work and programs that enable them to go to school in order to improve the financial future of their families. We can work together on these kinds of shared goals even when we cannot agree about other aspects of the issue.

WIDENING THE CIRCLE: HOW WE REACT WHEN *WE* ARE MISUNDERSTOOD

We misunderstand others, but they also misunderstand us. What judgments do we make when someone else is unable to see *our* perspective? Well, we round up the usual suspects. We decide that if the people who fail to see our viewpoint aren't stupid, then they are flawed in some way. If, for example, they make a remark that insults us, and we can't attribute their remark to ignorance or "stupidity," then we decide that they must be insensitive, mean-spirited, or self-absorbed.

A friend warned me that people would treat me differently if I let my hair go gray. A few months after I had stopped coloring my hair, I had nearly forgotten her remark when I met a young nurse during a visit to my doctor. I was carrying a copy of a book written for children by Louis

Sachar, the author of the prize-winning novel *Holes* that was made into a popular movie.[11] I had been so taken by *Holes* that I decided I wanted to read more of Sachar's work, so I was carrying another book of his that day. The title of this book—*There's a Boy in the Girls' Bathroom!!*—and the picture on the cover made it clear that this was a children's book. The nurse spotted it and commented, "I see you're reading something." I started to tell her about Sachar. "Yes," I responded, "it's really a children's book . . ." But before I could finish my sentence, she patted my hand and said, "That's all right, dear. Whatever keeps your mind active."

Now, it's very tempting to label her behavior as rude, insensitive, or insulting. Yet it was clear to me in her other words and actions that she was trying to conduct herself in a considerate, caring manner. She acted as she did, not because she was uncaring, but because she had a blind spot. Empathy requires two elements: a genuine caring about the other person and the ability to see the world through the other person's eyes. It's perfectly possible to be empathic but still trip up because we are blind to another person's perspective. We can see this demonstrated in research involving children.

Preschoolers can be very empathic. Young toddlers barely out of babyhood will try to help another child who is crying.[12] But since they are also trapped in their own viewpoint, the actions that they take to help can be a bit off the mark. In one study, a thirteen-month-old baby, Lisa, tried to help another child who was in distress. Both of their mothers were sitting nearby. Which mother do you suppose Lisa tried to lead the crying child to? As adults, we'd understand that the crying child would want his own mother. This was lost on Lisa; she kept steering the little friend toward her own mother instead of the little friend's mother. Lisa couldn't grasp the other child's perspective, but she clearly was not self-absorbed or lacking in empathy.

In their daily lives, many people are quick to conclude that someone who fails to appreciate their perspective is insensitive or uncaring. In her books on communication, Deborah Tannen argues that women often seek what she calls "troubles talk."[13] In a troubles-talk conversation, I would tell another person about my problems simply so that I won't feel so alone with my situation, so that I would have the sense that someone else understands how I feel. In contrast, men often react to "troubles talk" by trying to help the person solve the problem.

If I'm a female seeking the comfort of "troubles talk" and my male colleague responds with problem-solving advice, I'm likely to feel frustrated or dismayed. I may find his response unfathomable—it is so clearly *not* what I need at that moment; it is obviously not the right response. He must, therefore, be stupid not to realize this. Or if not stupid, then insensitive, arrogant, or so full of himself that he holds forth with advice at every opportunity.

Similarly, if I'm a male who comes to a meeting hoping to make headway in solving a problem at work, I'm likely to feel frustrated if the female team leader spends time sympathizing with the people describing the problem instead of trying to do something about it. I may well find *her* behavior inexplicable. Hand-holding is so clearly *not* what we need at this juncture. It's obvious to me that the team needs to spend time solving the problem, not commiserating. *She*, therefore, must be stupid not to grasp this—or, if not stupid, then a poor team leader, inefficient, or unproductive.

What I won't usually assume is that the other person simply has a blind spot. Even more rarely will I appreciate that while *they* are missing something important (what I see, what I realize) *I*, too, may be missing something important (what they see, what they realize). I once caught a brief segment of a documentary on communication in which Deborah Tannen's ideas about troubles talk and problem-solving talk were highlighted. In one scene, a dismayed man stared at the camera and declared, "I don't understand why she would get mad when I'm trying to help her. If you love someone, why *wouldn't* you want to try to help them solve the problem that they're telling you is troubling them so much?" In his words, you could see his blind spot to his wife's need for "troubles talk," but you could also see her blinders. She could not see how his advice giving and problem solving reflected his caring. Acknowledging that, at times, we all have the blind spot of not seeing the perspective of another person can make it easier for both of us to keep listening.

GLITCHES: THE DANGER OF UNDERSTANDING THOSE WHO ARE POLES APART

In one of my courses, students are required to write what I call a "poles-apart" paper. For this paper, students are instructed to investigate a way of life, an attitude, or a set of beliefs that is poles apart from their own. I give them free rein in choosing a topic. As a result, a public school teacher discussed home schooling, a born-again Christian explored Scientology, an Iowa farm boy wrote about city pimps, a teacher investigated the use of drugs for children's hyperactivity, a staunch supporter of President George W. Bush's decision to wage war on Iraq considered the opposing views of Quakers, and a pro-choice woman explored the issue of abortion.

The first time I introduced this project, I was taken aback by the resistance of the students to doing this assignment. Here I was, faced with the same highly motivated, intelligent graduate students I had always encountered, students who I knew from experience could churn out papers comparing and contrasting different points of view without blinking an eye. Why were they so leery of this assignment?

The answer was in the way this assignment differed from typical research papers. As in traditional sorts of papers, the students had to be sure that they fully understood the topic, in this case the position that was poles apart from their own. For example, the student who wrote about Scientology had to learn about the Church of Scientology and its history, philosophy, rationale, and major beliefs. But the poles-apart paper was different in that the primary goal of learning about the opposite pole was not to evaluate it in an analytical way, but to try to grasp how it was possible for someone else to see the world so differently. To use Nel Noddings's phrase about the mathematics teacher and the bored pupil, the goal was for my students to try to grasp the reality of "the other" for themselves.

This meant that they needed to locate published personal accounts of people's experiences or to conduct personal interviews with others in order to try to see the world through other eyes: the eyes of the home-schooling parent, the member of the Church of Scientology, the pimp, the parent who opposed Ritalin, the person who opposed abortion, or the anti-war Quaker. In contrast to a more typical assignment, the aim of the paper was not to create a debate that one or the other side could ostensibly win, but to search for ways to understand how someone very different from oneself views the world.

It was this aspect of the assignment that triggered my students' uneasiness. On some level they recognized, as I had not when I first conceived of the project, that to really see the other side is potentially dangerous. Because they sensed this danger, people who could sail through a traditional paper in which the pros and cons of a controversial issue are dissected were very hesitant about undertaking the poles-apart assignment. Slowly I began to understand why they felt so cautious. If we actually succeed in understanding how someone else could believe, think, live in ways that are deplorable or offensive to us, what will that do to the values that led us to pass judgment on these opposite poles in the first place? If their perspective actually makes us realize that we have been somewhat off in how we have seen the world, what else will that realization call into question? How will that change *our* lives?

What many of my students feared was that they might be jeopardizing the values that they held most precious, including the ethical system or faith to which they adhered. They had the intuition that the more clearly they were able to grasp the pole apart, the more difficult it might be for them to judge that perspective as wrong. Once we really see the world from a viewpoint that is poles apart from our own, once even the most repellent actions or lifestyles or beliefs become understandable to us, how can we judge them to be wrong? Will we lose the capacity to conclude that one position is more morally acceptable than another? If we live in the gray world of multiple perspectives, will we utterly lose our moral compass?

This appears to be what happened to a college student who was asked, in an interview, if she believed that what Hitler did was morally right or wrong:

> STUDENT: Well, from my point of view I would say that what Hitler did was morally terrible. . . . Are you asking me if what he did was morally right or wrong?
>
> INTERVIEWER: Yeah.

> STUDENT: Well, I could say it would be morally wrong from my point of view. . . . They . . . it's terrible to say this, but they were doing what they thought was right.
>
> INTERVIEWER: Was he right or was he wrong? He believed he was right, so was he?
>
> STUDENT: No—'cause I'm looking at it from my point of view. But if you asked Hitler, he would say yes. You can't . . . see . . . there's no absolute. It depends on your frame of reference.[14]

This student, as clear as she is about her personal conviction that what Hitler did was terrible, is unable to pass a more general moral judgment on his actions. It's as if her realization that an action or a belief can look different to another person has led her to a sort of moral paralysis.

It seems to me that the student struggling with the Hitler question is in exactly the same position as the individuals who declare, "One man's terrorist is another man's freedom fighter." Such individuals have experienced the startling realization that others can view the world very differently from the way they do, and that realization makes it seem impossible to pass judgment on any person, ideology, or action. Harvard professor and educational researcher William Perry found that students sometimes experience this moral paralysis as they develop intellectually and ethically.[15] Fortunately, the paralysis is usually temporary. Eventually, most students move beyond it. They realize that they can understand the worldview that made Hitler's actions seem right to him, without agreeing that his actions actually were therefore defensible or right.

We can have empathy for the serial murderer, the rapist, the child molester, the inside trader, the accountant who shreds documents, the government official who lies under oath, or the spouse who deceives, without deciding that the person should not be held accountable for those actions. It is possible for us to go to great lengths to understand perspectives different from our own without necessarily endangering the moral compass that guides us. In fact, some moral philosophers have argued that our capacity to see another person's perspective is the true basis both of our emotional connection to that person and of our own morality.

In her book *Upheavals of Thought*, University of Chicago philosopher Martha Nussbaum argues that emotions are essential to morality because emotions are linked to empathy. Nussbaum writes, "All normal humans can imagine what it is like to be in the shoes of another. . . . [This kind of thinking] is fundamental to human emotional and moral life . . . [because it is] fundamental to our capacity for compassion and love."[16] An empathic understanding of others can lead to moral action rather than to moral paralysis.

Living in Gradations of Gray

It's much easier to make ethical decisions in a world where the good guys and the bad guys are clearly marked. When our granddaughter, Claudia, was three years old, she and I were browsing through a store when she spotted a Civil War display of soldiers. The blue soldiers and the gray soldiers were lined up in a glass case, arranged to attack one another in this "game" of war. Claudia asked me, "Which ones are the good guys?" How could I answer such a question? In real life, soldiers on both sides generally see themselves as the good guys. It takes great courage to come to grips with the reality that our cause may not consist of pure righteousness and that our enemies do not represent pure evil.

In the current Israeli-Palestinian conflict, for example, some Israeli reservists began to refuse to fight in areas beyond the 1967 borders of Israel. As of March 6, 2002, 314 reservists had signed a document that began, "We, reserve combat officers and soldiers of the Israel Defense Forces, who were raised on the principles of Zionism, sacrifice, and giving to the people of Israel and the State of Israel, who have always served in the front lines, and who were the first to carry out any mission, light or heavy, in order to protect the State of Israel and strengthen it . . . hereby declare that we shall not continue to fight this War of Settlements. . . . We shall not continue to fight beyond the 1967 borders in order to dominate, expel, starve, and humiliate an entire people."[17]

To take such a stand—a stand that will be seen by many Israeli citizens as disloyal, as endangering the liberty of Israel, as playing right into the hands of the Palestinian enemy—is extremely difficult. You can hear how tortuous the route to arriving at this decision must have been in phrases like

"We, whose eyes have seen the bloody toll this Occupation exacts from both sides. . . . We, who sensed how the commands issued to us in the Territories, destroy all the values we had absorbed while growing up in this country." No, it's not easy. It's not easy to know what is the right thing to do in such situations, and it's not easy to do it once you believe that you know it. Through such actions, you may estrange yourself from your own family and alienate yourself from the people who were your closest friends.

On the other hand, overcoming my-side bias so that we can see the other perspective more clearly can be a great source of hope. The empathy that we acquire can help us resolve chronic conflicts whose toll in human suffering is incalculable. The broader perspective that we gain can reveal the common ground that we share with those poles apart from ourselves. It takes effort to hold onto the different viewpoints, to juggle them rather than let one go in favor of another. But the insights we gain from doing this can be tremendously freeing, even revolutionary, in their impact.

Juggling Perspectives

Psychologist Michael Basseches uses the term *dialectical thinking* to describe the ability to juggle two contradictory realities while trying to make sense of them.[18] One example that he offers shows how juggling different perspectives can be liberating. Basseches describes a situation in which an adult daughter has rejected some of the values that her mother tried so hard to impart to her. How might the mother react? She could decide that her own values are right, while her daughter's new values are wrong. In this case, she's likely to grieve: "I have failed as a mother, since I have failed to impart my most treasured values to my daughter." Or the mother could decide that her daughter's values are right, while her own values are wrong. In this case, she is faced with the depressing conclusion that her own life has been misguided.

What if, instead, this mother places her perspective and her daughter's perspective on the same page and steps back from both of them, no longer trapped by either? She may discover that her daughter's values, while different from her own, have incorporated many of her ideals in a different form, one perhaps more adapted to the times or the life that her daughter leads. The mother may be able to see her own values as valid for her life and times, while at the same time realizing that in some ways those values were too narrow or limited. She might also learn something from her daughter's values, something that leads her to transform the values that she holds, deepening them rather than abandoning them.

When I read the poles-apart papers that my students had written, I was struck by the courage and the integrity with which they grappled with this assignment. One student, who was a staunch believer in sexual abstinence as the solution to teen pregnancies and sexually transmitted diseases, described how she went about trying to understand the other pole. When she found materials advocating safe sex rather than sexual abstinence, she realized that she was discounting all the arguments proposed in these appeals because she suspected that their authors held biases that fueled their contentions. For example, despite the claim of the safe-sex advocates that they wanted to protect adolescents from disease and unwanted pregnancies, she suspected that their real agenda was to advance a secular view of sexuality as a pleasure that should be indulged in without any moral restraints. It dawned on her that the only way she would truly be able to be open to the opposite pole would be if those views were espoused by someone whom she genuinely respected. So she searched for, and found, such a person to interview—a fellow teacher at her school. This student genuinely sought to understand the other pole. My experiences with students like her convince me that people can and do come to terms with positions poles apart from their own in ways that transform them—without necessarily sacrificing the values most dear to them.

What did happen to the students whose values seemed threatened by the very act of carrying out the assignment? In most cases, these students found that the ground shifted, but the foundations of their worlds didn't crumble entirely. Indeed, those foundations were often strengthened as they became more thoughtful about why they believed what they believed and more aware of the complexity surrounding those beliefs.

IN A NUTSHELL

The story of the radio show audience members raising their hands to answer questions illustrates the blind spot of not being able to see another person's perspective. Overcoming this blind spot involves the ability to gain experiential knowledge. In contrast to simply knowing factual information, we need to grasp through our imagination what the world is like to other people. The strategies that can help us do this include really listening, engaging in simulation exercises, and entering alien worlds through film, fiction, or other art forms. This blind spot has an especially powerful impact on our relationships with others since it influences how we understand or fail to understand them. It seems that being more understanding would be a good thing, yet we sometimes strongly resist truly experiencing the viewpoint of another person. We do this because we fear that to genuinely understand a view poles apart from our own might call our own ethical beliefs into question. Once we understand what is at stake for us, we can discover ways of resolving that dilemma.

SNEAK PREVIEW

When the nurse patted my hand to assure me that it was okay for me to read children's books to "keep my mind active," she was clearly operating under a stereotype of ageism. She apparently viewed anyone with gray hair as likely to be declining in intellectual keenness. We wouldn't engage in ageism if we didn't classify people as old. This leads some people to argue that we should never classify people—yet it is just as natural for us to classify people as it is for us to classify types of pasta or breeds of dogs. In the next chapter, we take a look at the strong inclination human beings have to classify what we observe. Gregor Mendel provides a great example of the upside of this tendency. Mendel noticed patterns in the offspring of the pea plants that he cross-pollinated. Wondering about those patterns ultimately led Mendel to his genetic theory of dominant and recessive genes. But as the nurse's misjudgment of me shows, categorization can also lead us astray. We can be trapped by the very categories that we create. That blind spot is the subject of the next chapter.

NOTES

1. John Flavell, *Cognitive Development*, 2nd ed. (Englewood Cliffs, NJ: Prentice-Hall, 1985).

2. Patricia King and Karen Strohm Kitchener, *Developing Reflective Judgment* (San Francisco: Jossey-Bass, 1995).

3. D. Perkins and S. Tishman, "Dispositional Aspects of Intelligence" (unpublished paper, 1998), pp. 1–45.

4. David Levy, *Tools of Critical Thinking: Metathoughts for Psychologists* (Boston: Allyn and Bacon, 1997), p. 4.

5. Alexander Solzhenitsyn, *Cancer Ward* (New York: Modern Library, 1983), pp. 449–50.

6. Tony Hillerman, *Coyote Waits* (New York: Harper, 1992), p. 149.

7. Nel Noddings, *Caring: A Feminine Approach to Ethics and Moral Education* (Berkeley: University of California Press, 1984), p. 15.

8. Brian Friel, *Molly Sweeney* (Old Castle, CO: Gallery Books, 1995).

9. Franz Kafka, *The Metamorphosis and Other Stories* (New York: Penguin, 1992).

10. Jim Wallis, *God's Politics: Why the Right Gets It Wrong and the Left Doesn't Get It* (HarperSanFrancisco, 2005).

11. Louis Sachar, *Holes* (New York: Farrar, Straus and Giroux, 1998).

12. Martin L. Hoffman, "Developmental Synthesis of Affect and Cognition and Its Implications for Altruistic Motivation," in *Social and Personality Development: Essays on the Growth of the Child*, ed. William Damon, 258–77 (New York: Norton, 1983).

13. Deborah Tannen, *You Just Don't Understand!* (New York: Harper, 2001).

14. B. Clinchy and C. Zimmerman, "Epistemology and Agency in the Development of Undergraduate Women," in *The Undergraduate Woman: Issues in Educational Equity*, ed. P. Perun, 161–81 (Boston: D. C. Heath, 1981), p. 167.

15. William Perry, *Forms of Intellectual and Ethical Development in the College Years: A Scheme* (New York: Holt, Rinehart, and Winston, 1970).

16. Martha Nussbaum, *Upheavals of Thought: The Intelligence of Emotions* (Cambridge, MA: Cambridge University Press, 2001), p. 146.

17. "Courage to Refuse—Combatant's Letter," http://www.seruv.org.il/defaulteng.asp (accessed April 25, 2006).

18. Michael Basseches, *Dialectical Thinking and Adult Development* (Norwood, NJ: Ablex, 1984).

Chapter 7
THINKING INSIDE THE BOX

BLIND SPOT #6: TRAPPED BY CATEGORIES

Imagine that a wealthy man who is part of a scavenger hunt rings your doorbell in the middle of the night. He asks if you have the final item on his list, a piece of wood that measures about three-by-seven feet. So intent is he on winning this hunt that he offers you ten thousand dollars if you can provide this item. Harvard professor and psychologist Ellen Langer describes this hypothetical scene in her book *Mindfulness*.[1] Would you be able to win the ten thousand dollars in this situation?

Langer's answer to this question is "probably yes." Nearly everyone has wood that meets these specifications in his homestead. But most of us would probably not get the ten thousand dollars, because we wouldn't realize that we were standing right next to the needed item. We'd fail to see that any wooden door in our home would work. We'd miss it because people are, as Langer puts it, "trapped by categories."

In his intriguing book, *Panati's Extraordinary Origins of Everyday Things*, Charles Panati tells the story of marine engineer Richard James.[2] James was experimenting with different delicate springs in an attempt to develop something that could be used to prevent sensitive nautical instruments from being affected by the pitching of ships. James was surprised by what happened when he accidentally knocked one of the springs off the shelf. Instead of falling to the floor, the spring crept, coil by coil, down a stack of books. James continued to see the spring as a coil that might help balance nautical instruments. His wife, however, saw something different. Not trapped in her husband's classification system, she saw the coil as something fun, and the Slinky was born.

Books on creativity are filled with stories like these to make the point that people would be more creative if they weren't so rigid in their thinking. In fact, creative thinking is often described as fluid, so creativity experts lament our tendency to think in inflexible categories. But categorical thinking is hardwired into human minds and tremendously useful to us.

"SORTING THINGS OUT" IS A NATURAL HUMAN TENDENCY

Human beings have a natural inclination to see patterns. One of the most basic patterns that we notice is "What is the same?" and "What is different?" We then group things that are the same together and separate them from things that are different. We see evidence of this skill in humans as young as twelve months old. At that age, babies spontaneously group similar objects together. In one study, researchers placed four different miniature horses and four different pencils in a mixed-up bunch in front of babies. The babies would begin to pick out all the members of one group, all the horses or all the pencils, and put them together in a pile. "By the time they were eighteen months old, babies would quite systematically and tidily sort the objects into two separate groups. . . . One particularly fastidious and precise little girl noticed that one of the pencils had lost its point. . . . [She made] a separate spot for this peculiar and defective object."[3]

This simple, basic process of noticing patterns and relationships—how things are similar, how they are different, what goes together—is a central component of our ability to think intelligently. Small children who have a category in their minds labeled "things that are hot" are less likely to get burned. Biologists able to create detailed taxonomies have helped us understand plant and animal kingdoms in new ways. If we were to encounter an alien culture, it would help us enormously if someone could relate what we were witnessing to categories that we already had in our heads. If someone would say, "Oh, that's a kind of food," or "That's a game they play," or "That's the way they appease their gods," some of what we were encountering would fall into place.

Noticing what is the same and what is different can be crucial in solving problems. In the story of kuru described in chapter 3, two anthropologists, Robert Glasse and Shirley Lindebaum, went to New Guinea to study what was causing this terrible disease. They sought the advice of epidemiologist R. W. Hornabrooke, and what he told them illustrates the usefulness of our ability to think categorically. Learning that the men of the village were unaffected by kuru, while women and children of both sexes were, Dr. Hornabrooke advised, "Find out what it is that adult women and children of both sexes in the Fore villages are doing that the adult men are not doing . . . and what the members [of adjacent tribes] are not doing either."[4] What is the same? What is different?—simple questions, the answers to which ultimately explained why adult Fore men and people of other tribes didn't suffer from this terrible disease, while adult Fore women and children of both genders did. We would lose an invaluable asset if we were to eliminate categorical thinking from our repertoire of intellectual abilities.

But there is a drawback to our impressive ability to sort things out. Our ability to categorize creates blind spots because classification systems are inherently reductionistic. The power of classification is precisely that it allows us to focus on one or two features and see something in terms of those characteristics alone. To classify plants and animals, we have to ignore all the variations that distinguish one plant from another and one animal from another. We have to focus only on those aspects that are shared by all plants and that differentiate them from all animals. We ignore the great variation that exists within each group and reduce its members to the common ground that ties all the members of that group together. As a result, we come to see objects in terms of their membership in a particular group, and we miss seeing that each is more than its group membership. Trapped by the category of doors, we become blind to the three-by-seven-foot pieces of wood that are right in front of us.

TACTICS: USING A SHIFTING KALEIDOSCOPE WHEN WE ARE TRAPPED BY CATEGORIES

Imagine that you are playing with Andy, a three-year-old boy, building towers out of painted blocks of different sizes, shapes, and colors. What will happen if you say to Andy, "Can you put all the blocks that are the same together?" Andy can do this. He is most likely to begin sorting the blocks by color, but he might use a different system. He might put blocks that are the same shapes or the same sizes together. However, a curious thing happens if, when he's finished, you once again ask Andy to put blocks that are the same together—"but in a different way." He doesn't get it. He can't figure out what it is that you want him to do. Trapped by seeing the blocks in terms of one category—color or size or shape—he can't shift gears and focus on a different perspective.

As children grow older, they become more able to shift perspectives. If we ask grade school children to tell us the different ways that these same blocks could be grouped, they'll have no problem. In contrast to young Andy, older children and adults are able to answer the question in fig. 7.1: "Now can you find two objects that are alike or go together, but *in a different way*?"

Fig. 7.1: Learning to Shift from One Category to Another

Find two objects that are alike or go together in some way.

Now can you find two objects that are alike or go together, but in a different way?

Tactic #1: Shift Categories—View the World through the Lenses of Different Classification Systems

In our everyday lives, we don't have that second question nudging us to look at objects or events in a different way. But if we would remind ourselves that the objects or events we are considering belong to various categories, then we could shift from one category to another and so restore some of the complexity that our first classification had oversimplified. There is a *Peanuts* cartoon in which Charlie Brown is chewing on his pencil as he squints at the history test on the desk in front of him. The question on the test is: "Explain the causes of World War II. You may use both sides of the paper if necessary." This cartoon is funny because we realize that it would be impossible to adequately explain the complicated causes of World War II on one sheet of paper—even if we were to use both sides! The causes of World War II are too complex; we know that we'd be ignoring all sorts of perspectives if we were to limit ourselves to such a tiny space. Whatever we wrote, even if it were correct, could not possibly capture the complex causes of that war.

In order to generate a more complete discussion of the causes of World War II, we could take the categories that we have learned about and, instead of being rigidly bound by them, use them like lenses that we can shift around in order to uncover multiple points of view. We can look through different lenses that reveal economic, social, historical, psychological, political, religious, and geographical factors. Once our awareness of the complexity involved has been restored, we won't mistake the first answer that occurs to us in response to fig. 7.1—that the horse and the zebra are alike or that the zebra and the striped shirt are alike—as the only answer. The big trick, I think, is to remember that we're intentionally ignoring different perspectives when we view anything through the lens of a classification system and to remind ourselves that there's likely much more complexity than we are focusing on at any one moment.

Tactic #2: Listen for the "Rhetoric of the Merely"

I once overheard a pilot "explain" how planes fly: "Well, that's just aerodynamics." Most of us talk like this at times, sometimes using a well-worn label that we've never really thought much about. For example, we may say, "That's just gravity," or "She's only doing that to get attention." Because we believe we've answered the question "What's that?" (That's "just" gravity) or "What's happening?" (She's "just" looking for attention), we don't bother to consider more deeply what we're trying to understand. We don't ask, "But what is gravity, really?" or "But doesn't everyone want attention? Why does she demand so much more attention than others do?"

Cultural anthropologist Mary Catherine Bateson describes this kind of talk as "the rhetoric of the merely."[5] She emphasizes that when people speak the rhetoric of the merely, they are discounting what they are referring to. By saying, "That's merely a ritual," or "That's just aerodynamics," they are ignoring the complexity of what they are discussing and reducing it to a label. If we listen for the rhetoric of the merely, we could let those little dismissive words ("That's *just* x," or "They *just* do that because . . .") become a warning flag. Words like *just* should remind us we may be reducing something very complex to a platitude or a simplistic label that hasn't been questioned for a long time.

In a BBC interview, theoretical physicist Michael Berry gave an example of the rhetoric of the merely among scientists. Sunlight creates a pattern of bright lines on the bottom of swimming pools. Berry argued that if someone had asked an optical scientist about those lines, the scientist would probably have begun by saying, "Oh! That's a rather trivial problem. It's just refraction of light. We all understand light refraction." But, Berry contends, if the questioner had pursued the issue, asking why the pattern was a particular way, with certain sorts of junctions of lines rather than others, the scientist wouldn't have been able to answer.[6]

Whenever we hear the brusque, dismissive tone of voice that rejects a question or an observation out of hand, our antennae should perk up. A voice in our head should whisper, "What if there's more to it than that? What if what everyone accepts isn't quite true? What if it didn't have to be this way?" Questions like these spur us to search for the complexity that our categorical label has temporarily concealed.

Tactic #3: Think "Outside the Box" by Seeing the Heart of the Matter

Finally, we can overcome the narrowness of the categories we use if we search for a more general answer to questions like "What is this?" and "What are we doing?" We want to find answers that go beyond the narrow confines of the little box we have used to classify objects or events. One anecdote describes a leader in the cosmetic industry asking her salespeople, "What does our company sell?" Cosmetics was not the answer she was looking for because the category of cosmetics didn't get to the heart of the matter. It didn't tap the more general idea of what the company was in the business of selling: the *real* products of the company were beauty and youth.

Often the most imaginative solutions to everyday problems involve overcoming narrow categories by seeing the heart of the matter. Felicity is unable to open her car doors after an icy rain freezes the door locks. She comes up with the idea of using her hair drier to direct hot air at the locks to melt the ice. She's able to do this when she thinks about the fact that what she really needs is a portable source of heat. This allows her to look at her hair dryer and see something more fundamental and more general than an instrument to dry hair. In the opening story of this chapter, the anecdote about the scavenger hunt is another example of how we could escape a narrow category by seeing to the heart of the matter. We'd be able to see that the doors in our homes were fundamentally pieces of wood.

When we are trying to solve a problem, asking the question "What do we *really* need here?" or "What is *really* going on here?" is useful. If we can reframe the situation and the objects we have at hand in terms of more general qualities that get to the heart of the matter, we won't be trapped so tightly in our categories.

WIDENING THE CIRCLE: TRAPPED BY CATEGORIES, WE CLASSIFY PEOPLE, TOO

A Jewish friend of mine living in a predominately Christian town volunteered to go to her child's school and explain Hanukkah to the children. The first grade teacher beamed as my friend entered the room, and then announced, "Children, I want you to welcome Aaron's mother, Mrs. Steinberg. Mrs. Steinberg is going to tell us today about Hanukkah, the Jewish Christmas."

Well, not quite. The teacher's comment may strike some people as ignorant, others as insensitive or demeaning. But this sort of comment about people is one downside of our tendency to think in categories. All of us use familiar categories to help us understand what is unfamiliar. To help them understand what zebras are, we tell children that a zebra is a horse with stripes. To help students grasp what free verse is, we tell them it is poetry that doesn't rhyme. Pigeonholing zebras and free verse in this way inevitably reduces their meaning, treating the new ideas as if they were merely different forms of what is already familiar to us. This is what the teacher did, reducing Hanukkah to nothing but a variation of what the children already knew, which was Christmas. It seems likely to me that her error was the result of a blind spot on her part, or an intentional attempt to simplify the concept for the children's benefit, rather than a deliberate slight to my friend or to her Jewish faith. Nevertheless, it's understandable that people react strongly when their group identities are reduced in this way.

Classification flattens our perception of individuals if we see them solely in terms of their group memberships: their identities as men or women, as blacks or whites, as Buddhists or Muslims, as Democrats or Republicans, as teachers or attorneys. That's why people resent it when others treat them stereotypically, even when the stereotype is a flattering one, like the stereotype of the Asian child as gifted in math. Moreover, classification ignores the complexity of the groups themselves. People label the groups that they create and then, speaking in the rhetoric of the merely, often act as though that group can be summed up in a few words. In addition, people resent being reduced to a group membership because there are always many ways in which they don't fit the stereotypes associated with that group. Even when a stereotype holds true statistically for the group as a whole, we don't want others to automatically assume that we, too, have that characteristic. For example, even if it is true that the great majority of CEOs of Fortune 500 companies are male, while the majority of their administrative assistants are female, female CEOs are understandably annoyed if someone assumes that they are administrative assistants.

Our annoyance at being stereotyped is, of course, greatest when the stereotype is negative. I once participated in a discussion with both sexes in which several women began their comments by saying, "*Men* . . ." And the tone of voice in which they said that word wasn't neutral; it had an eye-rolling, head-shaking, disdainful tinge, as in "Men always . . . ," or "Men think that . . ." After a while, one man in the group spoke up: "I would like to make a plea during this meeting. I'd like to ask the women here not to say *men* do this, and *men* do that, *men* are like this, and *men* are like that. Would you please say, 'some men,' or 'many men,' or even 'every man I've ever met'—but not just *men*? Would you please not lump all of us into one group?" He was reminding us that our classifying all males into a group that we called *men* blinded us to the individual differences among them. That's a major hitch related to our penchant for creating categories and classifying people.

Novelist Amin Maalouf writes in *In the Name of Identity*, "I don't know any two Lebanese Christians who are identical, nor any two Muslims, any more than there are anywhere in the world two Frenchmen, two Africans, two Arabs or two Jews who are identical. People are not interchangeable." Maalouf notes that nearly everyone would agree with this statement, yet we often act as though it were not true. For example, he writes that we says things like, "'The Serbs have massacred . . . ,' 'The English have devastated . . . ,' 'The Arabs refuse . . . ,'" thereby lumping together all members of these groups and ascribing to them "collective crimes, collective acts and opinions."[7]

Maalouf is acutely aware that every individual is complex and that no one's identity can be captured by the identification that he or she has with a single group. Maalouf was born in Lebanon and lived there until he was twenty-seven; he has lived in France for more than twenty years. As he expresses it, "Arabic is my mother tongue. . . . It was in Arabic translation that I first read Dumas and Dickens." Yet his identification with France is equally strong: "I drink her water and wine. . . . I write my books in her language; never again will she be a foreign country to me."[8] Maalouf describes how he would try to explain all this to people who would ask him whether he felt "more Lebanese" or "more French." But sometimes after hearing his remarks, his listeners would dismiss his insistence that he was both Lebanese *and* French. They would say, "Of course, of course. But what do you really feel, deep down inside?"

Maalouf no longer smiles in response to such comments because to him they seem to reflect a dangerous view of people's identities. They presuppose, he writes, "that 'deep down inside' everyone there is just one affiliation that really matters, a kind of 'fundamental truth' about each individual, an 'essence' determined once and for all at birth . . . [as if everything else that followed]—in short his life itself—counted for nothing."[9] This thinking is behind the demand that people choose who they really are when the different groups to which they belong are at odds with one another. In the American Civil War, young men in southern states were forced to choose between their allegiance to their country as a whole and their allegiance to the South, at times pitting brother against brother.

We humans have a long history of using our ability to differentiate one group from another in order to discriminate against, persecute, and demean members of all sorts of groups in unspeakable ways. The main thrust of Amin Maalouf's book is his contention that grounding our identities solely on our membership in a particular group—such as our German or French nationalism, or our Christian or Muslim religion, or our Hutu or Tutsi ethnicity—fuels the atrocities that are done in the name of patriotism, religion, or ethnic allegiances. We hear of terrible massacres, ethnic cleansings, and persecutions and wonder how human beings can be capable of such atrocities. Yet when we buy into the idea that our allegiance must be to a single group to which we see ourselves as first and foremost belonging to, we inadvertently, Maalouf writes, "contribute to the tragedies by which, tomorrow, we shall be genuinely shocked."[10]

"If Only We Could Stop Classifying People!"

Because our natural tendency to see people, including ourselves, in categories and groups can have such devastating effects, many well-intentioned people wish that we could somehow eradicate it. "If only," they say, "we could just see people, not different sorts of people whom we pigeonhole because of their gender, or race, or whatever." They reason that if we couldn't detect differences, or if we could somehow train ourselves not to see those differences, then we wouldn't diminish people by focusing solely or primarily on their membership in a particular group. For example, in an attempt to prevent race from affecting how they treat the children in their classrooms, some teachers declare that they don't see black and white at all. "We see only children," they assert.

Perhaps some are able to pull this off. But skin color—like gender and age—is such a conspicuous aspect of individuals and one that seems to matter so much in the United States that intentional efforts to ignore it feel contrived and unconvincing. Imagine a situation in which a child, Chris, has run from my classroom into the hall. I go into the corridor and glance in both directions but don't see Chris. I spot another teacher standing there. "Did you see Chris?" I ask her. Imagine that the teacher responds, "There were a few kids here a moment ago. Is Chris a boy or girl?" and I say, "I don't know. I don't notice gender. I just notice children as individuals." Such a response would strike us as bizarre. Like race, gender is conspicuous and gender matters—we can't eradicate the potential negative effects of noticing it by pretending that it's an insignificant aspect of who we are.

"We're all just people" represents a well-meaning, bighearted attempt to avoid the terrible repercussions that have too often been the offshoot of seeing differences among people. It does so by emphasizing our common ground. But it not only seems to be an impossible goal to attain, given our predilection for thinking categorically, but also defeats the very goals at which it is aimed. How can we embrace or celebrate diversity if we are trying, at the same time, to deny its existence? How can we validate the individual identities of each person if in the process we are panic-stricken at the thought of acknowledging the group memberships that are fundamental to most people's identities?

Instead of allowing us to see people more as individuals, this approach risks turning a blind eye to aspects of our identities that may be crucial to us. As author and law professor Harlon Dalton comments, "Personally, I don't want to be treated as a raceless individual. So much of who and what and how I am is the result of growing up Black and male in America. You can't begin to know me without taking my race into account."[11]

The child we classify as male or female, African American or Caucasian or Hispanic or Asian, won't be diminished by that label unless we reduce the child to nothing but that group—and reduce that group to nothing but a caricature of it. If we were able to make finer and finer cuts, if we were able to look at any given group of people in all its complexity, including its positive and negative features, we would restore the members of that group to a fuller version of their humanity. If we were able to look at any given child through a set of lenses that reflected *all* the different groups to which she belongs—such as "super reader" or "shy" or "pizza lover"—and all the variation within those groups, we would eventually end up with a unique individual. This would happen not because we had somehow pared the "real" child away from all the categories that describe her, but because we can now see her as a synthesis of the hundreds of facets that constitute her identity, that make her who she is.

Using Shifting Categories as Lenses to Look at People

It's impossible to do this completely. None of us can hold all the complex aspects of another person in mind simultaneously. Nor can we remain acutely and clearly aware of all the complexity that a label such as "Christian" or "Muslim" covers. What we can do, first, is use the same tactics described earlier that help us recover the complexity of objects and events and apply them to classifying people. We can notice when people are speaking the rhetoric of the merely. When someone explains another's actions by saying, "Well, what do you expect? He's a man, isn't he?" or "Just like a woman!" we can go on red alert that a person is being diminished.

Second, we can try to shift more often from one perspective to another. Just as we can overcome the narrowness of classification by viewing World War II through multiple lenses, we can use the identities of different groups to which people belong as lenses. I had a powerful personal experience of this kind when my college organized discussions among faculty, staff, and students and set up the discussion tables to ensure that each included African Americans and Caucasians, males and females. In the course of our conversation, a white male student asked the group to help him understand why a black student had gotten angry at him. He described an incident in which he and the black student, both members of the college track team, were in a buffet line. Watermelon had just come into season, and the white student said to his black comrade, "Hey! Look, watermelon! Aren't you glad to see that?" Based on the innocent confusion with which he told this story and asked his "What did I do wrong?" question, I was sure that this nineteen-year-old white student was genuinely baffled about why his remark might be offensive. Unlike me, he had no memory of the old *Our Gang* television programs and the films that portrayed simpleminded black folk playing harmonicas at picnics and savoring wedges of watermelon. I felt sympathy for him because I believed him to be genuinely ignorant, well intentioned, sincere, and even brave in his desire to learn what he had done wrong.

But he wasn't viewed sympathetically by one of the black females at the table. She reacted to him with disdain: "If you don't understand why your remark is insulting, there's no use trying to explain it to you." I felt angry at her; she was dismissing him without giving him a chance to learn or to change. She had made her judgment. If he couldn't grasp why his comment was offensive, he must either be stupid or irredeemably flawed. Either way, she thought, he was a hopeless case.

I thought this young black woman was wrong to treat the white student in this way—but suddenly, in her tone, I also heard my own voice echoed. Often, similar words had rung through my mind when men had protested that they didn't get it, such as when some men stated that they couldn't understand why women objected to being called girls. For the first time, I truly understood the frustration that some of these men clearly felt when women would turn their backs, claiming that if they didn't get it, there was no sense in trying to talk further. Frustrated by the unfairness of the black student who didn't want to explain what faux pas the white student had committed, I was able, for the first time, to see how unfair I myself had been toward a different group—men.

What if we viewed these moments in which the other person doesn't get it as a valuable opening rather than as a reason to shut the door to further communication? In his book *Racial Healing*, Harlon Dalton advises that when we look at one another in confusion, recognizing that there's some fundamental misunderstanding occurring, we should "relish these moments . . . for they have the potential to teach us much about how race affects our lives."[12] During the same mixed-race, mixed-gender discussion, a white male student complained about a recent women's retreat that the college had sponsored. I had been instrumental in developing this weekend, so I felt encouraged when a female student began defending our right to have time away. A black male then remarked, "I think that you have the right to go off on your own for a retreat. I just think that you ought to tell us what you're going to be talking about, and then when you return, you should submit some kind of report on what was discussed." All the women at the table, black and white, were flabbergasted by his suggestion. In contrast, all the men at the table—black and white—were nodding in agreement. Then one of the white women said, "How would you feel if all the black students wanted to go on a retreat, and all of us white people said, 'Sure, you have the right to do that. Just tell us what you're going to talk about and give us a report when you get back.'" Her remark clearly took the black males aback, as they could suddenly see what their blind spot had prevented them from apprehending earlier.

One way to think about what happened in both of these examples is that our dual, simultaneous memberships in two groups—male and female, black and white—became lenses through which we could grasp the reality of the other. The black males who saw their attitude toward the women's retreat through the race lens suddenly grasped the female perspective clearly. Because our memberships crossed over, we were able to feel our affiliation with the same people (women or men, black or white) from whom, at other moments in the conversation, we had been estranged. We could use our shifting perspectives from these different categories to understand realities that had previously eluded us.

GLITCHES

"Just a minute," you may be thinking. "I'm uneasy with what you're saying here. It sounds fine in some ways, but . . ." Statements like the following often trail that "but . . ."

- Sometimes people *are* ill intentioned; they dislike certain groups and they belittle them on purpose.
- Even if they're not doing it on purpose, I don't want people to think that what they did is all right just because it was inadvertent.
- I don't want to be so understanding of people's blind spots that I don't challenge them to change. If I say, "Well, that person just has a blind spot; that's why they are saying something insensitive," I'm afraid that I'll be aiding the very behavior that I deplore.

These are understandable and valid concerns. The idea of a blind spot, applied to the ways we classify people, could be misused to support attitudes that harm others. If someone intentionally wanted to demean a group of people, that person might use the idea of a blind spot to justify or excuse what he or she was doing. But rather than trying to counter this problem by ignoring differences that actually exist, I'd rather see people call others on what they are doing. Any blind spots discussed in this book could be used to try to excuse bad behavior. When people use the idea of a blind spot in this way, we should take them to task.

Imagine, for example, that the young man who made the watermelon remark responded, "Well, I didn't know! No one should take offense!" He needs to learn that others *will* take offense and to understand why they will. He needs to avoid repeating this same mistake in the future. And he may need to learn more about what offends black people in order to relate to them more sensitively, in the same way that people involved in international business will learn about Scandinavian or Vietnamese culture so that they don't inadvertently offend the people they are trying to do business with.

In fact, helping someone become aware of a blind spot can be the first step in helping him do something about it. Once I recognized how I, too, had been complaining about men, lumping all men into a single stereotype, I saw that I needed to change. Once I realized that I had been trapped by a category, I couldn't go blithely on my way. Instead, I had a responsibility to behave more sensitively in the future and to try to make up for ways that I had inadvertently insulted or hurt some men in the past.

IN A NUTSHELL

The opening story of the scavenger hunter who needed a three-by-seven-foot piece of wood but failed to see that any wooden door in the house could be used to meet this requirement shows how we can be trapped by categories. Classifying objects and events creates a blind spot because it inevitably reduces the complexity of what we are categorizing. The tactics suggested for countering this blind spot, such as shifting categories, are all aimed at restoring that complexity. A particularly thorny downside to our ability to categorize is that we classify people as naturally as we classify other objects and events. When our classification of people leads us to ignore *their* complexity, we can end up insulting and demeaning them without realizing what we are doing.

SNEAK PREVIEW

One of our great powers of thinking, the one that logicians call *deductive reasoning*, rests partly on our ability to see the world in terms of categories. If I ask you, "Is there water in Lake Erie?" or "Does the ostrich lay eggs?" you can probably answer these questions correctly even if you have never been to Lake Erie or have never actually seen a real ostrich in your life. You know the answers because you can deduce them from what you know about the groups we call lakes and birds. Deductive reasoning can take us far beyond these simple conclusions, as the stories of Sherlock Holmes so delightfully illustrate. But if we have such a great capacity for classification, the cornerstone of many deductions, why aren't more of us like Sherlock Holmes? Why do so many of us make logical errors or miss the obvious conclusions that Sherlock seemed able to deduce so easily? These are the questions we'll look at in the next chapter.

NOTES

1. Ellen Langer, *Mindfulness* (New York: Perseus Books, 1989).

2. Charles Panati, *Panati's Extraordinary Origins of Everyday Things* (New York: Harper and Row, 1987), pp. 380–81.

3. Alison Gopnik, Andrew Meltzoff, and Patricia Kuhl, *The Scientist in the Crib* (New York: HarperCollins, 2001), p. 82.

4. June Goodfield, *The Quest for the Killers* (Boston: Birkhauser Press, 1985).

5. Mary Catherine Bateson, *Peripheral Visions* (New York: HarperCollins, 1994).

6. Lewis Wolpert and Alison Richards, *A Passion for Science* (New York: Oxford University Press, 1988), p. 27.

7. Amin Maalouf, *In the Name of Identity: Violence and the Need to Belong* (New York: Arcade, 2001), pp. 20–22.

8. Ibid., pp. 1–2.

9. Ibid., p. 2.

10. Ibid., p. 29.

11. Harlon Dalton, *Racial Healing: Confronting the Fear between Blacks and Whites* (New York: Doubleday Anchor Books, 1995), p. 47.

12. Ibid., p. 73.

Chapter 8
THINKING BY THE SEAT OF YOUR PANTS

BLIND SPOT #7: JUMPING TO CONCLUSIONS

In the early 1930s, Russian psychologist Alexander Luria interviewed illiterate Russian peasants. Luria was studying how the peasants reasoned, so he gave them logical puzzles. For example, he would say, "Cotton only grows well where it is hot and dry. England is cold and damp. Can cotton grow there or not?" Here is how one thirty-seven-year-old villager responded:

VILLAGER: I don't know.

INTERVIEWER: Think about it.

VILLAGER: I've only been in the Kashgar country. I don't know beyond that.

INTERVIEWER: But on the basis of what I said to you, can cotton grow there?

VILLAGER: If the land is good, cotton will grow there, but if it is damp and poor, it won't grow. If it's like Kashgar country, it will grow there too. If the soil is loose, it can grow there too, of course.

The interviewer continued his questioning: "Cotton only grows well where it is hot and dry. England is cold and damp. Can cotton grow there or not?" He then asked, "What can you conclude from my words?" The villager responded, "If it's cold there, it won't grow. If the soil is loose and good, it will."

The interviewer persisted and asked, "But what do my words suggest?" The villager responded, "Well . . . we Kashgars, we're ignorant people; we've never been anywhere, so we don't know if it's hot or cold there."[1]

Why is the villager having so much difficulty producing the answer that the interviewer is seeking? Transcripts like these always left me with the feeling that these adults just don't get it. But what exactly is it that they don't get? What are they failing to grasp?

THE IDEA OF *LOGICAL NECESSITY*

It seemed to me initially that these adults failed to understand that people can know things even when they have never observed them directly. They didn't seem to grasp the idea that people can know information by logically deriving it from other facts that they know or have been told. That's what makes me want to say to the Russian peasant, "But if cotton can only grow where it is hot and dry, can't you see that cotton cannot grow in a country that is cold and damp?" It seemed to me that these adults didn't understand what philosophers call *logical necessity*, the idea not only that certain things *are* true but also that they *must be* true. For example, the fact that as long as we both are living, my older sister Jane will always be older than me is a fact that not only is true but also must be true.

Here is another example of logical necessity. Imagine that I have two hats, one white and one red. I blindfold you and put one hat on your head. I then tell you that I am putting the other hat on my own head. I remove your blindfold so that you can see me, and I ask you if you can tell me, for sure, the color of the hat on your head. Can you do this without looking in a mirror or otherwise directly seeing the hat you are wearing? If you look at me and see that I'm wearing the red hat, then you know that you must be wearing the white one, unless I am deceiving you in some way. That fact necessarily follows from the information given earlier.

We "know" that such facts "must be true" because they are dictated by logic. We don't have to observe them directly, because we can derive them from what is already known. Yet the Russian peasants seemed to insist that there was no way to know about cotton in England except by going there and seeing for themselves. As a result, Luria and his associates concluded that the peasants were deficient in their reasoning. But in their everyday lives, these same people, in Luria's own words, "made excellent judgments about facts of direct concern to them, and they could draw all the implied conclusions according to the rules of logic revealing much worldly intelligence."[2] So why couldn't they pass Luria's logic tests?

ARE LESS EDUCATED ADULTS UNABLE TO THINK LOGICALLY?

The interpretation that Luria offered to explain what was going wrong with the Russian peasants was similar to explanations offered by researchers during the same period who studied other groups. For example, when British anthropologist E. E. Evans-Pritchard studied the Azande tribe in Africa, he concluded that despite their success in practical reasoning about everyday life situations, the Azande seemed unable to grasp basic logical arguments. For instance, the Azande believed that they could detect by autopsy whether or not a deceased person had been a witch based on the presence or absence of a substance in the intestines.

Following this determination, they should theoretically have been able to apply other beliefs they held about the inheritance of spiritual witchcraft powers in order to conclude whether or not relatives of the deceased were witches. Knowing whether or not someone was a witch was a crucial concern to the Azande. But when Pritchard pressed them to recognize that their questions about who was or was not a witch could be answered on the basis of their own belief system and its logical implications, they treated his remarks as irrelevant. The Azandes' rejection of Pritchard's logic led some philosophers to raise the question: Are the Azande irrational? Or at least less rational than the social scientists who were studying them?

Phrases like "less rational" always struck me as a more academic, polite way of saying that these less educated people weren't as smart as the rest of us. Yet both the Azande and the Russian peasants were capable of competent reasoning in their daily lives. For example, they were astute at identifying the best areas to plant one crop rather than another, based on their knowledge of soil conditions, weather, and so forth. So why couldn't they solve these logic problems?

This question was even more perplexing to me when I considered the research that shows how capable even young children are of thinking logically. When they are presented with the white hat/red hat problem described earlier, virtually all kindergarten pupils know that you can tell you must be wearing the white hat if you see that your friend is wearing the red hat.[3] These children can also reason about purely hypothetical creatures. You might recall the study mentioned in chapter 1 in which preschoolers heard stories about make-believe animals such as "merds." They were told, "Merds laugh when they're happy. Animals that laugh don't like mushrooms." Then they were asked, "Do merds like mushrooms?"[4] The children were capable of using their reasoning to arrive at the correct answer. It didn't seem sensible to me that adults, no matter how limited their formal education, would be incapable of doing the same. So what could be going wrong here?

THINKING IN EVERYDAY LIFE

Imagine that I tell you, "I'll give you a raise if you work overtime for the next three months." In everyday conversation, we assume that the opposite is also true—that if you refuse to work overtime, you won't get the raise. This is, most likely, exactly what the speaker means. It's a reasonable inference to make. It is what some linguists call an *invited inference*, one that isn't logically necessary but is the interpretation commonly arrived at for such sentences in conventional conversation.[5]

In everyday conversation, assuming that the reverse statement is also true generally serves us well. But it trips us up in logic tests because the reverse statement is not *necessarily* true. For example, we know that all mothers are women, but that doesn't mean that all women are mothers. Our tendency to assume that if a statement is true, then its reverse must also be true leads to many mistakes that adults make when they try to solve logic problems. The very strategy that serves us so well in daily life misleads us when we play the logic game.

In fact, the logic game is governed by a set of rules that is exactly opposite to those that help us interpret what people say in our everyday lives. Normally, we draw upon our general knowledge of the world in order to intelligently interpret what is being said. But the logic game requires that we ignore that general knowledge and base our conclusions only on the literal meaning of the words. For example, I overheard an eight-year-old boy comment on a sign over the entrance to the liquor section of a store. The sign said: "You MUST BE 21 years old to buy beer." He thought about it for a moment then announced to the adults with him, "None of us can buy beer here!" His literal interpretation of the words allowed him to make a joke: clearly, based on the situation, the intended meaning of the sign was that you had to be *at least* twenty-one years old to buy beer, not that you had to be *exactly* twenty-one. But this literal way of interpreting statements is exactly what is required in formal logic problems.

Here is one final example of how the ideas that apply to solving logical problems are opposite from the thinking that helps us reason competently in everyday life.

All poisons are bitter.
Arsenic is not bitter.
Therefore, arsenic is not a poison.

If you are asked on a logic test whether or not the conclusion that arsenic is not a poison is valid, you would have to say yes to get the answer correct. On a logic test, *valid* doesn't mean true in the real world. It simply means that the conclusion follows logically from the first two statements. In this logic game, it's as if someone were saying to you, "I know that the first two statements might not be correct. But ignore that for now. Just ask yourself: Does the conclusion necessarily follow from them? If so, then the conclusion is valid—even if it's not true in the real world. If not, then the conclusion is invalid—even if it is true in the real world."

It's not natural for people to ignore the truth of the statements that they are reasoning about and to focus solely on the logical relationship between the statements. Similarly, when trying to understand what others say, it's not natural for us to ignore what we know about the real world and focus solely on the literal meaning of the words themselves. This brings us closer to understanding the central puzzle posed in this book: how is it that adults make logical errors in reasoning, yet even preschoolers seem capable of logical feats?

What we share with children is a sort of *natural logic*—a term that cognitive psychologist Martin Braine uses to describe how people think.[6] Even members of preliterate societies, Braine contends, naturally use logic to deduce facts about their worlds. But when formal logical puzzles require people to think in ways that run counter to how they normally interpret language, or normally reason in everyday life, people will be tripped up.

In everyday life, a person usually poses a question because they *don't* know the answer to it. But as psychologist and author Margaret Donaldson points out, what happens in the classroom is different. The expert, the trainer, the teacher who poses the question already knows the right answer, and the students know that the teacher knows it. The students understand that they are playing the classroom game.[7] Students tailor their answers to classroom questions accordingly.

This explains what was going wrong in the study I described in chapter 1. In that study, the researchers would point to a box on the table and announce, "If there's a cat in this box, there's an apple." After peeking inside the box, the researcher would then declare, "There is a cat!" and proceed to ask the adult in front of them, "Is there an orange in here?" About half of the adults answered no.[8] Logically, there is no reason why there couldn't be an orange in the box, based on the information provided. So the correct answer to the question, "Is there an orange in the box?" is simply "I don't know. I'd have to look."

What kept half the adults from giving the "I don't know" answer? Why did many adults need several examples of the same problem before they got it? The adults in this study realized that the researcher was asking a classroom question. He wasn't inquiring, "Is there an orange in the box?" because he had abruptly experienced an alarming deficiency of vitamin C. They knew that the researcher already knew whether or not there was an orange in the box. They knew that they were being tested. And one thing that we have all learned through experience about classroom questions is that "I don't know" is rarely the right answer. So these adults needed to have several problems in which "I don't know" and "I can't tell" turned out to be the right answer before they considered it as a possibility.

LEARNING HOW TO SOLVE LOGICAL PUZZLES

Logical puzzles are often viewed as a good test of whether or not people are "smart." They appear in publications such as *Games* magazine and occasionally on the place mats that restaurants provide to keep children occupied. A child of six or seven, even a very bright child, might be stumped the first time he sees the sort of puzzle shown in fig. 8.1. "How can I know where Peter lives?" the child might well ask. "It doesn't even tell me anything about Peter!" But if you say, "Well, look here, first let's figure out where Joan lives and write her name on the line below that house," he'll begin to catch on. He just needs to learn the strategy that will reveal the answer.

Similarly, learning to play the logic game is at least partly a matter of

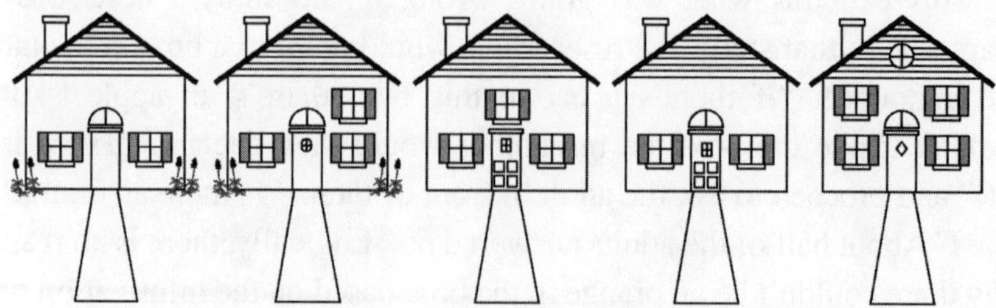

Joan, Salvador, Miranda, Derrick, and Peter all live on the same block.
Can you figure out which house belongs to each of them?

Here are some clues:

Joan has more windows than anyone else on her block.
Salvador is allergic to flowers and would never live next door to a house with flowers.
Miranda doesn't like Joan so she moved as far from Joan as she could.
Derrick and Salvador have the same designs on their front doors.
Where do Joan, Salvador, Miranda, and Derrick live?
Where does Peter live?

Fig. 8.1: A Child's Logical Puzzle—"Where Does Peter Live?"

learning the strategies, such as creating a grid, that help us organize the information and make the relationships among the different facts clearer. Once those relationships are clear, no genius is required to deduce the answer: it becomes obvious, just as the location of Peter's house becomes obvious. The challenge lies in figuring out the best way to represent the information so that the answer *will* become obvious.

In formal logic classes, students learn how to use Venn diagrams and Euler circles to represent complicated information. Our ability to do this depends at least as much on our experience with various puzzles and the strategies that work well with them as it does on our capacity for logical reasoning. Once we are familiar with the methods and have some practice in applying them, we can follow a method by rote and see the answer revealed.

People who have little or no experience with these methods will be stymied by these kinds of logical puzzles. Until someone shows them the methods they need, they won't know how to take the steps that will make the answer obvious. It's probably clear that in my view the problem is not that these people are dumb but that they are inexperienced. They possess the same natural logic that all human beings appear to have innately. They just need to learn how to play the logic game.

In everyday life, we can also miss seeing something if we haven't found a way to organize the relevant information, especially when we're trying to understand something that involves changeable conditions. Have you ever tried to work out the logistics of sharing cars among different people? Imagine that a husband and wife are trying to share their two cars with their son. The needs of each person for the cars are changeable. The husband, for example, travels a great deal, sometimes by plane but sometimes by car. When he's traveling by plane, his car is available. The son needs a car to get to his job, but his hours vary. He's able to take a train to his classes, except for the days when he must drive straight from class to work. If you were to overhear a discussion among these people, you would probably hear, "Oh, wait a minute" a lot, as in, "Oh, wait a minute, no, it doesn't matter on Tuesday, because Dad's flying then." Working out such logistics usually ends up being more complicated than anyone had anticipated, not because the three people aren't logical and smart, but because the changing conditions make it hard to create any sort of schedule that can be routinely followed.

"Well . . . just a second," you may be thinking. "It's all well and good to contend that we are naturally logical and have trouble because we don't understand how to play some obscure logic game or because we've got a lot of information that's hard to organize. But don't we make mistakes that can't be explained away in this fashion? Don't we make logical errors even when we're reasoning about the real world, even when we're juggling just a few facts? Why do people make mistakes when they reason about everyday, relatively uncomplicated, issues?"

THE BLIND SPOT OF JUMPING TO CONCLUSIONS: UNCOVERING THE INVISIBLE CHAIN OF REASONING

In everyday life, we reason about all sorts of practical matters, but most of the time, this process of reasoning is implicit. It happens automatically so that we arrive at conclusions without much awareness of just how we got there. We are a little like the mathematician in the Sidney Harris cartoon below.

This cartoon makes us smile because we know that in a mathematical proof it's not acceptable to make a logical leap and explain the solution as a miracle. We expect to see the various steps that lead to the answer to the problem. Remember the school assignments in which you were required to explain your reasoning? The purpose of this instruction is to help students see where they are going astray by making each reasoning step that they take visible. In the way that people naturally think, our reasoning processes are frequently invisible to us. Blind to that chain of reasoning, we are also blind to any errors we may have made.

"I think you should be more explicit here in step two."

Reprinted with permission from ScienceCartoonsPlus.com

TACTICS: OVERCOMING OUR TENDENCY TO JUMP TO CONCLUSIONS

It's unusual for people to make a conscious effort to trace the invisible chain of reasoning that led to their conclusions. It's only when we are wrong, only when we discover that we've been mistaken, that we typically step back and wonder, "Now what made me think that?" The antidote for this particular blind spot, then, is to make the invisible chain of reasoning visible to us—and then to examine that chain to see if it makes sense.

Tactic #1: Make the Chain of Reasoning Visible

Asking questions about our own reasoning can help us to overcome this blind spot. We need to ask ourselves questions like, "What are my reasons for believing that?" Often we *do* have reasons, but because so much of our thinking is implicit, it may not be easy to articulate them. It helps simply to ask ourselves questions like the following.

"What are my reasons?"

What makes me think that? How do I know that? It often helps people to jot down notes or to create some sort of chart or diagram to represent the ideas that their conclusions are based on. In whodunit mysteries, detectives sit down to organize the information they've gathered. They may have a hunch that *x* did it or that *y* is innocent, but they ask themselves what their hunch is based on and put their thinking on paper. This not only helps them keep track of various bits of information but also makes it easier for them to take a look at the chain of reasoning involved to make sure their hunch is solid. Once we have made our own reasons explicit, we can scrutinize them and ask more questions.

Imagine that you and your colleagues at work are discussing Bob's proposal for implementing a new delivery method. Here are some opinions that they voice.

Laura

When I ask Laura why she is voting against Bob's plan, she says, "Bob is a jerk!"

That is Laura's reason for voting against Bob's proposal. The crucial question I need to pose here is:

Is this reason relevant?

I need to ask myself, "Is the fact that Bob may be a jerk really relevant?" This question will help me see that the jerk comment is distracting me from the real issue—whether the plan that Bob proposes is better than what we do now and worth implementing.

Audrey

"Why change?" asks Audrey, pointing out that some problems in the current delivery system will continue under the new plan.

I need to ask myself:

Is this thinking logical?

Audrey's reasoning seems to be that we shouldn't adopt the new system because it isn't perfect. But does it necessarily follow that we should reject a new system whenever it doesn't solve all the problems?

Instead, I might argue that the real question is whether or not the new system would be enough of an improvement to warrant the costs of changing systems.

Koji

Koji says, "Either we stay with the old system, or we move to Bob's. The old system has so many problems with it, I'd vote for Bob's plan."

Whenever I hear someone suggest that there are only two options—yes or no, this plan or nothing—I need to ask myself:

Is this reason a false dilemma?
Does it present me with a false choice?

I might disagree with Koji's reasoning, pointing out that this isn't an either-or situation. There are more than two alternatives here.

Trisha

Trisha says, "I'm going to vote for Bob's proposal. He's worked on this new plan for months. If it's rejected now, he'll be crushed. How will he ever be motivated to work on another problem at this company?"

Whenever someone is tapping my sympathy to persuade me, I need to ask myself:

Is this reason an appeal to my emotions?

Trisha wants to spare Bob's feelings, reasoning that a rejection will discourage him. I might disagree with her reasoning, arguing that Bob will be even more discouraged if we adopt his plan and it fails spectacularly.

How Should I Respond to My Colleagues?

When others offer reasons that seem flawed to you, you can bring their attention to the problems by asking the "So you think that . . ." question.

Imagine that I said to Audrey, "So you think that unless a new system is perfect, eliminating every problem in the old system, we shouldn't even consider it?" Or to Koji, "So you believe that we have no other choices but to stay with the old system or move to Bob's?" Or to Trisha, "So you think that we should adopt Bob's proposal, even if it fails in the future, in order to protect his feelings now?" It's very likely that all these people would backtrack in the face of such questions—or they might bring up better reasons that we could consider.

Tactic #2: Using Common Fallacies as Clues

Philosophers have identified numerous logical fallacies, the most common reasoning errors that people make. Another way that you can identify mistakes in reasoning is to practice listening for these common fallacies. Here are four.

Common Fallacies

1. Attacking the person rather than evaluating the person's ideas.
   Example: The proclamation that "Bob is a jerk!" clearly falls in this category.

2. Rejecting a solution on the basis that it isn't perfect.
   Example: The objection that Bob's plan doesn't solve all the problems is an example of this error.

3. Thinking in either-or terms rather than seeing multiple options.
   Example: Koji's contention that either they must vote for Bob's plan or that they must live with the old system falls into this category.

4. Using emotional appeal rather than reasons to support our position.
   Example: Trisha's objection that Bob will be crushed if his proposal is rejected is an example of an emotional appeal.

This handful of fallacies is only the tip of the iceberg. Entire books have been devoted to describing these fallacies, such as philosopher and logician T. Edward Damer's *Attacking Faulty Reasoning*.[9] Damer's book has the unusual feature of describing constructive ways that people can react, in everyday conversations, when they hear others using false reasoning. *Asking the Right Questions* is another useful book.[10] The authors emphasize the key words or phrases that function like clues to alert us to the likely presence of fallacies. I have found these two books to be especially useful. But every standard logic text, as well as self-help books such as John Chaffee's *The Thinker's Way*, spends some time outlining the common fallacies.[11]

If we become attuned to these fallacies, then every time we hear them—every time we hear a person attacked, an emotional appeal made, an idea rejected because it isn't perfect, or a phrase like "we have only two choices"—our antennae will go up. This doesn't mean that we should necessarily reject what the person is saying but that we should reason more carefully about the issue before deciding what we believe should be done.

Tactic #3: Watch Out for "Common Sense"

In his book on *Moral Politics: How Liberals and Conservatives Think*,[12] cognitive psychologist and linguist George Lakoff notes that politically liberal individuals often find the views of politically conservative people illogical and vice versa. For example, most pro-life conservatives do not support government programs that provide prenatal care for low-income mothers. This seems illogical to liberals. "If conservatives are so concerned about protecting fetuses," they ask, "why wouldn't they support programs that have been shown to reduce infant mortality rates?" On the other hand, conservatives see some liberal stances as equally unreasonable. For example, they wonder how liberals can claim that they believe in the American Dream when they punish financial success through a progressive income tax.

To both liberals and conservatives, the positions of the opposite group seem illogical. But are they? Lakoff believes that both groups are being perfectly logical. Both groups reach conclusions that follow logically from the metaphors that they embrace. What are these metaphors? Lakoff argues that both camps view nations as families, with governments acting as the head of the family. Differences in views come because politically conservative individuals favor a family model in which the government acts like a "strict father," while politically liberal individuals favor a model in which government acts like a "nurturant parent." Lakoff shows how many of the apparently contradictory stances of both conservatives and liberals actually flow logically from the underlying family model that they are using as a metaphor for government and how it should work. However, their ideas *seem* illogical because the metaphor that those ideas are based on is hidden.

Lakoff argues that most of us are unaware of the metaphors that underlie our reasoning. Arguments that are based on metaphors seem like common sense to us. They appear obvious. In order to evaluate such commonsense ideas, we need to become more aware of the metaphors that underlie them and then consider how well a particular metaphor reflects the reality of the situation. For example, for many years the relationship between physicians and patients was based on a parent-child metaphor. Patients were expected to unquestioningly accept the assumed wisdom of their physicians and obey their orders. During this same time, the relationship between physicians and nurses was based on a master-servant metaphor in which the nurse, even one with decades of experience, was expected to obey whatever order a physician wrote out—even when a physician was an inexperienced resident in training. Both of these underlying metaphors have been called into question in recent years as patients increasingly insist on actively participating in medical decisions about their own health and nurses press for a working relationship with physicians that is a genuine partnership. The recognition of an underlying metaphor, such as the master-servant metaphor assumed to apply to physicians and nurses, is the crucial first step to questioning its validity. This questioning not only leads to disputing the common practices that have flowed from that paradigm for decades but may trigger a paradigm shift. What was once viewed as simple common sense is now rejected, and new models arise regarding what the relationship between physician and patient, or between physician and nurse, should be.

Notice when you find yourself saying, "It's just common sense!" Take a moment to see if a metaphor is fueling your reaction. See if what seems obvious to you appears self-evident because it flows logically from a metaphor that you've taken for granted and make that metaphor visible. Then ask yourself, "How well does this metaphor really apply to this situation?" If the metaphor is a poor fit, then you want to be cautious about accepting the beliefs that are based on that metaphor, no matter how logically those beliefs may flow from it.

Tactic #4: Your Enemy Can Be Your Friend: Let Someone Who Disagrees with You Find the Holes in Your Reasoning

One shortcut through the process of painstakingly attempting to analyze your own reasoning is to seek out the criticism of those who disagree with you. It's likely that they will be more adept at spotting the weaknesses in your position than you are. Their comments and questions will force you to clarify your reasons. Find a sounding board who talks back, someone who essentially says, "So let me try to understand what you believe and why you believe that." As they paraphrase their view of your position, you will probably find yourself correcting them, clarifying what you meant. But you may also discover the spots where there are problems with your thinking, and that will allow you to think the matter through more carefully. You might end up advocating the same position you originally held, but you'll be able to defend it more forcefully.

WIDENING THE CIRCLE: WHEN BEING UNREASONABLE SUCCEEDS—THE CASE OF POLITICAL CAMPAIGNS

If you study the books designed to help people become better critical thinkers, you'll find that the authors provide many examples for readers to analyze. They typically draw these examples from real life, using newspaper and magazine articles, speeches, and advertisements. Very often they quote political material: election ads, speeches by governmental leaders, political editorials and articles. It's no accident that so many authors go to political material for examples of illogical thinking. Just consider the four fallacies mentioned earlier. How often does a candidate, of whatever party, appeal to emotions to sway voters? How often do candidates attack the character of the person opposing them rather than arguing with their opponent's ideas? How often do opponents of proposed programs dismiss those programs on the basis that they are less than perfect? How often do writers of editorials or articles present issues in either-or terms?

In addition to using approaches like these, astute politicians capitalize on our tendency to be swayed by underlying metaphors that will make their statements seem like common sense to us. Especially in campaign ads and speeches, where time limits reduce most of their points to sound bites, politicians have learned to intentionally cast issues in terms of underlying metaphors, emotional appeals, and either-or alternatives. Politicians do this because they have recognized that these messages are often more effective in influencing public opinion than longer, more complex arguments are.

One researcher I know described how he used to go in front of school boards to make presentations regarding a particular reading program that he hoped the school district would adopt. In his early days, he would go armed with statistics and research results that showed how effective the program was. As time went on, however, he said he learned that "one powerful story about an individual kid, preferably with a photo and a quote from the kid's parents, was worth ten research studies, as far as convincing the board members." The more he pares down his approach to eliminate the research supporting the program and stresses a more emotional appeal, the more he is using *argument-by-fallacy*. This doesn't mean that the statements he's making are false or that the program isn't as good as he claims. It does mean that he's using one of the fallacies to convince others rather than trying to use persuasive methods based more on logic and evidence. Like the politicians, he's doing this because it works. It helps him accomplish his purpose of persuading board members to adopt the program that he believes in.

It's not only in politics that argument-by-fallacy works. In a business where proposals are carefully considered and presented in some detail, or in a setting where staff members are encouraged to debate the advantages and the disadvantages of proposed plans, people are likely to think critically about them. But in a time-pressed organization where a proposal's fate is primarily a matter of influencing key decision makers, the situation is more like a political election. In this setting, the careful thinker who tries to gain support by offering a more in-depth analysis of the issues may well be at a disadvantage. The person who instead uses argument-by-fallacy, such as relying on emotional appeal or by downplaying conflicting information, may be more persuasive.

Ultimately, of course, the wisest long-term decisions for a school board, a company, or a nation will occur when they rest on solid reasoning. But it's not easy to establish an atmosphere in which careful thinking is the norm, while jumping to conclusions is suspect. This is one challenge that we face in our age, where sound-bite advertising, three-sentence executive summaries, and two-minute news capsules tend to replace, for many people, longer articles, books, and reports that could provide a more complete analysis of the issues.

GLITCHES: LOGIC LEAVES ME COLD

I was once introduced to a very intelligent woman whom I'll call Miriam. Upon learning that I taught classes in critical thinking, Miriam exclaimed, "Oh! That's good—yes, I had an excellent education in critical thinking at [here she named a prestigious university]. It really made me aware of how rarely people think! I would come home from college, and my mother would make these off-the-wall statements, and I'd say, 'But what makes you believe that?' I drove her nuts. Because she couldn't answer me—just like my colleagues at work now, they don't like it much when I question them. They can't defend the stuff they say either!" Here she grinned victoriously. She didn't add, "I drive them nuts, too!" But it was clear from the glances exchanged by the people in the circle that this is what we were all thinking. In the brief span of this two-minute conversation, Miriam revealed her smug sense of superiority over others, her brusque impatience with people who could not defend their opinions, and her dismissal of them as stupid.

One reason that some people are less than enthusiastic about critical thinking and logical reasoning is that they have encountered the Miriams of the world. People who have had lots of experience in critiquing arguments or deducing facts can often run circles around the rest of us. Sometimes such people are very smug. They are the Sherlock Holmeses of the world, brilliantly deducing what must have happened, while the rest of us are, at best, the Watsons, the hard-working but plodding members of the team. Like Miriam, many logical thinkers tend to be suspicious of intuition.

They are quick to judge people who say that they are sure of something "just because I am" or "because I have a feeling about it." But is intuition necessarily a sign that what we believe has no logical basis?

Intuition as a Sign of Implicit Knowledge

It's often hard for people to articulate the reasoning that their beliefs or practices are based on. That doesn't necessarily mean that they have no reasons. Maybe they have what is sometimes called *implicit knowledge*, knowledge based on their experience that guides them, but without much conscious awareness on their part. They act intuitively, automatically, "by the seat of their pants."

I once heard a talk by English professor Tori Haring-Smith, in which she described a pivotal moment in her teaching career. She was lecturing to a large group of students in an auditorium, discussing the meaning of a poem. She was talking about how funny the poem was, how ironic. As she put it, "I was on a roll. So when I saw a hand waving in the front row, I tried to ignore it. I didn't want to stop to answer any questions. But the waving persisted and finally I interrupted my lecture to call on the student. That student asked me the most important question anyone had ever asked me in my teaching career. She said, 'Professor Haring-Smith, if you were not an English professor, how would you know that this poem is funny?'"

That question was so important because Tori Haring-Smith couldn't answer it: "I realized that I was like a magician, pulling rabbits out of hats, showing—in my analysis of the poem—how clever I was. But I didn't have a clue as to how I went about doing that, and so I couldn't teach my students how to do it."

Tori Haring-Smith isn't alone in being skilled at doing something but unable to articulate just how she does what she does. Many gifted professionals find it very difficult to express the implicit knowledge that guides what they do. Indeed, in his best seller *Blink*, journalist and author Malcolm Gladwell[13] argues that the decisions we make intuitively, "in a blink," are often just as accurate or even *more* accurate than those we arrive at through painstaking analysis, even though we cannot explain how we know what we know.

So we need to be cautious about belittling someone's ideas simply because the person in question attributes them to gut feelings or intuition. In their book *Sparks of Genius*, physiology professor Robert Root-Bernstein and his author-scholar wife, Michele Root-Bernstein, describe how Barbara McClintock, who would eventually earn a Nobel Prize for her work in genetics, thought about the results of a genetic experiment that had puzzled her colleagues. Half an hour later, she shouted, "Eureka! I have the answer! I know what is causing the 30 percent sterility [we saw in the experiment]." When challenged to provide proof for her explanation, she was unable to do so at the time, but she had no doubt that she would be able to. As she wrote, "The answer came fast . . . [but later] I worked it out step by step—it was an intricate series of steps—and—it worked out exactly as I'd diagrammed it."[14] The authors give other examples of creative people who had insights that they couldn't defend at the time. Even the mathematician Carl Friedrich Gauss admitted he often had an intuitive way of knowing ideas that he could not immediately prove mathematically.

These examples are useful reminders that people get labeled as dumb for jumping to conclusions only when those conclusions turn out to be wrong. When they're right, the fact that they were able to jump to the conclusion is interpreted as a sign of their genius. But this doesn't mean that intuition is always superior to painstaking analysis or that all intuitions are equal. In *Blink*, Gladwell includes examples of intuitive judgments that were disastrous as well as fortuitous, and he suggests that our intuitive decisions are most likely to be correct when we are drawing, however unconsciously, on a deep well of experience. When people argue that they "just know" something intuitively, we need to avoid both romanticizing their intuitive thinking as unassailable and rejecting it outright as unfounded. Intuitions should be respected, but it is also reasonable to expect people to trace the invisible threads of the thinking that led to their conclusion, as Barbara McClintock did.

Cold Logic: Are Emotions the Enemy of Logical Thinking?

The other aspect of logical thinking that has given it a bad name is the way logicians have traditionally viewed emotions. Emotions are usually seen as impediments to reasoning. Being very angry, for example, may make it more difficult for us to think clearly. When this view is taken to an extreme, emotions are considered the enemy of rational thinking. From this perspective, it would be better if everyone were like Mr. Spock, the *Star Trek* character who feels no emotion but determines what to believe or do based solely on logic. This leads to a picture in which reasonable thinking is not only objective but downright cold.

What if emotions are not only *not* the enemy of logical decision making but instead its friend, absolutely essential to it? Neurologist Antonio Damasio argues that emotions play an indispensable part in rational thinking—so essential that human beings are unable to think rationally when a brain injury has impaired their ability to feel. For example, here is how Dr. Damasio describes one of his patients:

> The instruments usually considered necessary and sufficient for rational behavior were intact in him. He had the requisite knowledge, attention, and memory; his language was flawless; he could perform calculations, he could tackle the logic of an abstract problem. [But his neurological disease left him] with a marked alteration of the ability to experience feeling . . . [the result was] a profound defect in decision making.[15]

The man in question, for example, would sit for hours in his office, helplessly sifting through various reports and materials because he experienced no emotional reactions that might suggest that a particular issue cried for immediate attention, or that one problem was more crucial than another, or that one course of action was clearly to be favored over others. Lacking the emotional experiences that alert the normal person to these factors, he was unable to decide what to do. While not denying that strong emotions can sometimes interfere with clear thinking and careful reasoning, Damasio draws on his studies of brain-damaged patients to support his contention that the ability to feel is as necessary to reasonable decision making as the ability to think. Mr. Spock, according to Damasio's research, would in fact be a very poor decision maker.

Not Every Problem Is a Logical Puzzle

The Mr. Spock image can also help us understand another reason why some people are wary of logical thinking. Mr. Spock, lacking those crucial emotions, treats every life problem as a logical puzzle. But can all of life's challenges really be reduced to logical puzzles? In the film *A Beautiful Mind*, Nobel Prize–winning economist John Nash is depicted as a brilliant man who flounders when he tries to understand love. John Nash tries to decide whether or not to marry on the basis of some sort of logical calculation. The movie is a reminder that a straightforward, linear argument, with impeccable logic, is not the only way to know something, especially to know something like, "Do I love this person?" or "Should I marry this person?" What to do about life's challenges cannot always be determined solely by logical reasoning. This is true not only in personal life decisions but also in thinking about what to do about social and political issues, such as US tensions with other nations or global climate change.

Today many problem-solving experts make a distinction between what they call *closed puzzles* versus *messy problems*. They point out that many logic problems that logically minded people enjoy solving as a pastime are in the form of closed puzzles. They usually have a single, logically necessary, right answer that can be deduced from the information given. In contrast, real life is full of messy problems, problems in which we don't have all the helpful information and there is no perfect or single correct answer. While thinking logically is helpful in dealing with messy problems, it isn't adequate by itself.

Don't Throw the Baby out with the Bathwater!

Because they feel alienated by the attitudes some logical thinkers express, people who consider themselves more intuitive sometimes have their own blind spots. They dismiss logical thinking out of hand. Yet it really isn't our ability to think logically that they reject. They object to the coldness of logic, or to the arrogant attitude of some logical thinkers, or to the belittling of feeling and intuition. They are throwing the baby out with the bathwater. It's possible to be a logical thinker without being cold and unemotional. It's possible to use rational deduction and still respect the intuitions of others who may not yet be able to support their ideas with a fully developed line of reasoning.

Instead of abruptly challenging others to defend a statement, which they may well have made off the cuff, it's possible to adopt a more inquisitive tone. Acknowledging that all of us have many beliefs and ideas that are based on reasons that are invisible to us, we could ask, "What makes you think that?" with genuine curiosity instead of with a sneer. Remember the three-year-old girl in chapter 1 whose aunt was playfully threatening to eat her up? It's the astonishing capacity for logical thinking that enabled that three-year-old to figure out that she could outwit her aunt by eating her aunt's mouth first. True, logic has been associated with coldness or arrogance in some logical thinkers, but I hate to see people who are more intuitive reject such a breathtaking ability.

IN A NUTSHELL

This chapter got to the heart of the question of why children can demonstrate such logical ability, while adults falter in trying to solve certain logic problems. The crux of the answer is that the natural logic that people use to interpret conversation and solve problems is, as the opening story of the Russian peasants illustrates, often at odds with the kind of thinking required to solve formal logic problems. The natural logic that serves us so well in everyday situations leads us astray when we are faced with logical puzzles.

But why do we have trouble thinking about everyday life issues where our natural logic ought to serve us well? People are blind to their thinking errors because the thread of reasoning that underlies what we think or believe is often invisible, blinding us to the mistakes we may be making. The solution to this blind spot is to use tactics that make our reasoning more visible so that we can critique it more carefully. Careful thinking is likely to lead to better problem solving, but it's often ignored when people are trying to persuade others. In fact, the approaches that are often most effective in politics rely on tactics such as character assassination and emotional appeals more than on reason. Finally, logical thinking has gotten a bad reputation among some people because it has become associated with a cold, linear way of thinking and with an arrogant attitude toward anyone who values more intuitive ways of knowing.

SNEAK PREVIEW

Even when we've uncovered our own reasoning and critiqued it thoughtfully, we can reach erroneous conclusions in real-life situations. The main reason is that the facts we base our thinking on turn out to be wrong. To be effective in thinking about real-world problems, we need to be as sure as we can that our facts are accurate. How can we do that? As Cynthia, a child featured in the next chapter, suggests, we can seek empirical evidence. We can act as if we were from Missouri and demand, "Show me!" But as Cynthia's story also illustrates, it's not quite that simple.

NOTES

1. A. R. Luria, *The Making of Mind* (Cambridge, MA: Harvard University Press, 1979), pp. 77–78.

2. Ibid., p. 79.

3. Frank B. Murray, "The Conversion of Truth into Necessity," in *Reasoning, Necessity, and Logic: Developmental Perspectives*, ed. Willis F. Overton, 183–203 (Hillsdale, NJ: Erlbaum Associates, 1990).

4. J. Hawkins, R. D. Pea, J. Glick, and S. Scribner, "Merds That Laugh Don't Like Mushrooms: Evidence for Deductive Reasoning by Preschoolers," *Developmental Psychology* 20 (1984): 584–94.

5. M. Geis and A. M. Zwicky, "On Invited Inferences," *Linguistic Inquiry* 2 (1971): 561–66.

6. Martin Braine, "The 'Natural Logic' Approach to Reasoning," in *Reasoning, Necessity, and Logic: Developmental Perspectives*, ed. Willis F. Overton, 133–57 (Hillsdale, NJ: Erlbaum Associates, 1990).

7. Margaret Donaldson, *Children's Minds* (London: Croom Helm, 1978).

8. B. Rumain, J. Connell, and M. D. Braine, "Conversational Comprehen-

sion Processes Are Responsible for Reasoning Fallacies in Children as Well as Adults: If Is Not the Biconditional," *Developmental Psychology* 19 (1983): 471–81.

9. T. Edward Damer, *Attacking Faulty Reasoning*, 3rd ed. (Belmont, CA: Wadsworth, 1995).

10. M. Neil Browne and Stuart Keeley, *Asking the Right Questions*, 6th ed. (Englewood Cliffs, NJ: Prentice-Hall, 2001).

11. John Chaffee, *The Thinker's Way* (New York: Little, Brown, 1998).

12. George Lakoff, *Moral Politics: How Liberals and Conservatives Think* (Chicago: University of Chicago Press, 2002).

13. Malcolm Gladwell, *Blink: The Power of Thinking without Thinking* (Boston: Little, Brown, 2005).

14. Robert and Michele Root-Bernstein, *Sparks of Genius* (New York: Houghton Mifflin, 1999), p. 2.

15. A. R. Damasio, *Descartes' Error: Emotion, Reason, and the Human Brain* (New York: Avon, 1994), p. xii.

Chapter 9

WHY IT'S SO HARD TO *FIND* THE PROOF IN THE PUDDING

BLIND SPOT #8: FUZZY EVIDENCE

Authors Robert E. Bartholomew and Benjamin Radford describe how some folks in Laredo, Texas, believed an article in the *Morning Times of Laredo* that claimed a three-hundred-pound, seventy-nine-foot-long earthworm was traveling down Interstate 35 near their town.[1] Not everyone in Laredo believed the story, and those who did soon realized it was false. But the fact that anyone believed it at all, even for a moment, astonishes people. Bartholomew and Radford relate many other examples of news stories describing unlikely events that were harder to disprove than the giant earthworm tale. In these cases, the headlines continued to influence people's beliefs for weeks and months. What made so many people believe the unlikely facts that were being reported? What made so many ignore evidence that could have made them question the outlandish claims being made? Paraphrasing the title of *Skeptic* magazine editor Michael Shermer's thought-provoking book, why *do* people believe weird things?[2]

CHILDHOOD CLUES

Twelve-year-old Cynthia was assigned to read an article describing how several people involved in opening or visiting the tomb of King Tutankhamen later died strange deaths. They were victims, some contended, of the so-called Pharaoh's curse. Before doing her assignment, Cynthia was asked a series of questions, including the following.

> INTERVIEWER: What do you definitely know about curses?
>
> CYNTHIA: There are good ones and bad ones. Good ones are like spells and only exist in fairy tales, but the bad ones definitely exist. It's like the Bermuda Triangle. I read about a ship that had a mummy on it in 1832 and it never returned. The mummy put a curse on the ship. People with ESP have the power to put curses on other people. I have ESP, but I don't think I could do it.
>
> INTERVIEWER: What don't you know about curses?
>
> CYNTHIA: How they really work. How do voodoo priests really place curses on other people? Do those dolls with pins really work? Did the lost ark have a curse? What was it?
>
> INTERVIEWER: Do you believe in the King Tut curse? (Cynthia nods yes.) What makes you believe this?
>
> CYNTHIA: I am just like Missouri—you know, the "Show Me" state. I have to see it or it doesn't exist. I believe in the King Tut curse because I've read about it in books and have seen it on TV.

THE PUZZLE: WHAT HAPPENED TO CYNTHIA?

Cynthia's remarks strike most people as naive. They assume that Cynthia thinks the way she does because she is young. But research shows that children much younger than Cynthia appear more sophisticated in their thinking than she does. In one study, preschoolers were shown a picture of two boys near a creek. The boys have just spotted something they've never seen before, an object hidden in the grass so that the children in the study cannot see what the boys are looking at. The children are told that one boy in the picture is saying, "Look at this thing. I don't know what it is, but I bet it can float." The other boy disagrees: "I think it would sink."[3]

The children were then asked a series of questions: Why do you think the two boys would disagree about this? Who do you think is right? Can they find out for sure who is right?

Asked this last question, one preschooler said, "I could just pick it up and throw it into the water and see if it can float." Over half of the preschoolers suggested that the way to resolve differences when two people disagree is to perform a test of some sort to see for themselves what the truth is.

Now back to Cynthia. What has changed to make the twelve-year-old shift from relying on the evidence of her own senses to now relying so heavily on statements she hears on TV? The answer can help us understand why adults sometimes unquestioningly accept evidence from the media, such as believing that a three-hundred-pound earthworm is moving down a local highway.

CHILDREN LEARN TO DISTRUST THEIR OWN PERCEPTIONS

One father told me what happened when he took his four-year-old daughter on her first plane trip. She loved airplanes, and they had often visited the airport to watch planes take off and land, so she was filled with excitement as the flight began. The plane rose in the sky. After a minute, the child looked up at her dad and asked, "When are we going to shrink?"

How clever she was! She had worked out what must happen inside the planes, which she could plainly see get smaller as they rose after takeoff and larger as they landed. Clearly the people riding in these expanding and contracting vehicles must themselves expand and contract in order to survive the experience! She was ingenious, but she was wrong. Like all young children, she was easily fooled by appearances. On her first plane ride, she learned that she couldn't always trust her own observations.

Children have repeated experiences in which they discover that things are not always as they appear. A little girl forgets her paints at her friend's house. "Never mind," says Grandma, "we'll get them when we go there next time." But the next day, the child is sure that her paints are somewhere back in her own home. "Mommy went during the night, when I was asleep," she insists, "and brought the paints back to our house." She is absolutely certain that this unlikely event has occurred, but Grandma begins to muse. "Maybe you just had a dream that Mommy went and got your paints," she says. And so the child has another experience of what is real versus what is just a dream, just pretend, or just a movie.

Learning that things aren't always as they appear, children face a fundamental question about how we can know anything. How can you tell what is real? How do you know what is true? If you can't rely on directly observing reality to determine what really happened, what can you rely on?

Quite reasonably, as children we decide to rely on the Big People to tell us what is real, to trust the adults who obviously know so much more about the world. We accept that the moon is not really following our car, though it certainly appears to. We accept that we must wash our hands to get rid of germs, even though we can't see these invisible critters. When adults tell us that the sun doesn't really rise, but rather that the earth is moving around the sun, we accept this counterintuitive picture of the world that they offer us. When our class watches a documentary showing what happened when immigrants first arrived on Ellis Island, or reads a book describing the first Thanksgiving, we believe the facts that are presented. School-age children learn to depend upon authorities—parents, teachers, books, films, TV programs—for the truth about what the world is like. And here is exactly where we find Cynthia, citing television programs as the basis for her belief in the existence of the King Tut curse.

THE ADULT REMNANTS OF RELYING ON OTHERS FOR THE TRUTH

In many ways, as adults we are in a situation similar to that of children. Like children, we want to know the truth about events that we cannot directly observe. We want to know about events reported in the media: television, radio, newspapers, news magazines, documentaries, and books. It's not usually possible for us to observe these events ourselves, so we must rely on the reports of others who were present at the time or interviews of people who were there. We are curious about events that occurred in the remote past, one hundred or one thousand or even a million years ago in our galaxy. These remote events are discussed in books and articles in specialized fields such as history, anthropology, archeology, and paleontology. It's not possible for anyone living today to witness them directly, so we rely on the writings of experts to interpret the clues that they find in older written documents and in other materials, such as fossils, bones, and ancient tools.

Only a handful of people can travel to the moon to establish for sure that it is possible to reach; most of us must rely on more indirect evidence from media such as photos and video clips of astronauts. Few people are directly privy to classified governmental information or to the closed meetings of top officials at major corporations. Beyond these human events, a host of phenomena in nature are invisible to the naked eye. We can't directly observe recessive genes, the exchanging of molecules, black holes, or colors beyond the spectrum accessible to human beings—much less subatomic particles such as quarks. Even scientists with sophisticated equipment can't just look directly at subatomic particles: they must infer their presence from the traces they leave, just as historians, archeologists, and geologists must infer what happened in the past from the signs left in rock formations, bones, clay pots, and ancient scrolls.

Here is our dilemma in a nutshell. It's not possible for us to directly witness for ourselves, or to test for ourselves, most factual claims that are made about the world. By ourselves, we have neither the time nor the ability to gather the needed evidence. We can't simply throw the rock into the water to see for ourselves if it will float; we must rely on the reports of other people. Yet it is just as impossible to exhaustively research the expertise and the credibility of every report, every author, every scientist, every documentary producer, as it is to investigate every claim directly ourselves. Moreover, even when people agree on the facts, we find that different conclusions can be drawn from those same facts. Different interpretations of the facts are often possible. So how can we decide what to believe? Like the children who learn to trust the Big People to tell them what is true, we naturally rely on experts and authorities. But when experts disagree, whom do we trust?

WHAT DETERMINES WHOM WE WILL TRUST?

What determines whom we will trust? Most of the time, people will trust those individuals and organizations that they have been taught to trust: those who share their values, their overall worldviews. If we are Christian, we accept the information offered to us in a Christian publication or radio program more easily than information offered in a Jewish or Muslim or secular publication or program and vice versa. If we are liberal in our political leanings, the books we find believable, the talk-show hosts we trust, the comedians whose statements we consider accurate as well as witty—all these will be different than they would be if we were politically conservative in our views. Whether our "bible" is the Christian Bible, the Koran, the *Tibetan Book of Living and Dying*, or the *New York Times*, we all accept information offered by those whose values and worldviews generally agree with our own more easily. We all reject, or at least are more skeptical of, information offered by those whose values and worldviews generally disagree with ours.

I had always rejected the idea that the deaths of Lord Carnavon and other visitors to King Tut's cave were in any way related to their visit there. My worldview has no place for curses, so I dismissed out of hand the idea that these deaths could possibly be related to the visits to King Tut's cave. Then I read an article from the British *Sunday Times* quoting three different scientists, all of whom speculated that some sort of long-lived pathogen—deadly bacteria, spore, or fungi—may have been present in the tomb and could have infected Lord Carnavon.[4] Is it possible that this pathogen might also have been implicated in the deaths of others who entered the cave that day? I was intrigued by the idea that what had been explained by invoking a curse might have a more scientific reason behind it.

Notice that I shifted in my thinking even though none of the facts had changed. The only thing that had changed was the explanation of those facts: the scientific explanation fit my worldview, while the curse explanation did not. This is the power of our worldviews and our belief systems to influence how we accept or reject evidence.

In some ways, it makes sense to let our general belief systems and our set of values influence how we evaluate information and evidence. This approach is a kind of shortcut. It enables us to bypass the work involved in trying to figure out the truth about a matter, such as seeking corroborating evidence before deciding what to believe, or seeing whether or not the statements being offered seem plausible, or investigating how reliable the source of that information is. Since it is impossible for any one person to have the time, energy, interest, and expertise to personally check out every claim that is made, it's understandable that we rely instead on our general sense of trust in particular groups of people whom we respect. It's understandable, but it does create a blind spot. At times, we blindly reject evidence that we should consider more seriously. At other times, we blindly accept evidence that we should scrutinize more carefully.

THE BLIND SPOT OF FUZZY EVIDENCE

Our worldviews and our beliefs create the blind spot of *fuzzy evidence*, fuzzy because this blind spot prevents us from seeing evidence clearly. Joel Best, sociology professor and author of the book *Damned Lies and Statistics: Untangling Numbers from the Media, Politicians, and Activists*,[5] provides a clear example of erroneous evidence that was blindly accepted when it should have been questioned. Best quotes a statement that was originally made in 1995 in a scholarly journal: "Every year since 1950, the number of American children gunned down has doubled." Best shows that it is impossible for this statement to be true. If even only one child had been murdered in 1950, that would mean that two children were victims in 1951, four in 1952, eight in 1953, and so forth. "By 1960, the number would have been 1,024. By 1965, it would have been 32,768 . . . in 1970, the number would have passed one million; in 1980, one billion (more than four times the total US population)." Why did so many educated and intelligent people—the editors of the journal, the reviewers of the article, the doctoral student who quoted it as part of his dissertation prospectus, the professors who reviewed that student's work—fail to question the statistic? I suspect that their values made them sensitive to violence in the world and that they were prone to support any social program aimed at decreasing that violence. As Best repeatedly points out in his book, we tend to accept unquestioningly the statistics that support the causes we advocate and to reject out-of-hand statistics that support an opposing view.

WHY EVIDENCE FAILS TO RESOLVE ARGUMENTS

When people disagree about issues such as "How serious a threat is global climate change?" the introduction of evidence regarding the issues often fails to resolve their differences. One reason is that proponents of the opposing sides ignore or discount the evidence that the other side offers. Often they assume that the counterevidence comes from an unreliable source, one that is either honestly mistaken or that is intentionally trying to deceive people. They decide that the group offering the evidence that contradicts their beliefs is part of some conspiracy, some attempt to suppress the truth for its own self-serving purposes.

Unfortunately, such allegations have all too often turned out to be true. Author and head of the American Physical Society Robert Park writes:

> If we have learned anything . . . in recent years, it is that we cannot . . . accept uncritically the soothing reassurances of authorities. We have seen tobacco companies suppress their own studies of nicotine addiction and the health effects of tobacco smoke; the nuclear industry, chemical companies, drug manufacturers, car makers—all at times have engaged

> in cover-ups. The federal government has conspired with civilian contractors to withhold information about the spread of radioactive contamination around nuclear weapons production facilities.[6]

Because we know that such deception can and does occur, it's very tempting to dismiss any claims we disagree with by arguing that those claims rest on deception and conspiracy.

A second reason that evidence has so little impact on some arguments is that what we know is incomplete. Many issues require us to fill in gaps. For example, Robert Park argues that the reason that scientists can differ among themselves about global climate change is not so much because they disagree about the actual data and physics involved, but because answering the question, "How serious a threat is global warming?" requires us to extrapolate into the future. This involves making assumptions based partly on the past, and our knowledge of the past is filled with gaps. How do we fill them in? Park suggests that we fill the gaps in with worldviews that we have absorbed much earlier, views "learned at our mothers' knees," so that the global climate change debate becomes "more an argument about values than [an argument] about science."[7] The grip that our worldviews can have on our thinking can lead us to ignore mounting evidence that global climate change is a critical problem. Indeed, we may reconsider such evidence only when those whose values are akin to our own begin to reverse their stance on the issue and concede that climate change is a reality.

MISSING EVIDENCE AND PARADIGMS

There are almost always missing pieces in the puzzles we are trying to solve. Trying to understand what happened in the far past is, as best-selling author, social scientist, and activist Riane Eisler wrote, like putting together "a giant jigsaw puzzle with more than half its pieces destroyed or lost. It is impossible to reconstruct completely."[8] Though fewer of the pieces are missing when we try to reconstruct what happened last week or last year, it is still a challenge to do so. It is even more daunting to try to determine what is happening in the invisible world of minute atomic particles or what has transpired in the minds and hearts of other people.

Yet Eisler writes that "the greatest obstacle . . . is not that we are lacking so many pieces; it is that the prevailing paradigm makes it so hard to accurately interpret the pieces we have."[9] The prevailing paradigm is that larger worldview that we have adopted, along with the set of values that it involves. All the bits of information that come our way are like little pieces of a puzzle that we try to put together in some coherent whole in order to make sense of the world. Our blind spot is that we toss aside those pieces that don't seem to fit the general outline of the picture we already have of what the world is like. And we unthinkingly accept as valid any pieces that do seem to fit that general picture. How can we offset this blind spot?

TACTICS: OVERCOMING THE BLIND SPOT OF FUZZY EVIDENCE

What can we do to address the blind spot that comes when we allow our worldviews and our values to determine, in an absolute fashion, which evidence and claims we take seriously and which we dismiss without a second glance? What can we do to help us see evidence more clearly?

Tactic #1 Slow Down— Question Our Automatic Judgments

The first step is to notice when this blind spot is happening, to notice when we are making a judgment without even considering the evidence. In July 2003 I read a letter to the editor about the rape accusation that had been leveled against basketball player Kobe Bryant. The author of that letter, Ryan Holeywell, began with, "I am growing more appalled each day with the coverage of the Kobe Bryant sexual assault allegation. It seems that everyone has made up his or her mind regarding this case, even though evidence has not been presented, a jury has not been selected, and lawyers have not made their arguments."[10] Holeywell noted that some people were "so intent on seeing Bryant's image crumble" that they automatically assumed he was guilty, while others had already concluded that Bryant's accuser was lying and simply after his money, "despite the fact that this young woman has not even offered testimony yet." Who is telling the truth? Kobe Bryant or the woman alleging rape? The author of this letter was pleading with the public to recognize that the best answer to that question, prior to the trial, was "impossible to determine," or "not sure," because we hadn't even looked at the evidence, the pieces of the puzzle that might help us reconstruct a picture of what did or didn't happen. So the first step in addressing the blind spot of not seeing evidence clearly is to slow down and ask ourselves, "What evidence exists? What evidence am I basing my views on?"

Tactic #2: When Our Minds Slam Shut, Ask, "What Would It Mean?"

In his work with parents of children who have physical impairments, clinical psychologist Ken Moses tells the story of Mary, a three-year-old girl who had been recently diagnosed with a severe hearing impairment. Mary's mother did not believe the diagnosis, insisting instead that Mary could hear her name whispered behind her back. The audiologist asked the mother to demonstrate this feat. She turned her daughter around so that the child's back was toward her mother then loudly whispered "Mary!" At the same time as she whispered, Mary's mother stamped her foot on the wooden floor. At the vibration, the child turned and beamed at her mom, who then shot the audiologist a victorious look.[11]

Now, the audiologist is likely to be astonished by this mother's "evidence" of her daughter's ability to hear. He will be tempted to try to argue her out of her position by pointing out the inadequacy of her hearing test and press her to acknowledge that his own testing is more accurate. He *might* change the mother's mind if he does this—but he might not. His opposition might instead cause Mary's mother to become even more entrenched in her position. What can he do?

Ken Moses suggests that the audiologist adopt the "What would it mean to you?" question. He might say something like, "The idea of Mary's being deaf seems almost impossible for you to accept. Can you tell me a little bit about what it would mean to you if somehow my assessment were even partially correct?" If the mother responds by saying that "it would mean that my child will never live a normal life . . . be happy . . . know the joys of love and children of her own . . . ," then he might say, "If you truly believe that, then I can certainly understand why you would not be able to accept that Mary might have a problem." Here the audiologist is walking a fine line: he is acknowledging the mother's viewpoint without agreeing with it. He is planting the seed that maybe there is another way to think about Mary and her condition. Maybe his diagnosis doesn't have to mean what Mary's mother fears it must mean.

"What would it mean to you?" is crucial because it reaches the heart of our resistance to evidence that is potentially painful to embrace. It may not make much *logical* sense for Mary's mother to take the stance she is assuming, but it makes perfect *psychological* sense that she would need to blunt the sharp reality of her daughter's condition—especially if "what it would mean" to her is so devastating.

"What would it mean to you?" is also key because it can help people identify the values they hold that they fear will be endangered by that evidence. Once we see how the evidence threatens something that is important to us, such as a value or a hope that we hold dear, we may be more able to face the challenge of evaluating that evidence with an open mind.

Tactic #3: Take a Closer Look at the Evidence on Both Sides

After we've identified the evidence offered and are committed to considering it with an open mind, we need to ask some hard questions.

When others make a factual claim that *contradicts* what we believe, we should ask:

- *Is it possible that there is some validity to this claim that opposes my own?*
- *Is it possible that there is some truth here, even if it is only a small part of the truth?*
- *How sure am I that there is nothing useful or true in these statements?*

When others make a factual claim that *agrees* with what we believe, we should ask:

- *Is it possible that some of what is being said here is on shaky ground?*
- *Is what's being claimed true as far as it goes but limited in some important ways?*
- *How sure am I that this evidence should be swallowed whole—that there are no qualifications that should be attached to it?*

When people answer "How sure am I?" honestly, they often find that they are not 100 percent sure. We need to figure out, like the jurors in a trial, whether the doubts that we have are significant enough to constitute a reasonable doubt, a sign that we should investigate further before deciding what we believe.

Tactic #4: Actively Search for Counterexamples, Evidence That Contradicts Our View

Imagine that you are acting as a chaperone for a field trip. At the end of the visit to the museum, the children pile back on the bus, and you count them. You expect there to be twenty-three children on the bus, but you count only twenty-two. Naturally, you re-count the children. This time you come up with twenty-three, the expected number, the one that confirms your expectation about how many children there should be. At that point, you tell the bus driver to take off and head for home.

But notice that there is no reason to assume that your second count would necessarily be more accurate than your first. You might just as easily have overcounted on your second try as undercounted on your first. Moreover, if you had come up with the expected number on your first try, you probably wouldn't have bothered to count a second time. Your answer would have confirmed your expectation, and you probably would not have sought out possible *disconfirming data* by doing a second check.

We human beings have a bias to seek only confirming evidence, a bias that you can see in everyday life. Imagine that I have recently joined a new company, and I'm warned on my first day about how contrary Marie is: she is accused of always being a naysayer, a pessimist, someone who is programmed to inevitably take an opposite position. Our bias to seek only confirming evidence means that people are likely to notice all the incidents in which Marie's behavior confirms this hypothesis but not to seek out disconfirming evidence. If I said to a group of Marie's detractors, "Is she really so negative?" they would readily supply me with examples that support this judgment. What if I interrupted this flow and asked, "But can you think of any times when Marie *didn't* act in this way?" If her colleagues genuinely thought about it, they might well recall such occasions. Logically, we *know* that a single incident in which Marie was not contrary is all that is needed to shake our faith in the belief that she is inevitably negative, yet we rarely seek that disconfirming information.

We can seek counterevidence and can keep those facts on file for future consideration. There is an old folk adage that proclaims, "the exception proves the rule," meaning that the only reason we notice those exceptions is because most of the time the usual behavior that reflects the "rule" prevails. Thus, our noticing of exceptions is offered as evidence that the usual behavior is typical and shows what the person is really like. When we seek counterevidence, we reject that folk wisdom. Instead, we assume that the exceptions *disprove* the rule or at least alert us that there's something more going on than the simplistic rule captures. Instead of tossing out information that contradicts the accepted view, we can put those facts into a box labeled something like "facts I don't understand yet." Like scientists who eventually return to the anomalies, the bits of evidence that don't fit their general theory, we can return to those pieces, add to them, and perhaps eventually change our understanding of an issue, a person, or an event in a way that allows more pieces to fall into place.

Tactic #5: Investigate the Reliability of the Source

Sometimes it is transparent that the source of the information is likely to be less trustworthy. Most people, for example, are suspicious of advertising endorsements when the spokesperson is getting paid or owns stock in the company whose product he is advocating. In contrast, when we believe that the person offering evidence and opinions is a disinterested party, we are more likely to see his ideas as trustworthy. Because the trustworthiness of the source of information is so crucial, critical-thinking texts often advise people to search for the most objective sources of information that they can find. A scientific report on the efficacy of a drug, for example, is generally considered more trustworthy than the remarks of a paid actor on a TV commercial about how his headache went away. But if the scientists conducting the research are working for the drug company that produces the medication, we once again become wary.

What's hard about taking the reliability of the source into account is that we can't automatically assume that the evidence is flawed just because the person endorsing it stands to gain if people believe the evidence. Similarly, we can't automatically assume that the evidence is accurate just because it emanates from a scientist who is presumably objective in her approach. What we need is what the investigative reporter seeks: corroborating evidence and statements from at least two independent sources. One advantage of scientific research is that it makes it possible to search for corroborating evidence by duplicating the original research. If numerous scientists replicate the research and discover the same outcome, we have more confidence in that evidence, even when it contradicts what we have long believed to be true.

Until we are surer, we need to state our claims tentatively. We also need to be more open to the possibility that others have at least a small piece of truth. The truth about many matters is complex. Often our beliefs are, in effect, our best guess. If truth can so often be interwoven with innocent mistakes, with plausible but incorrect interpretations, with intentional deception, then we need to be cautious about assuming that the truth is ever so clear-cut that it can be associated completely with one worldview while being utterly absent from the opposing worldview.

LIVING WITH AMBIGUITY

In their studies of creative people, psychologists report that creative people are more able to live with ambiguity than the rest of us are. To keep holding in our hands all those puzzle pieces that don't fit our worldview, to keep trying to juggle them, isn't easy. This way of considering evidence brings us into a grayer, more complicated world, a world in which there are often more questions than answers. The good news is that this world also holds more possibilities. Being willing to look at the anomalies, the pieces of the puzzle that don't fit what we expected, can lead to creative discoveries. Those discoveries can help us revise our worldviews to reflect more accurately or more completely the complexity that we are trying to understand.

WIDENING THE CIRCLE: WHAT HAPPENS WHEN WE DISCOVER THAT WE WERE WRONG?

On September 17, 2003, President George W. Bush confirmed that, counter to the beliefs of nearly 70 percent of the US citizens polled at the time, the United States "had no evidence that Saddam Hussein was involved with [the terrorist attacks of] September 11." Earlier that week, Defense Secretary Donald Rumsfeld had made a similar statement at a Pentagon news conference. Bush's statement seemed to disagree with the earlier statements of the administration, and it certainly contradicted what most US citizens had come to believe.

Now, how are we likely to react to about-faces such as this one? Well, it depends upon which side we initially favored, doesn't it? The people who had supported the president's war in Iraq, believing that a strong terrorist link existed, were likely to feel stunned, confused, and perhaps disillusioned or even betrayed by the admission from the White House. If the president had allowed people to believe in this link while he knew that such a connection did not exist, was it possible that the administration had also allowed or even encouraged the public's confidence in other erroneous beliefs? Was it also possible that Iraq—as Hussein had protested from the outset—had not had weapons of mass destruction? When the statements and honesty of those whom we once believed are called into serious question, our faith can tumble like a house of cards.

And that collapsing house of cards makes us afraid that our whole worldview might also fall to pieces. It takes a very courageous person to face the counterevidence offered and try to come to grips with its implications, rather than minimize it or deny that it makes any difference. One host of a conservative radio talk show was clearly turned upside down by the president's statement. "But didn't they tell us that they had proof of this?" he protested. He then vowed to search the station's news files to trace the statements that had led him, along with so many other US citizens, to believe unquestioningly in that link. Clearly distraught, he wanted to discover the truth about these matters, wherever that truth might lead.

It is the rare person who is able to react in the way that this talk-show host responded. More commonly, we scramble to deny the significance of what's been revealed. Why do we do this? One reason is the way that our adversaries respond to the same news that has so disillusioned us. Those who opposed President Bush and the war in Iraq reacted with a combination of anger and glee at the president's admission. The anger came from their belief that a war that they opposed had been sold to US citizens under false pretenses. But the glee came from having been right, from being able to crow their triumph to the co-worker at the desk next to theirs or to the neighbor over whose backyard fence they had so often argued politics. As one person who called into that same talk show began, "I don't like to say I told you so, but . . ." He then went on, clearly relishing that he could "tell them so."

It's very, very hard to engage in coming to grips with information that shakes our world up when our adversaries are essentially ridiculing us. They are telling us that we were stupid to have believed what we did. I don't suppose that the vast majority of Americans, the almost 70 percent polled who believed that a link existed between the 9/11 attacks and Saddam Hussein, were stupid. They simply did what most of us do, most of the time. They believed the claims made by those who belonged to groups whose views and values they shared. They rejected out of hand counterclaims made by other groups, such as antiwar groups, whose philosophies and worldviews differed from their own. Those who ridiculed the believers after the truth emerged wanted the believers to revise their thinking. Yet the jeerers had their own blind spot. They ignored the fact that their derision makes it that much harder for others to reconsider their old belief systems.

GLITCHES: THE SCIENTIFIC WORLDVIEW AS THE ONLY VALID WORLDVIEW

One glitch in using empirical, scientific approaches to evaluate evidence is that it can make it seem that the only questions worth investigating and the only answers worth considering are those that can be tested by the scientific method. Scientific thinking has allowed us to make such unprecedented strides in understanding the material world, so much so that we're seduced into believing that it's only a matter of time before we understand everything. Confronted with questions that we can't answer, we think, "Well, we just need more time or more research or more advanced technology, and eventually we will know . . . how the universe began . . . what causes cancer . . . how to regenerate spinal cord cells, etc." Why is this attitude a glitch?

Critics of this thinking are afraid that we have become so enthralled by what science can accomplish that we act as if nothing matters but matter. We act as if the material world, and the questions that we have about it, are the only questions that are worth our attention—because they are the only ones that can be definitively answered. This attitude can blind people to philosophical and religious worldviews that attempt to address existential questions, ones that cannot be answered using scientific methods. What is the meaning of life? Why are we here? How should we live? These are among the issues that philosophy and religion attempt to address.

Religious studies scholar Huston Smith, author of *Why Religion Matters*, argues that our modern attitude of viewing science as a god has created a kind of tunnel vision.[12] In this tunnel vision, a question such as "What is the meaning of life?" is not worth pursuing because the answers we come up with can't be tested scientifically. Unlike the cause of cancer, the meaning of life doesn't exist "out there," waiting to be discovered. Any meanings that people propose must then be merely their own ideas—ideas that cannot be evaluated because the measuring stick of scientific experimentation cannot be applied to them. Smith deplores this attitude as a negative side effect of our scientific age.

Religion, along with some philosophical views, deals with a reality that cannot be seen, measured, or "proven" scientifically, a reality that scientific methods cannot detect. Smith urges us not to dismiss the idea that such a transcendent reality exists simply because science cannot detect it. He urges us not to speak the rhetoric of the merely when we refer to ideas about the existence of God or the meaning of life, not to dismiss these as *merely* quaint childhood beliefs or *just* fantasies to comfort those who cannot cope with the reality of death.

Contrasting with the view that nothing matters but matter is this statement commonly attributed to Einstein: "Not everything that can be counted counts, and not everything that counts can be counted." We will have a blind spot if we let the breathtaking power of scientific thinking lead us to forget its limits or to act as if speculation about, or faith in, any reality that isn't detectable through scientific methods is inevitably foolish.

IN A NUTSHELL

Fans of critical thinking urge people to make sure that their beliefs are based on solid evidence. It turns out, however, that evaluating evidence is trickier than it first appears. As a result, rather than basing our beliefs directly on the strength of the evidence itself, we often simply accept any evidence offered by those whose views are similar to our own, and we reject all evidence offered by those whose views conflict with our own. This causes the blind spot of fuzzy evidence—we fail to see the evidence clearly. To compensate for this blind spot, we need to take a closer look at the available evidence, using such tactics as actively seeking evidence that might disconfirm what we believe to be true. Ultimately, this will enable us to modify our worldviews so that they are more complete and more accurate.

SNEAK PREVIEW

When we try to understand the world around us, one of the most important questions we try to answer is "Why?" In every area of knowledge, from science to history to our personal lives, we have "why" questions. Why docs thc occan havc tidcs? Why can't we solve the problem of world hunger? What caused World War II? Why am I so disturbed by what my boss said yesterday? It makes sense to most people that existential "why" questions such as "Why do we exist?" are challenging to answer. Human beings have been wondering about such questions since time immemorial. But even scientific "why" questions about the material world are often very hard to answer. In the next chapter, we look at *why* that's so.

NOTES

1. Robert E. Bartholomew and Benjamin Radford, *Hoaxes, Myths, and Manias* (Amherst, NY: Prometheus Books, 2003).
2. Michael Shermer, *Why People Believe Weird Things: Pseudoscience, Superstition, and Other Confusions of Our Time* (New York: Freeman/Owl Books, 2002).
3. Annick Mansfield and Blythe Clinchy, "The Early Growth of Multiplism in the Child" (paper presented at the Fifteenth Annual Symposium of the Jean Piaget Society, Philadelphia, PA, June 1985).
4. Steve Farrar, "Fatal Steps," *Sunday Times* (UK), August 23, 1998. See also Australian Skeptics, "King Tut's Curse 'A Killer Bug,'" http://www.skeptics.com.au/features/weird/media/mw-tutbug.htm (accessed October 11, 2003).
5. Joel Best, *Damned Lies and Statistics: Untangling Numbers from the Media, Politicians, and Activists* (Berkeley: University of California Press, 2001).
6. Robert Park, *Voodoo Science* (New York: Oxford University Press, 2000), p. 146.
7. Ibid., p. 34.
8. Riane Eisler, *The Chalice and the Blade* (New York: HarperCollins, 1987), p. 29.

9. Ibid.

10. Ryan Holeywell, "Don't Judge Him Yet," *USA Today*, letter to the editor, July 28, 2003.

11. Kenneth Moses and Madeleine Van Hecke-Wulatin, "A Counseling Model re: The Socio-emotional Impact of Infant Deafness," in *Early Management of Hearing Loss*, ed. G. T. Mencher and S. E. Gerber, 243–78 (New York: Grune and Stratton, 1981).

12. Huston Smith, *Why Religion Matters* (San Francisco: HarperCollins, 2001).

Chapter 10
THE USUAL SUSPECTS
Why We Miss the Real Culprit

BLIND SPOT #9: MISSING HIDDEN CAUSES

In the summer of 1993, a total of five thousand people gathered in small groups across Washington, DC, to participate in the National Demonstration Project to Reduce Violent Crime. Staggered over a two-month period and working in two-week shifts, these groups tried to reduce crime by practicing group meditation across the nation's capitol. The organizer of this project, John Hagelin, predicted a 20 percent reduction of crime as a result of their efforts. Instead, reports Robert Park in his book *Voodoo Science*, "the murder rate for those two months reached a level unmatched before or since."[1] Nevertheless, in a press conference, Hagelin claimed that the meditation had been a success, reducing crime by 18 percent. "Compared to what?" a reporter from the *Washington Post* asked. Hagelin replied that the incidence of violent crime was 18 percent lower than it would have been had the participants not been meditating in the city at that time. "But how can you know what it would have been?" wondered the reporter.

Is it *possible* that the DC crime rate was lower than it would have been without the meditation project? Perhaps. But is it *likely* that the meditation project reduced crime? To believe that, you would have to believe that without the meditation the rate of violent crime would have been 18 percent higher that summer than it actually was—despite the fact that the height it did reach set a record that remains standing today.

The story of the Washington, DC, meditation group is a great illustration of the main point made in chapter 9: our worldviews can make it difficult for us to evaluate evidence objectively. By group leader Hagelin's own prediction, the project had failed: they had not reduced crime by 20 percent compared with the average summer crime rates. In fact, the reverse happened, as the crime rate soared to a record high. Yet Hagelin claimed success, maintaining that he could figure out what the rate would have been without the meditation through complex computations related to other factors. When we really want to believe that something causes something else, we can find a way to do so.

CHILDHOOD CLUES TO ADULT THINKING

But in this chapter I want to focus on a different aspect of the meditation group story: on how it is possible—in fact, all too easy—for people to feel sure about the cause of something and be wrong. Once again, the way that children think gives us some clues. Four-year-old Desmond was watching his babysitter, Claire, make a salad. As Claire sliced a carrot over the bowl of greens, Desmond reached for a piece just as Claire brought the knife down to make another cut. Fortunately, the small paring knife barely nicked Desmond's finger. But as Claire was washing the cut under the faucet, Desmond protested, "I only wanted to get a piece of carrot!" Astonished, Claire realized that Desmond thought she had intentionally cut his finger as a punishment.

What would Desmond say if he were able to explain his reasoning to us? He'd probably say something like, "When one thing happens, and then another thing happens, the first one caused the second one." This sort of intuitive reasoning is common among three- and four-year-old children. It reflects the logical assumption that causes precede their effects.

As adults, we continue to use this sort of reasoning; it's effective in many situations. But it also has flaws. The first of these is that it's too simplistic. When we think in this way, we act as if a single, apparent, and immediate cause can account for what occurs. As adults, we know that a single cause is often inadequate to explain what happens. The folk saying about the final straw that broke the camel's back reflects our hunch that an accumulation of minor incidents can cause major events, ones that could not be explained if we focused only on the final event that was the last straw. Yet we often lose sight of the fundamental idea of *multiple causation* and instead accept a simplistic explanation for what has happened.

There is a second limitation to the intuitive idea that when two things happen together, the first is the cause of the second. Desmond doesn't entertain the possibility that his finger cut was a chance event, a fluke that had nothing at all to do with Claire's feelings about his actions. Whenever two things happen in proximity, we need to have some way of determining whether the two events are meaningfully connected before deciding that one caused the other. That they occurred together could be simply a fluke, a chance happening: literally, a *co*incidence.

HOW CAN WE TELL WHICH PATTERNS ARE MEANINGFUL?

Our minds are programmed to find patterns, and the pattern of what causes what is a particularly important one to human beings. When we encounter some unusual event, we immediately try to explain it by seeing what it might be connected to. We search for causes using the simple method of asking what happened earlier. If we wake up with an upset stomach, we wonder about the curry that we tried for the first time the night before. It's apparently quite natural for us to glom on to the first likely cause that we suspect and less natural for us to ask whether that event is really adequate, by itself, to explain what has happened. It's apparently also not usual for us to consider whether the curry might be utterly unconnected with our upset stomach, that it might be merely a fluke. As with other blind spots, this natural inclination of ours to see patterns wherever we look, so useful in many respects, is also the source of our dilemma. How can we distinguish which patterns are really meaningful?

For example, people who believe in numerology read great meaning into various numbers, such as measurements or the number of words in a passage. And the meanings they read into the relationships are not commonplace meanings, such as saying that those numbers are proportional to one another because the builder intentionally made them proportional in order to design a particular type of arc. No, numerologists search for hidden meanings that hint at causes outside the mundane. For example, some people read the sixteenth-century writings of Michel de Nostredame (known popularly as Nostradamus) and conclude that he was a prophet, foreseeing the future in his cryptic quatrains. But are the numerical relationships identified by interpreters of such works meaningful or simply coincidental?

In his book *Why People Believe Weird Things*, author Michael Shermer provides a vivid example of why it is easy for people to interpret coincidental numerical relationships as meaningful.[2] Shermer describes how mathematician Martin Gardner decided, on a lark, to analyze the measurements of the Washington Monument. Gardner discovered that the number 5 emerged prominently in the monument's features. The height of the monument is 555 feet and 5 inches; the base is 55 square feet; the windows are set 500 feet from the base; multiply the base by 60 (which is 5 times the number of months in a year), and you'll get 3,300—the exact weight of the capstone in pounds. To top it all off, the name of the monument, Washington, has ten letters, which equals 5 times 2, and if the weight of the capstone is multiplied by the base, the answer is close to the speed of light in miles per second.

These facts are peculiar, but should they leave us breathless with wonder? They might make us curious about the conscious intentions of the monument's designers, but should they trigger faith in prophetic visions or in the power of unseen forces? As a mathematician who understands how easy it is to find patterns in numbers, Gardner would say no.

Two steps, then, are crucial when we are trying to avoid the blind spot of hidden causes. First, we need to ask: Are the causes more complex than the simple or single cause that we have identified? Second, we need to wonder: Is the occurrence of these events or factors meaningful—or is it a fluke? We'll look at each of these in turn.

THE NEED TO SEARCH FOR MORE COMPLEX CAUSES

Like Desmond, most people use a simple, single-cause model to explain events. Imagine that in recent weeks, Mom has been nagging her son to start applying to the colleges he's interested in. Their arguments about this issue have escalated. What's causing this escalation? Mom might say that she's nagging more because her son still hasn't taken action. The son, however, might make exactly the opposite interpretation. He might say that the more she nags, the less motivated he is. And the father in this family might think that Mom is nagging and the son is dragging his feet because they are both worried about his job security, which has become precarious. "She's just generally more crabby," he might say of his wife, "because she's afraid I'll be out of work soon. And I think Josh is afraid that in that case, there might not be enough money for college, so why bother?"

The point of this example is that even when events are meaningfully connected, it's not always easy to tell whether A is causing B, or B is causing A—or whether both are being caused by a different factor, C. It's quite possible that all three explanations of what's going on in the household above are correct and that there are multiple causes working together.

To muddy the waters further, the relationships among various causes are often complex. When there are multiple causes, do all the factors contribute equally? For example, when someone asserts that the cause of alcoholism is one-third hereditary, one-third learning the drinking patterns of a culture, and one-third reacting to stress in an individual's life, he is claiming that each factor contributes about equally to the development of alcoholism. But causal factors don't necessarily contribute to the same degree or in an additive way. For example, small-boned women are more likely to develop osteoporosis. In this case, being small-boned is a predisposing cause rather than a factor that adds up in equal proportions with other factors to cause the disease.

Because people tend to ignore the fact that causes are often complex, they get irritated when researchers appear to change their minds, especially about health issues. People grumble, "First they said that eggs were terrible because of cholesterol; now they say it's okay to eat eggs!" The ubiquitous "they" in these references typically refers to scientists whose research has been reported in the news. When new research repeatedly seems to invalidate old beliefs, people who have followed those old beliefs are understandably disgruntled. Why not just toss a coin to decide what to do about health issues if research is so unreliable?

Perhaps one of the most disconcerting disillusionments occurred when the Women's Health Initiative (WHI) contacted the women participating in their huge nationwide study and told them to stop taking hormone replacement medication. The WHI study was testing the idea that hormone replacement therapy not only decreases the discomfort of menopausal symptoms, such as hot flashes, but has other beneficial effects, such as preventing osteoporosis and heart disease. However, the data that WHI had been accumulating over the initial years of its study indicated that the women taking the hormone replacement therapy instead not only had a *higher* incidence of the disorders the therapy was supposed to prevent—heart attacks and strokes—but, in addition, had a higher incidence of breast cancer.[3]

Some people reacted to this report by wondering how earlier scientists could have been so wrong in the first place. If the current research is right, then the earlier researchers were wrong, and the physicians who wrote the forty-five million prescriptions that pharmacists filled the previous year for estrogen were in the wrong for giving bad advice to their female patients. You can see the stupid-versus-flawed dichotomy at play here: either the scientists were stupid for being mistaken about this matter, or they were in the wrong for encouraging practices that might have harmed people.

It's hard not to make harsh judgments like these when you believe your health or the health of people you love has been endangered. But the reality is that the workings of our bodies involve complex processes, many of which are difficult or impossible to observe directly. The causes of many diseases must be inferred from what we can observe, and they are multiple and multilayered. In the case of the kuru disease, for example, having the infectious agent in your body seemed to be both a necessary and a sufficient cause for developing the disease. That is, you would not get kuru if you didn't have the agent, and everyone who had the agent eventually would develop the disease. In contrast, many other illnesses such as Legionnaires' disease involve a viral agent, but the virus alone is not sufficient to cause the disease. Many people who had antibodies to the virus *Legionella pneumophila* in their bloodstream, showing that they had been exposed to it, never became sick. Thus, Legionnaire's disease is caused by a combination of a necessary cause (the invasion of the body by the virus) without which the person will not get the disease plus a secondary cause. The secondary cause can vary; it might be a specific condition such as emphysema or a more general factor such as a weak immune system.

TACTICS: HOW CAN WE OVERCOME THE BLIND SPOT OF HIDDEN CAUSES?

Tactic #1: Ask the History Teacher Question

One high school history teacher tried to counter his students' natural tendency to ignore complex causes by describing a situation in which a man, driving home from work late on a rainy night, had an automobile accident and hit a tree. The teacher would ask his class, "How many different possible causes for this accident can you come up with?" The students would generate lots of potential causes, from the slickness of the road to the possibility that the man was distracted because he was angry at having to work late in the first place. Then the teacher would ask them, "Do you think the causes of World War II would be more or less complicated than the causes of this man's automobile accident?"

This is a great question. It takes us aback and gives us pause. One way to overcome our tendency to seize the first cause that occurs to us is to ask, "Would the causes of what I'm trying to explain likely be more or less complicated than the causes of a car accident?" If our answer is that they'd likely be more complex, then we'll stop and think more about what the multiple causes might be.

Tactic #2: Analyze the Causes

Once we've generated a list of what the multiple causes might be, we can ask ourselves whether some might work together in ways that are more complicated than A causing B. Applying our knowledge of the different causal relationships that can occur, we can ask:

- Is there a main cause, a root cause that is more fundamental than the others?
- Is it possible that instead of A causing B, it is actually B causing A—or that A and B are in a kind of vicious cycle, each continually triggering the other?
- Could there be a third, hidden cause that is responsible for both A and B?
- When we are sure that A is a cause, can we tell if it is a necessary cause, without which B will not occur?
- Can we tell if A alone is sufficient to cause B or if other conditions must be present as well? What might these conditions be?
- And finally, that all-important question: Is it possible that the coincidence of A, B, and C is simply a fluke—that these events really have nothing to do with one another?

The last question is crucial. If we think something is meaningful when it is really a fluke—or if we think something is a fluke when it is really meaningful—we'll be blind to the actual cause of what we're trying to understand. Why is it so hard to determine whether or not something is a fluke?

THE FLUKE FACTOR: A FLUKE OR FRAUGHT WITH MEANING?

Remember Cynthia and the article about the King Tut curse? The interviewer also asked Cynthia the following questions:

> INTERVIEWER: Suppose at the exact moment someone died, there was an electrical blackout in the city. Could there be a connection between these two events? Explain why or why not.
>
> CYNTHIA: Yes, there is a connection. No, probably not because I know the blackout in New York was the result of an electrical storm. A person's death causing a blackout is rare—it would be beyond phenomena. I'd have to go to a lot of books to find out for sure.
>
> INTERVIEWER: Suppose when this same person died, there was not only an electrical blackout, but also at that exact moment a dog howled. Could there be a connection between these three events?
>
> CYNTHIA: Could be the person's dog senses that its master was dead. Dogs can sense things miles away. More than likely there is a connection.
>
> *The interviewer repeats the question about the howling dog again—only this time she adds, ". . . and the dog died."*
>
> CYNTHIA: Definitely a connection. Something like that would not happen without a reason, so there must be a connection. The person who died had to have some influence over the storm and the dog.

Cynthia's answers show that she is trying hard to distinguish between events that could have happened simply coincidently from events that are meaningfully connected. Her comments capture the dilemma we all face. How can we tell whether the connections that we see represent a meaningful pattern—or whether they reflect a coincidence, an accident, a fluke?

The same challenge of how to distinguish meaningful connections from coincidences is faced by scientific researchers. Author and statistician David Salsburg opens his book *The Lady Tasting Tea* with an anecdote about a university gathering in Cambridge in the 1920s in which one guest proclaimed that tea tasted different to her depending upon whether the tea was poured into the milk or thc milk into the tea.[4] While others poked fun at her assertion—how could the order in which the elements were combined possibly make any difference to the taste?—one guest proposed a way to test the lady's assertion. He presented her with a cup of tea that had been made outside her view and asked her which way it had been prepared. She sipped, then declared that it was one where the milk had been poured into the tea. Imagine, for a moment, that she was correct. Should the guests at the party now be convinced that she could tell the difference?

Salsburg points out that she would have a 50/50 chance of being right if she were merely guessing and couldn't really tell the difference. So perhaps we shouldn't be convinced by her correct answer. What if we changed the test a bit and presented her with two cups of tea—one prepared with milk added to tea and one with tea added to milk? Now the odds of her guessing correctly the first time are still 50/50—but if she is correct on the first cup, then the odds of her correctly identifying the second cup rise to 100 percent.

The key question, as Salsburg notes, is how many cups of tea prepared in these two different ways does the lady need to identify correctly in order for us to be convinced that she can really tell the difference? If she guesses correctly three times in a row, is that enough? How about ten times? What if she guesses correctly twenty-three times but misses on two occasions? Do we decide that her errors prove she can't tell the difference or that her twenty-three correct responses prove that she can? What are the odds that her correct guesses are a fluke? At what point should we conclude that coincidence alone can, or can't, account for the lady's level of accuracy?

As Salsburg's book recounts, various statistical theories and methods were developed in an attempt to answer questions like these. Statistical tests help scientists decide the odds that a particular research result could have been a fluke rather than resulting from the factor under investigation. For example, in many published studies, the researchers will state that their findings are significant at the .05 level. This means that if the same study they had done were repeated a hundred times, the same results would occur only five times in that hundred—*if* the results were merely a coincidence or a fluke. The odds, then, are that the study is one of the other ninety-five. The odds are that its results are meaningful rather than coincidental. But we are still dealing in probabilities: this study *could* be one of the five flukes—in which case the results are meaningless. This is why scientists become more convinced of research results when similar studies are conducted that arrive at parallel results: the odds that the results of several different studies are all fluke events are so small that we become confident of their findings.

If you feel you are stumbling as you try to follow the rationale underlying these ideas, you're not alone. Many people find their eyes glazing over when they are presented with detailed descriptions of statistical tests and the theoretical concepts that underlie them. Neither the tests nor the theories are intuitively obvious. Entire college and graduate courses are devoted to statistics, probability theory, and research design.

Many intelligent people who are uneducated in math or not mathematically gifted struggle with mathematical concepts. In fact, Gregor Mendel's paper on genetics that would have shed invaluable light on Charles Darwin's theory of evolution was found untouched on Darwin's bookshelves. In her biography of Gregor Mendel, author Robin Henig suggests that Darwin would probably not have grasped the significance of Mendel's findings even if he had read the paper, because Mendel's work relied heavily on mathematics, and mathematics were not Darwin's strength.[5]

So it's not surprising to me that people who are untutored in these areas find it hard to follow the explanations offered to explain why one particular set of events should be suspected of being mere coincidence, while another set should be accepted as meaningful, or why the results of a particular study are taken seriously, while the results of another are viewed as flawed, likely to be a fluke.

In fact, the mathematical area called *probability theory* that underlies statistical inference is not easy even for highly educated mathematicians and scientists. Columnist and author Marilyn vos Savant relates a question sent to her by a reader. The reader described a situation in which a game-show contestant is given a choice of three doors, one of which has a car behind it, while the other two have goats behind them. Marilyn's reader wrote, "You pick a door, say number 1, and the host, who knows what's behind the doors, opens another door, say door number 3, which has a goat. He says to you: 'Do you want to pick door number 2?' Is it to your advantage to switch your choice of doors?" Marilyn advised, "Yes, you should switch."[6]

If you think that Marilyn is wrong, you are not alone. PhD mathematicians and Nobel Prize–winning physicists were among those who were sure she was in error. Frequently, those who disagreed with Marilyn argued that once the host had eliminated door number 3, the odds of picking the correct door become 50/50, so that the chances of winning the car are the same whether or not the person switches. Many of the authors of letters disagreeing with Marilyn were condescending in their tone. One professor wrote, "Your answer is in error. But if it is any consolation, many of my academic colleagues have been stumped by this problem." After Marilyn responded to their objections in another column, explaining her rationale in more detail, she continued to receive letters such as the following: "May I suggest that you obtain and refer to a standard textbook on probability before you try to answer a question of this type again?" Another reader protested: "I am in shock that after being corrected by three mathematicians, you still do not see your mistake."[7]

Often, the proof of mathematical problems lies in a series of equations or other mathematical representations, such as matrices, which will ultimately demonstrate the correctness of the answer. These complex and abstract proofs are often beyond the ability of nonmathematicians to grasp. But in the case of the game-show problem, there is a simpler way to determine whether or not Marilyn is right. Marilyn's answer can be empirically tested by simply seeing how often the contestant wins when he switches compared with how often he wins when he sticks with his original door choice. All we have to do is replicate the situation and have the contestant switch his choice every time for, say, one hundred trials and then stick to his initial choice during a subsequent hundred trials. If her detractors are correct, the person should win the prize roughly 50 percent of the time, regardless of whether he switches or sticks. But if Marilyn is correct, the individual should win the prize about 66 percent of the time when he switches and only about 33 percent of the time when he sticks. When computer programs—and schoolchildren throughout the United States—conducted tests like these, Marilyn's answer was supported.

Many of the experts who initially disagreed with Marilyn's answer eventually came around to her way of thinking. But the fact that this problem, which appears simple on the surface, could stymie and confuse highly educated scientists and mathematicians is a powerful reminder to me of how difficult it is to grasp probability theory. No wonder it's often not easy to judge whether events are connected in a meaningful way or whether they are more likely the result of coincidence. What might help us do this, despite the challenge?

TACTICS: PART II

These two tactics both involve asking yourself questions in order to consider the fluke factor when trying to decide the cause of something.

Tactic #1: What Are the Odds That This Is Sheer Coincidence?

Sometimes things happen by sheer coincidence. For example, you take a class in woodworking and discover that of the six women in the class, four who have never met before can all speak Italian. Or you think about calling a friend to suggest that you go to a concert together and come to work the next day to find she's already bought tickets for both of you. Or you run into someone you haven't seen for years while you are traveling in Europe, at a café that bears the name of the street that the two of you once lived on. Are these events meaningful in some way or simply flukes?

Most people won't see any great meaning in these sorts of occurrences; instead, they accept that they happened by chance or by a combination of chance and factors such as both of us enjoying similar musicians. Before we ascribe meaning to *co*incidences, that is, to two events that happen to occur at the same time, we need to ask another question.

Ask Yourself, "Was This Coincidence Predicted Ahead of Time?"

If we predicted the coincidence *ahead of time*, we'd be much more likely to think that the coincidences were more than meaningless flukes! Imagine that we had said, "I'm taking woodworking, and I just have a feeling that there will be four women in the class who can speak Italian," or "I bet my friend will arrive at work tomorrow with two tickets for the Bruce Springsteen concert in her pocket," or "I have an uncanny feeling that when I go to Europe, I'll run into someone I knew from the old neighborhood at some spot that has the same name as the street we lived on." If we made these predictions *ahead of time*, and they came true, that would be quite impressive fortune-telling. But after the fact, these same events could so easily be a matter of chance that we should be leery of assuming they are meaningfully connected. Before you decide that the connection is meaningful, you need to ask the next question.

Tactic #2: Ask Yourself, "What Are the Odds That Some Coincidental Events Will Occur during a Person's Lifetime?"

If the coincidence we experience involves a friend getting tickets for a concert or running into someone from the old neighborhood while on a trip, most people won't see anything portentous in the event. But what if the coincidence involves experiences like the following:

- Two friends give me the same book on the same day—a book that just happens to be about mother-daughter relationships, something that I've been having trouble with lately but haven't discussed with either friend.
- I find myself sitting next to a member of a dance company on an airplane, just days after I've decided that I want to pursue dance as a career.
- I have a dream in which my sister is upset, then I receive a call from her the next day telling me that she was in a car accident the night before.

In these cases, many people are strongly tempted to see the coincidence of these events as meaningful rather than a fluke or chance occurrence. But before coming to that conclusion, we need to ask, "What are the odds that some coincidental events will occur during a person's lifetime?" How often, for example, would you expect some purely coincidental events to occur during the lifetime of an individual who lives into her seventies? Would you expect coincidences to happen twice? Ten times? Given all the different experiences that people have, is it possible that people might have occasion to exclaim, "What a coincidence!" twenty or even a hundred times in a fifty- or sixty-year span of adulthood? If so, then two friends giving me the same book on the same day, finding myself sitting next to a dancer on an airplane, or dreaming about my sister the same evening she had a car accident might all be sheer coincidence. They might constitute one of those ten or twenty or fifty times that we'd expect things to happen by chance alone during a person's lifetime.

GLITCHES: BUT I DO BELIEVE THAT MEETING THE FRIEND IN EUROPE COULD BE MEANINGFUL!

Some people argue that there are no chance events, that everything is meaningful. As the bumper sticker proclaims, "There are no accidents." Many of the ideas associated with the New Age movement have the quality of seeing meaning everywhere and of doubting that *any* meaningless or fluke events ever occur. For example, Julia Cameron suggests in her popular book *The Artists' Way* that we live in a caring universe, one that is concerned about us all and is constantly opening doors for us to enter.[8] From this perspective, it is not a coincidence that a dancer happens to sit next to me on an airplane just at the time that I have been thinking about professional dancing. It is not merely a fluke that two different friends offer me a copy of the same book on the same day: it is the universe trying to tell me something, some important message that this particular book holds for me.

When I argue that coincidence, rather than the intervention of a caring universe, may explain events like these, some students balk. "But what's so terrible about assuming that these patterns are meaningful? What does it hurt to take it on faith that somehow the universe is looking after us?" It may not do any harm to take on faith the idea that the universe is a benevolent place. But there is a major drawback to accepting on faith that all is meaningful, that nothing happens by chance. Given the way our minds naturally work, it's all too easy to see meaningful patterns. The patterns we detect are patterns in our minds, imposed on reality, rather than being out there, an intrinsic aspect of that reality. Those patterns are not always benevolent. As a result, the belief that there are no accidents can be used to justify negative ideas as well as positive or harmless ideas.

For example, when the *Columbia* space shuttle disintegrated over Texas in February 2003, a Saudi Arabian newspaper emphasized that the ship had collapsed over a Texas town named Palestine. As far as it went, this statement was accurate. But in reality, the debris from this flight covered several different towns. Focusing on a single town, the article implied that the link between the *Columbia* disaster and the town of Palestine was meaningful: presumably it showed that some higher power was sending a message to the United States about the Middle East conflict and our involvement in it.

We might want to argue against that newspaper's claim by saying that it was just a fluke that some debris landed on a town called Palestine. But we don't have this option if we insist that all events are meaningful. If we maintain that there are no coincidences, we deprive ourselves of the ability to argue on that basis against whatever meaningful interpretations anyone wants to make—interpretations that may not be so innocuous as a belief in synchronicity or in a benevolent universe.

The Desire to Believe

Most people can identify with Mr. Boffo's dilemma in the following cartoon. Objectively, Mr. Boffo knows that his odds of winning are better if he doesn't bet on the horse that happens to have his dog's name, but emotionally he has a strong pull to believe that this coincidence is not accidental but meaningful. One reason that people believe weird things is because they *want* to: the beliefs console them, give them hope, or make them feel they can control what happens in their lives.[9] It's seductive to believe that the universe has special messages for us, but that belief can also lead us astray if we insist that there are no flukes, that all is fraught with meaning.

MISTER BOFFO

Reprinted with permission from Joe Martin.
Originally published by Tribune Media.

IN A NUTSHELL

This chapter opens with the story of the Washington, DC, meditation group leader who argued that meditation had reduced crime in DC, despite the all-time high that crime rate reached that summer. This story illustrates the blind spot of hidden causes. Often we come to the wrong conclusion about what's causing what because the causes we are searching for are hidden and complex, and we settle for the more apparent and simplistic explanation. We also get it wrong because it's difficult to determine whether a relationship we see is meaningful or merely a fluke. Strategies for addressing this blind spot include ways to search for more complex causes and intentional efforts to consider the possibility that the relationships we detect are simply flukes. Finally, the risks in insisting that there are no accidents were discussed.

SNEAK PREVIEW

Our blind spots are often caused by our narrow focus. As we've seen, when we narrow our focus by acting as if the label we've given something is all that there is to it, we are trapped by categories. When we focus solely on our own perspective, we fail to see other people's point of view. When we focus too narrowly on the most obvious and most immediate causes, we fail to accurately identify what's causing what. If only we could step back far enough to gain an aerial view that would enable us to overcome our narrow focus and see the big picture! Instead, in one way or another, we often miss the forest for the trees. That's the final blind spot we'll consider in this book.

NOTES

1. Robert Park, *Voodoo Science* (New York: Oxford University Press, 2000), p. 30.

2. Michael Shermer, *Why People Believe Weird Things* (New York: Freeman/Owl Book, 2002).

3. Geoffrey Cowley and Karen Springen, "The End of the Age of Estrogen," *Newsweek*, July 22, 2002, pp. 38–45.

4. David Salsburg, *The Lady Tasting Tea: How Statistics Revolutionized Science in the Twentieth Century* (New York: Freeman, 2001).

5. Robin Marantz Henig, *The Monk in the Garden* (New York: Houghton Mifflin, 2000).

6. Marilyn vos Savant, *The Power of Logical Thinking* (New York: St. Martin's Press, 1996), p. 6.

7. Ibid., p. 7.

8. Julia Cameron, *The Artist's Way* (New York: Putnam, 1992).

9. Shermer, *Why People Believe Weird Things*, pp. 301–302.

Chapter 11

"HE CAN'T SEE THE FOREST FOR THE TREES"

BLIND SPOT #10: MISSING THE BIG PICTURE

I once owned a cat that never figured out if it was raining at the front door, it would be raining at the back door. No matter how many times I demonstrated this, as Boots meowed pitifully to be let out, she never got it.

Tiger was different. Spotting a rabbit or cat moving toward the west end of our yard, out of his field of vision, Tiger would race through the house to whichever bedroom window would allow him to maintain a vigilant eye on the interloper. Tiger grasped what eluded Boots. He understood that the outdoor scenes he viewed from the windows were all connected. He could connect the dots.

In contrast, Boots apparently experienced the front door to our house as unrelated to any bigger picture that would connect the front door to the back door or to the rainy conditions outside. The weather at one door was an isolated event to her, irrelevant to the weather at the other. It's as if Boots's encounters with the outside world were, to her, isolated "dots" of experience—and she was unable to connect the dots to see the larger outline, the bigger picture.

We sometimes refer to our tendency to miss the big picture as not seeing the forest for the trees. I like this phrase since it reminds me that this blind spot doesn't occur because we fail to see different components. Rather, we do see at least some of the trees—in fact, it's focusing on the individual trees that causes us to miss the forest as a whole. In order to see the forest, we need not so much see the trees as detect the connections among them and grasp how those trees are connected to some larger whole. That's what it means to get the big picture. Our blind spot is that we have a tendency to focus on just a couple of dots, ones that are up close, and we fail to consider the larger system of which they are a part.

WHY IT'S HARD TO SEE THE FOREST: SYSTEMS ARE DYNAMIC AND CHANGING

Since I tend to stay warm on winter nights, while my husband gets cold, I was happy to discover dual-control electric blankets. The first time we used one, I put it on the bed one chilly November night and set Greg's temperature control to 12, while leaving mine at 6. During the night, I woke up feeling awfully warm, turned my control down to 3, and fell back asleep. An hour later I woke again, sizzling. Frustrated, I turned off my side of the blanket completely, but this didn't seem to help. After a while I threw the blanket off. The next morning over breakfast, I was about to complain that the blanket didn't seem to be working right when Greg grumbled that he'd been freezing the night before. No matter how high he turned his control up, he became, if anything, colder.

If you're familiar with this sort of blanket, you can guess what happened here. There are two plugs that need to be inserted into a double outlet at the foot of the blanket. But it's not easy to tell which of these plugs control which side of the blanket. When I told Greg about my experience, we realized that these plugs had been reversed in the outlet. As a result, I'd been controlling the temperature on his side of the bed, while he had been controlling mine. The warmer I got, the more I inadvertently lowered his setting, which then led him to get colder and raise my setting.

Being mistaken about how things are connected can lead us to act in ways that make things go awry. Moreover, the big picture that we need to grasp is usually not a stagnant picture, like Boots's dilemma with understanding how the two doors of the house were related to the rain outside. Rather, the big pictures that are most crucial for us to grasp are more like Greg and me affecting one another's actions: they are dynamic systems in which one element affects another.

CAUSES: SEEING UP CLOSE AND PERSONAL CLOUDS THE BIGGER PICTURE

After I stood back from the electric-blanket experience and tried to consider all the elements involved, the cause of the problem became obvious to me. But it doesn't seem natural to us to stand back and think in terms of larger systems. An older friend of mine recalled one of her college professors setting aside his planned lecture one morning in order to tell the class about a revolutionary idea that he had just read about. This professor wasn't an excitable person. But that day he was animated—he saw the idea he had discovered as a whole new way of thinking that could radically alter our understanding of nature.

What was that groundbreaking notion? That we could think of the biological world in terms of systems, with each organism and its activities having its own niche but inevitably affecting numerous other organisms. This remarkable new way of looking at nature had a name, he told the class: it was called ecology. Today, of course, concepts like "ecology" and "ecological system" no longer seem groundbreaking: they are taught to second graders. Today, it hardly seems earth shattering to recognize the interdependence of biological systems. It seems obvious to us that these interrelationships exist. Yet at one time people like this professor were amazed to recognize this interdependence. Even today, we continue to be intrigued as scientists uncover in more detail the curious ways in which events that seemed unrelated turn out to be intimately connected after all.

Why was the idea of ecology such a breakthrough? Why did it take so long for someone to notice and describe what seems obvious once it is pointed out? We seem programmed to home in on what is most immediate: the present moment, the detail that's right in front of us. We don't seem to naturally assume a *systems perspective*. As a result, it's easy for us to fail to consider how the larger system as a whole might be affecting what we're experiencing.

At a meeting intended to discuss how to improve communication at a major corporation, one manager raised the question, "Is there anything about our company as a whole that makes it more difficult for honest communication to occur here?" His question silenced the room, both because it was important and so unusual. It's the rare person who considers a problem from a systems perspective, as this manager did. Conversely, it's easy for us to ignore how our actions might be affecting the system as a whole. We often see only our little piece of a much larger scheme. It might not occur to us, for example, that the crabby mood we were in last night reverberated for days to affect every other member of our family, even those who weren't home at the time.

"DOT" PEOPLE

Years ago, psychologists K. W. Fischer and S. L. Pipp presented a diagram (fig. 11.1) that is useful to represent different levels of getting the big picture.[1] When we are considering only what is closest to us, most immediate, it's as if we are thinking only in terms of isolated elements, the dots of our experience. Usually our bosses want us to see more than this; they want us to see the bigger picture. Supervisors don't want us to simply grasp the immediate situation in front of us, the single dot of our own duties. They want us to understand how what we do relates to others and to the process as a whole.

Imagine Pete, who's just been hired at a fast-food restaurant. He is being trained to take the fries out of the oil and place them in containers. His initial focus is on the hot oil, the basket he needs to lift, and the timer that tells him when the fries are ready. These dots are Pete's focus of attention. Given his inexperience and the care required to do his job safely, he probably *should* devote most of his attention to this narrow range of objects and events.

But even on his very first day, Pete is probably not functioning solely as a dot person. He's not focused exclusively on fries. He's gone to fast-

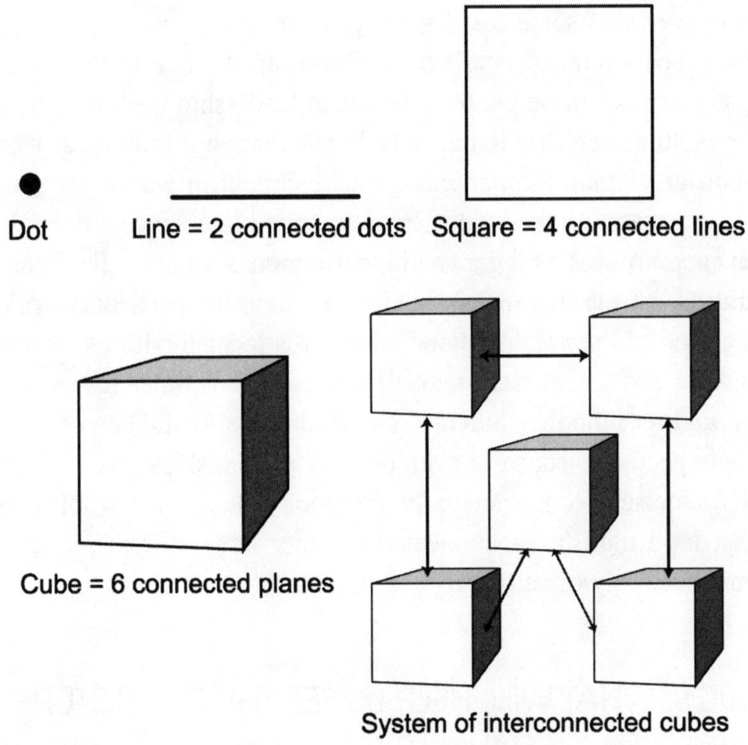

Fig. 11.1: "Dot" People Fail to See the Connections

food restaurants and observed the system to some extent. He grasps the connection between what he does and what the order takers are doing, between his role and the job of the people who assemble sandwiches or fill drink cups. As time goes on, Pete will come to understand even more clearly how the many parts of his work situation relate to one another, how what one person does—or fails to do—affects everyone else.

Most people can grasp this bigger picture easily because the elements in it are familiar and readily observable. We can directly see the different workers and their activities; we can openly observe the overall process they are involved in. As long as we have some familiarity with what's going on in this setting, we'll get the bigger picture. Understanding how the system works at this concrete level is all that we need to perform our piece of the process effectively and all that our boss expects of us.

However, this same fast-food organization expects something more of Pete's boss—and of Pete's boss's boss, up the line to the CEO. The company expects those people who are in leadership positions to grasp a bigger picture, one that is not only larger than any individual worker's task but larger than the particular establishment in which we work. As Pete is promoted up the ladder, he is expected to achieve an aerial view, which encompasses a bigger and bigger region. As a manager, Pete needs to think about the national franchise to which his particular workplace belongs and of the neighborhood where it is located with its own particular ethnic and social class makeup, its numerous other restaurants and stores, and its schools, churches, and traditions. At the corporate office, Pete is expected to consider even broader relationships, such as how the entire franchise is connected to the fast-food industry as a whole and how the fast-food industry is connected to other large systems, such as the national economy or cattle farming.

TACTICS: WHAT WILL HELP US SEE THE BIG PICTURE?

Because we don't naturally think in terms of systems, a major antidote to the blind spot of missing the big picture is to intentionally consider how a system as a whole may affect the smaller detail that is our current focus.

Tactic #1: Use Charts, Graphs, and Models to Make the System Visible

To increase our awareness of how the different elements of a system relate, it's often helpful to represent this visually, in some sort of graphic form. For example, a flowchart representing what happens when a claim is filed with a health insurance company might clarify where the bottleneck in processing claims is occurring and why things get stuck at that point. From a Tinkertoy model of the solar system to the double-helix representation of DNA, representing complex systems in simpler ways can help us grasp how those systems work. Simply thinking about what the dot, line, or cube graphic itself might represent in the organizations that we are a part of can sharpen our awareness of the bigger picture.

Tactic #2: Ask, "How Is the Larger System Affecting This Particular Piece?"

Business guru W. Edwards Deming argued that managers often place the blame for problems in quality control or production rates on individual workers rather than consider that the system itself might be faulty.[2] One company required that the amount of raw material used in making its product be monitored to ensure that excessive raw material was not being used. Author Joseph Jablonski tells the story of this company, whose accounting department had determined how much money ought to be spent for raw materials.[3] When the bill for these materials exceeded the set limit, the managers would be criticized for using more material than necessary. The wastage happened because the quality of the raw material varied. Some rolls of that material were of lower density, which would result in a defective product unless the machine operators compensated for the low density by adding additional material. But since there was no way to tell which rolls were lower in density, the operators routinely added additional raw material. This, of course, got them into trouble since they then used more raw material than the company allowed.

As Deming's perspective might have predicted, the problem of wasting raw materials was a systems problem. It turned out that the raw material was always of the high density needed when it had been purchased from a particular vendor and was of low density when purchased from others. But the reason that the poorer raw materials were purchased in the first place was that the director of purchasing had been told to obtain materials at the lowest possible price. The purchasing requirements established by the company's leaders made it impossible to achieve the quality that the leaders themselves demanded. But the blame for the failure had been placed on the machine operators and their supervisors.

As Deming repeatedly stressed, it is extremely demoralizing to be blamed for outcomes that are essentially out of our control because they result from policies or constraints imposed by the larger system. Moreover, when we take action in an attempt to resolve a systems problem on a dot level, we create other problems. For example, if the machine operators had tried to contain costs by reducing the amount of raw material they used, the quality of the product would have declined, since they'd often be using the lower-density raw material.

Tactic #3: Think of Relationships among People in Terms of Larger Systems

Years ago, I was intrigued to learn that carpooling contributed to the development of family therapy. Three colleagues carpooled to the mental health clinic where they worked. Discussing their cases during this commute, they lamented two facts. First, it seemed extremely difficult to make a big change in the children they treated; only rarely did the therapists believe that their efforts had been markedly successful. Second, in the few cases where they felt their attempts had been successful, another child from the same family—one who to all appearances had previously been doing well—often developed symptoms. The parents would appear once more at the doorstep of the clinic, this time with a different child in tow. The therapists' conversations about this phenomenon led to the theory that the individual child's problems were connected to a bigger system—the system of the family.[4]

Family therapy was viewed as an incredibly innovative approach forty years ago precisely because, up until that time, therapists engaged in treating children had been blind to this dimension. Reminding ourselves that people function as part of systems can open our eyes to the different roles that people play. For example, in a particular department of one high-tech company, one colleague was called "Mom" by all his coworkers because he tended to look after the others. Clues revealing how members of a particular group interact won't usually be so obvious. It takes a conscious effort to view people from the perspective of a larger, interactive group. We need to ask questions such as, "How does the presence—or absence—of Lydia affect how others behave at a meeting?" Or "What triggers Dwayne's withdrawal from the conversation?" We need to think about the group as a system and be observant in order to identify the impact that people have on one another.

Tactic #4: Ask, "When Did That Change?"

Our focus on the present moment can blind us to the bigger, historical picture. Teachers hope that studying history will make their students more aware of this larger picture. They want them to deliberately pay attention to time as a big-picture framework that holds events and that can help us make sense of them. So they use time lines to trace the rise and fall of nations, the development of cultures, the dawning consciousness of different systems of thought. But we don't seem to naturally continue this historical view when we leave the classroom or to transfer it to our everyday lives. Without prodding, most of us focus only on the present dot of time. We are literally shortsighted. For example, we easily forget to look at the past in an attempt to make sense of current political developments.

Indeed, we find it hard to keep a historical view in mind even when we are looking at events that occur in the much more limited time span of our own personal lives. I'm repeatedly struck by people's reactions to questions about when something changed. A friend complains that her relationship with her husband isn't what it used to be. "When did it begin to change?" I ask, and the friend realizes with surprise that there *was* a demarcation: "After he started his new job . . . after he promised that we'd visit Israel and then said we couldn't . . . after we moved closer to my parents."

In one of the creativity classes that I taught, a student disclosed, "I used to write poetry all the time—I wrote literally hundreds of poems in high school and college—but I haven't written anything for years." A few weeks into the course, she realized with a start that "the last poem I wrote was the week before my wedding." Here was a connection whose import hit her hard, yet she had never placed this crucial event, the cessation of her writing, into a longer time line to see how it might be related to other events. If we can so easily miss a change that is this abrupt, this defined, how much more likely is it that we'll miss gradual changes? As a result of our blind spot, we fail to see the emerging pattern of a parent's signs of Alzheimer's disease, to notice just how much our workload and stress have increased over recent months, or to realize that our ten-year-old has matured over the past year and can be entrusted with more freedom and greater responsibilities.

Tactic #5: Consider the Law of Unintended Consequences

Sometimes we are so focused on the present that we are oblivious to the future. As a result, we fail to consider the long-term consequences of our decisions. A docent for a tour of a small cemetery in Key West, Florida, illustrated the law of unintended consequences by describing what had happened decades earlier to the Jewish street vendors of that town. In the early 1900s, the shop owners wanted to get rid of the street vendors, so they passed a law that goods could be sold only from stores, not from street carts. Apparently the intent of the law was to hinder the Jewish entrepreneurs in the area. But as a result of the law, the Jewish street vendors grouped together and pooled their funds to buy or rent store space, a move that ultimately made their trade more dominant. The docent told this story with a wry smile on his face, and we smiled in appreciation. This was a case in which we were glad that the law of unintended consequences had come into play.

But there are instances when we'd like to avoid the law of unintended consequences, times when we don't want to be blind to the possible outcomes of our actions or decisions. It would help if we asked ourselves two questions:

1. What are the possible outcomes of this action or decision?
2. Can I think of outcomes that would be the reverse of what I hope to accomplish? (Is there any way in which my action or decision might actually make those undesirable outcomes more likely to occur?)

THE ROLE OF ABSTRACT THINKING: WHY THE BIGGER PICTURE IS SOMETIMES HARD TO GRASP

Theories are like maps that can provide a particularly useful bigger picture because they show us how pieces fit together, how elements work together. We need theoretical models that capture the complexity of the system as a whole. This can be a tall order to fill. Rarely is the bigger picture a stagnant map of a stationary area, like a map that shows how our front door is connected to our back door. Instead, it is more like an ecological system that is in constant flux and that involves processes, such as changes in the air or soil, that aren't easy to detect.

All this complexity makes it harder for us to see the big picture and more understandable that we sometimes miss it. But another factor affects our ability to see the big picture: our capacity to think more abstractly. As we move from dot to line, line to square, square to cube, we frequently also move from what is more simple, immediate, and concrete to what is more complex, far-reaching, and abstract. For example, if the manager of a particular fast-food restaurant considers how his establishment affects the economy of the neighborhood and is, in turn, affected by it, he is thinking not of a concrete object but of a more abstract idea: the economy of the neighborhood. Similarly, the manager thinks about abstractions when he considers how his restaurant might relate to other broad systems in that larger set of cubes, including ones that might appear, on the surface, to have nothing much to do with a fast-food establishment—such as the moral responsibility of the restaurant.

In her book *No Shame in My Game*, anthropologist Katherine S. Newman describes how minority business owners in New York's Harlem neighborhood see their mission in broader terms than simply making a profit. One teenager at a Harlem food franchise described the impact that her job, and her manager's interest in her, had:

> I don't think I could have made it [in school] without a job, because that was my inspiration . . . you know, if you have one thing going for you . . . it's like a chain reaction. See, when I first started working, I didn't like to go to school at all. But see, my manager told me "I wanna see your report card." I was failing my first period class cause I was late . . . my manager said: "Well, I think I should cut your hours at work cause maybe you're not getting enough sleep." They just pushed me. If I wanted to keep this job, I had to go [to that class]. They tried really hard; [they'd] say "We don't want you to work here forever. We want you to move on."

In order to act in this way, these minority business leaders had to think about their businesses in the bigger picture, in contexts broader than the bottom line of the business world. But they also had to think in concepts more abstract than the day-to-day activities in which their employees were engaged, concepts such as the moral role of their restaurants. A manager might, for instance, ask himself how his establishment could play a role in advancing the cause of social justice or in expressing Buddhist or Christian or humanitarian values. The ideas of social justice and values are themselves abstract concepts. If we fail to think in these more abstract terms, we'll be blind to the deeper and broader connections that would give us insights into a more meaningful big picture.

IF CONCRETE THINKING SERVES US WELL, WHY THINK ABSTRACTLY?

One reason we often fail to think in this more abstract and broader way is simply that more concrete and immediate thinking serves us perfectly well in many situations. So even though we have learned to think in more abstract terms—for example, in some of our school subjects—we don't exert the effort to do so because we don't realize that there's an advantage to applying this kind of thinking to everyday situations. One of my students, Leanne, told me about a dilemma her twenty-one-year-old stepdaughter Dawn was having.[6] Dawn had been working for her boyfriend's father, an electrical contractor who needed some office help. Deciding that this might not be such a good idea after all (a little trouble was brewing on the boyfriend front), Dawn began working on her resume and asked Leanne to look it over.

Dawn's list of her job skills was very concrete; she described activities such as answering the telephone, shelving materials, writing checks, and typing letters. Realizing that Dawn needed to think of her skills in more general, abstract terms so that they'd be more applicable to a variety of jobs, Leanne had Dawn list specific skills from *all* her previous jobs, then asked her to group those that seemed similar and to name those groups. As a result, Dawn placed shelving materials, filing, and entering information into a database in a group, which she labeled "organizing according to a system." This is a more abstract way of viewing what she'd done, one that moved her from concretely matching her specific skills to specific jobs to thinking more deeply about the underlying processes that her work involved.

Dawn began to see the work she had done in increasingly more abstract terms, and she also began to use a similar system to analyze the jobs she might apply for. Eventually, this led her to move from thinking that her background made her a good match for secretarial and receptionist positions to realizing that she would be a strong candidate for managing a small office.

This example may seem simplistic: Dawn may seem to be doing something that most people would automatically do without even thinking about it. But is that the case? In his book *Managing in a Time of Great Change*, business guru Peter Drucker comments that "remarkably few Americans are prepared to select jobs for themselves. When you ask, 'Do you know what you are good at? Do you know your limitations?' they look at you with a blank stare. Or they often respond in terms of subject knowledge, which is the wrong answer."[7] It's not just that a candidate needs to show she understands how her knowledge would be actively applied to a particular job. It's also that listing our concrete knowledge and skills doesn't illuminate the connections between our competencies and the underlying nature of the jobs we are applying for. It shows that we haven't grasped the big picture.

Most people are more than capable of doing what Dawn did; we are capable of the abstract thinking that is necessary in order to think of our skills in this more theoretical way. Yet we often don't engage in this sort of analysis. It takes some reflection to figure out the more abstract ideas, such as "organizing according to a system," that could help us understand what we're good at in a different way. Shifting our thinking in this manner involves discovering an underlying common thread, abstracting a deeper concept that in some way ties together the different concrete skills that we have.

It seems that people repeatedly fail to do this, sometimes with serious consequences. In 1960 Theodore Levitt pointed out that the railroads lost business to trucks and planes because they thought of themselves as being in the railroad business rather than as being in the transportation business.[8] The bigger picture, the more abstract conceptualization of their work that the idea of transportation conveys, might have led them to adapt what they were doing to changing times.

CHILDHOOD CLUES TO OUR STRUGGLES WITH ABSTRACT THINKING

It's not surprising to me that as adults we so often neglect to think in more abstract terms, because this way of thinking is still fairly new to us. Thinking more abstractly is an ability that develops slowly and only begins to emerge in its adult form during adolescence. You can see its development if you think about how children answer the question, "What is this story about?" Imagine that you are reading "The Three Little Pigs" to first graders. This familiar fairy tale is about events that children can easily understand. You finish the story and ask the children, "What is this story about?" Their little heads buzz with answers, but they can only address that question in a very literal way. They retell the concrete details about what each of the pigs did, how the wolf behaved, and how it all ended. But they will have a hard time if you say, "Okay, that's all the specific stuff that happened in the story. But can you tell me in just one sentence, what is the story *about*?"

To answer that question, the children would have to look at all the concrete events in the story and then abstract the general theme from these details. They won't find the answer written in so many words anywhere in the story, a fact that frustrates older students when teachers insist that they must read between the lines. Not only must they conjure up an abstract idea that is logically related to the story's events, but also they have to discover a theme that captures the tale's most significant underlying meaning. As Richard Frey points out, "The Three Little Pigs"—despite its many references to the topic—is not a story about home construction.[9]

Grade school children continue to think concretely. If we ask fourth or fifth graders, for example, what justice is, they'll give us concrete examples about being fair when playing a game or having a teacher who doesn't play favorites when grading essays. Or they will say that justice is about bad guys and good guys and judges and courts and jails. Not until the advent of adolescence will these children begin to think like adults about justice, to define justice in terms that are more abstract.

It is exactly because we recognize that adolescents are more capable of abstract thought that we expect more of them academically. High school and college teachers expect their students to be able to think in more abstract ways, increasingly so as they move to advanced studies in a particular field. In physics, for example, we want students to not only recognize that certain objects will float while others will not but also to understand the more abstract, underlying laws that govern whether or not an object will float.

UP THE LADDER OF ABSTRACTION

In addition to the challenges involved in learning to think more abstractly, sometimes it's hard for us to think in this way because the concepts are themselves abstract in nature, higher up the ladder of abstraction. When we figure out what "The Three Little Pigs" is about, or how the various job roles we've performed are connected, we are looking at fairly concrete elements and learning to discover more hidden, underlying relationships among them. We are thinking about abstract relationships among those dots, but the dots themselves—the events in the story, the duties that we have performed—are not abstract. At the next level, however, we no longer take facts, observable events, or historical evidence as the objects of our thoughts and reason about these. We no longer consider concrete elements to arrive at conclusions about their more abstract meaning. Rather, we take the abstract meanings themselves as the object of our thoughts and reasoning about those: their meaning, their relationships, their significance.

To take a simple example, school-age children can grasp the underlying pattern that we call *symmetrical.* If we show children examples of symmetrical objects and point out how the two sides are alike—how our bodies are roughly symmetrical, for example, with two eyes, two nostrils, two ears, two arms, and two legs—children can grasp, in a concrete way, the underlying notion of symmetry. They can learn to identify sets of objects as symmetrical versus asymmetrical. They can think about what developmental psychologist Margaret Donaldson calls "things in relation" or "events in relation." They can identify the relationship of symmetry as connecting different things or events. However, as Donaldson points out, this thinking is not the same thing as thinking about the *relationships themselves*: "It is one thing to be interested in one's own body, or even in bodies in general, and another thing to be interested in symmetry *per se.*"[10]

What would it mean to be interested in symmetry per se? Well, for one thing, it would mean that we are no longer thinking only about concrete examples of symmetry. We have gone beyond even subtle concrete examples of symmetry, such as noticing that power relationships among people can be more, or less, symmetrical. To think about symmetry itself would mean that we consider, for instance, various conceptualizations of what it means to be symmetrical. Things in the relationship that we call *reciprocal* could be symmetrical, as could things in the relationship that we call *balanced*, or *circular* or even *opposite*. When we think about symmetry in these ways, we are thinking about abstractions: the abstract idea of reciprocity, of balance, of circularity, of oppositeness, rather than thinking solely about concrete examples of these abstractions.

Thinking on this top rung of the abstraction ladder is not easy. This sort of thinking involves what Margaret Donaldson calls "disembedded reasoning"—reasoning without the supportive context of meaningful events.[11] It's very hard for us to reason without the context of meaningful events. That's why we find concrete examples so helpful; that's why, when someone presents unfamiliar ideas to us, we find it useful to link those new ideas to more familiar concepts. When we focus on relationships rather than the concrete things or events that are in relationships, we have arrived at a very high level of abstraction, far above the actual objects and events in our lives.

To return to Fischer and Pipp's model, we could say that going from dots to lines, from lines to squares and squares to cubes, from cubes to systems, we are moving not only to bigger and bigger pictures but also often to more complicated and more abstract relationships among the elements involved in those pictures. When those relationships are very complex or very abstract, it becomes more and more difficult for us to grasp the big picture that they represent. When the elements are themselves abstract, it's even more difficult. Fortunately, it seems that we don't need to function at the upper, stratospheric rung of the abstraction ladder in order to be effective thinkers, even to be extremely competent thinkers.

IS GENIUS POSSIBLE AT THE LOWER RUNGS OF THE ABSTRACTION LADDER?

You might think that Nobel Prize winners always function on that top rung of the abstraction ladder when they make their discoveries. Some concepts that scientists work out as part of their Nobel Prize–winning discoveries *are* highly specialized and abstract. Professionals in a field will sometimes acknowledge that only a handful of scholars in their own field can really understand a new, complicated theory. However, other people who achieve Nobel Prizes do so not because their work involves this highest level of abstraction but because they overcame blind spots that others in their fields succumbed to. These innovators were able to see possibilities that others rejected out of hand, or they were able to grasp a different perspective that no one else had considered. This is what happened to Dr. Gajdusek in his discovery of the slow-acting virus that caused kuru. Some prizewinners differed from their colleagues simply in stopping to think, for a long time, about phenomena that others took for granted. Others had their insights because they refused to speak the rhetoric of the merely and thought more deeply about concepts that others had taken for granted.

WIDENING THE CIRCLE: BLAMING THE SYSTEM

Certain courses in high school and college emphasize a systems perspective. Sociology professors, for example, want their students to grasp how larger societal forces, such as the economy of a nation or the social class into which they are born, affect them. But even when people have learned this lesson as part of their formal studies, they often fail to think in terms of systems in their everyday lives. Instead, they read about events in the newspaper as if they were isolated dots. They attribute the difficulties they have finding a job to their own background without sufficiently taking into account broader factors, such as outsourcing, changes in their industry, or international importing and exporting patterns. People have to intentionally step back from the more local areas—the small geographical area in which they live, the narrow slice of the knowledge pie that they call their college major, or the bit role that their department plays in the company as a whole—to consider how those areas might relate to a broader system.

Applying the systems perspective in this way, however, raises a question: To what extent can people reasonably hold "the system" responsible for what happens, or fails to happen, in their individual lives? Here are two sample scenarios.

> SCENARIO #1: *A middle-aged man realizes that some employees at his paint plant cut corners when carrying out the safety policies so that at times fumes from the paint-producing process become hazardous and*

the risk of fire or explosions rises. He explains his inability to improve the situation: "I've tried. I've talked to the people involved. They argue that they could never meet production deadlines if they didn't cut a corner now and then. I've talked to my boss. He says that he can't change the deadlines that put the pressure on the line people; he's caught between a rock and a hard place, too. What can I do? I can't change the whole system. So I do my best to minimize how often this happens, and keep my fingers crossed."

SCENARIO #2: *A middle-aged woman is disappointed that she is cannot devote enough time to developing her small entrepreneurial business. She realizes that a big part of the problem is that she spends too much time doing things for other people. "When you work at home," she laments, "everyone thinks that you should be available to them all the time." She explains her inability to say no to others and puts her own work first: "Women are raised to be 'nice,' to help others." In response, another female entrepreneur answers, "Well, I was raised the same way. But I'm fifty-five years old now, and I think it's time that I got over it."*

When we take a systems approach, we acknowledge that systems seriously impact our lives. But to what extent can we legitimately blame the system? Here different attitudes surface. The first is the extreme attitude that the system is so powerful that individuals cannot be held responsible for their actions, beliefs, or feelings. Here we find the man at the paint company who cannot see any effective way to change the system that encourages lax safety policies. Here we also find the woman who cannot find a way to counter the upbringing she has had as a female in order to act differently now.

The second extreme attitude is reflected in the second woman, who says, "I was raised the same way, but I got over it." This person is impatient with anyone who uses the system as an excuse, and she believes that if people are motivated enough, they can overcome the obstacles imposed by the system. She believes that if society limits people's opportunities because of their ethnicity or race or religion or gender, they ought to be able to pull themselves up by their own bootstraps. If the past has shaped them, they ought to be able to get over it.

The powerful influence of the social systems into which each of us has been born, and in which we live our daily lives, is undeniable. No one is immune to the strong influence exerted by one's social class, gender, race, or ethnicity. Similarly, all of us are influenced by the smaller systems in which we work and live: the company of which we are a part, the family that we go home to each night. At the same time, most of us believe that individuals have to take some responsibility for how their lives turn out, that they can't simply blame the system for what they do or fail to do. Whatever the constraints of the systems we find ourselves in, each of us has some degree of freedom, some possible choices for us to make. Within that space, we are responsible for what we do. That space will usually be greater once we've grasped how our personal lives are connected to larger social factors.

In fact, once we recognize the influence that a particular system has had on our lives—once we've seen where we personally have failed to grasp the big picture—then we have the possibility of doing something about it. We might work to change the system; we might work to counter the negative impact the system has on others or on us; we might decide to leave the system. Whatever we do, the first step is to recognize the blind spot that we've had so that we can detect the systems that are and have been such a powerful influence on our lives.

IN A NUTSHELL

If it's raining at the front door, it's also raining at the back door. My cat that couldn't grasp this idea represents the blind spot of not being able to see connections, not being able to see the big picture. Too often, we act as dot people, who only see what is most immediate, right in front of us. The ways that we can compensate for our tendency to miss the forest for the trees include intentionally taking a systems perspective, sometimes by graphically representing the relationships among all the elements. One reason that it's easy to miss the big picture is that aerial views of a larger system often require that we think about what we're looking at in a more abstract way. Finally, acknowledging the power of a system to influence its components means that we also recognize the power of social systems to influence and shape people. This raises the question of how much or how little individuals can reasonably blame the system for their personal behavior and decisions.

SNEAK PREVIEW

The last line of this chapter is not quite the final word of this book. In the afterword, I do what I've so often suggested that you do. I step back from the book I've written and reflect on what I hope its place might be in the broader scheme of our times.

NOTES

1. K. W. Fischer and S. L. Pipp, "Processes of Cognitive Development: Optimal Level and Skill Acquisition," in *Mechanisms of Cognitive Development*, ed. R. J. Sternberg, 45–80 (New York: Freeman, 1984). I have modified Fisher and Pipp's original graphic to add a fifth component, the constellation of systems.
2. W. Edwards Deming, *Out of the Crisis* (Cambridge, MA: Massachusetts Institute of Technology, 1986).
3. Joseph R. Jablonski, *Implementing TQM*, 2nd ed. (Hoboken, NJ: Pfeiffer Wiley, 1993).
4. Salvador Minuchin, *Families and Family Therapy* (Cambridge, MA: Harvard University Press, 1974).
5. Katherine S. Newman, *No Shame in My Game: The Working Poor in the Inner City* (New York: Knopf, 1999), p. 129.
6. Thanks to Leanne Schau, who gave me this lucid example when she was a graduate student in my critical-thinking class.
7. Peter F. Drucker, *Managing in a Time of Great Change* (New York: Truman Talley Books/Dutton, 1995), pp. 5–6.
8. Theodore Levitt, "Marketing Myopia," *Harvard Business Review* 38, no. 4 (1960): 45–56.
9. Richard Frey, *How to Write a Damn Good Novel* (New York: St. Martin's Press, 1994).

10. Margaret Donaldson, *Human Minds: An Exploration* (New York: Penguin, 1993), p. 127.

11. Ibid., p. 75.

Afterword
BLIND SPOTS AND HOPE

Sometimes when I hear people urging that we celebrate diversity, the reasons they offer seem a little weak. They refer vaguely to the richness that different cultural heritages have to offer, then they declare that it's great to be able to go to a Korean restaurant, a tapas place, or a French bistro. Well, yes. But surely there is more to gain from different cultures than a varied menu. Other proponents of diversity take a more serious tone. "We're all interdependent," they declare. But their tone isn't celebratory; it's cautionary. They want us to appreciate that we can't afford to ignore other cultures, or worse, to deprecate them. They warn us of the grim price we will ultimately pay for our tunnel vision. I agree. But it seems important to recognize that the value of diversity is deeper than culinary variety and more positive than avoiding retaliation.

Becoming more aware of our blind spots, as individuals and as groups—organizations, businesses, ethnic and religious communities, political parties, states, and nations—deepens our understanding of the issues we grapple with and often points the way toward their resolution. The most direct path to discovering our blind spots is to intentionally bring perspectives other than our own to the table. This means that we absolutely need other people, people who are unlike ourselves, to help us see what we cannot see on our own. The contribution that diversity can make is both unique and invaluable.

From this perspective, other people and their differing viewpoints—

however blind they may be in some ways—truly have something priceless to offer. From this point of view, our own perspective—however blind it may be in some ways—always has something to contribute as well. It's easy to nod in agreement with the general concept that everyone has something to contribute. But taken to heart, this attitude reminds us that *our* way of looking at things is not necessarily the best way and certainly not the only way. This attitude annihilates the conviction that our own particular nation, culture, religion, political party, class, race, gender, or species is superior to all others. This attitude explodes ethnocentrism.

Lecturer and scholar Jim Kenney sees ethnocentrism as an essential blindness, one that props up what he views as the old wave of values, assumptions, and habits of thought that have "harbored racism, tolerated injustice, nurtured patriarchy, presided over the rape of the planet, and refined the art of war." If we can overcome or at least compensate for this essential blindness of ethnocentrism, then we might hope for a very different world.[1]

Kenney believes that the world is already changing in this direction. He contends that the old wave of ethnocentric attitudes, with its accompanying hatreds and injustices, is being challenged by a new wave—a world-centric view. As evidence of this, Kenney points to such changes as contemporary attitudes about the equality of women and our growing ecological consciousness. "Perhaps the clearest mark of the steady progress of cultural evolution," Kenney writes, "shows itself in the reaction we begin to feel in the presence of stark ethnocentrism. The unapologetic hater—the racist, sexist, homophobe, eco-predator, war hawk, or cultural despoiler—every day becomes more of an anomaly and an embarrassment to those who realize that they live in an age of transition."[2]

Are there grounds for hope? Kenney uses the image of two ocean waves to explain his optimism. One wave is "powerful but subsiding, the other just gathering momentum and presence but not yet cresting."[3] Imagine, Kenney says, that these two waves meet when they are nearly the same strength and amplitude. What will happen? In the resulting chaotic crash, it may be impossible to tell which wave is rising and which ebbing. This picture, Kenney argues, is a metaphor for our times. Because we are at a point in history in which these two waves are converging, a point at which it's difficult to tell which is ascending and which is waning, it's easy to be cynical. It's easy to believe that the new wave doesn't stand a chance and to dismiss all evidence of its presence as nothing but puny ripples. The skeptics point to the proof, and there is lots of it, that shows that old values persist: racism and hate, the oppression of women, the exploitation of the earth, the recourse to war.

But Kenney isn't surprised that we see many signs that the old wave is still here: after all, he's assuming that the two waves are nearly equal in strength at this point. The old wave, though losing momentum, is still robust. The crucial point to Kenney is that the newer wave is on the rise. He points to a growing consensus about these issues: that fundamental human rights exist and should be respected by all peoples, that we need to work together as a global community to protect our air and water, that we must find alternative ways of resolving our conflicts other than war. To Kenney, these changes are not insignificant ripples but signs of the gathering strength of the new wave that one day could clearly establish itself as the dominant force.

To me, the idea that we can liberate ourselves from the narrow perspectives that our blind spots impose is another source of hope. If we can become aware of our blind spots, including the "essential blindness" of ethnocentrism, won't we then also be more able to achieve the genuine mutual respect that would make a cooperative, peaceful, global community possible? If we stop labeling those who disagree with us as stupid or evil, won't that enable us to have the discussions essential to building a different world?

I won't live long enough to see that new world emerge fully. It hasn't been my lot to exist in that coming era when that newer wave may embrace our world more completely. But I hope that I have lived at a time in which what I've written can contribute to that change. It's my hope that this book will ease the ascendance of that new wave. If we can have more compassion for others as they struggle with their own blind spots; if we can more often hold others as worthwhile people in their own right, even as we challenge them to see further; if we can detect and contain our own arrogance toward those who are riding the old wave, perhaps we can lessen some of the undertow that seems unavoidable in the clash of these two mountains of water. Perhaps the period in which each forward movement is countered by a backlash can be shortened if we work with others to preserve the good that the old wave contains, even as we rise—buoyant with hope—on the new.

NOTES

1. Jim Kenney, "The Coming Giant Wave of Change," *Conscious Choice*, August 2003, p. 26.
2. Ibid.
3. Ibid., pp. 26–27.

BIBLIOGRAPHY

Abagnale, Frank W., and Stan Redding. *Catch Me If You Can: The Story of a Real Fake*. New York: Random House/Broadway Books, 2003.

Bandler, Richard, and John Grinder. *The Structure of Magic*. New York: Science and Behavior Books, 1990.

Bartholomew, Robert E., and Benjamin Radford. *Hoaxes, Myths, and Manias: Why We Need Critical Thinking*. Amherst, NY: Prometheus Books, 2003.

Basseches, Michael. *Dialectical Thinking and Adult Development*. Norwood, NJ: Ablex, 1984.

Bateson, Mary Catherine. *Peripheral Visions*. New York: HarperCollins, 1994.

Bean, J. C., and J. D. Ramage. *Form and Surprise in Composition*. New York: Macmillan, 1986.

Belenky, Mary Field, Blythe McVicker Clinchy, Nancy Rule Goldberger, and Jill Mattuck Tarule. *Women's Ways of Knowing: The Development of Self, Voice, and Mind*. New York: Basic Books, 1986.

Best, Joel. *Damned Lies and Statistics: Untangling Numbers from the Media, Politicians, and Activists*. Berkeley: University of California Press, 2001.

Braine, Martin. "The 'Natural Logic' Approach to Reasoning." In *Reasoning, Necessity, and Logic: Developmental Perspectives*, edited by Willis E. Overton, 133–57. Hillsdale, NJ: Erlbaum Associates, 1990.

Browne, M. Neil, and Stuart Keeley. *Asking the Right Questions*. Englewood Cliffs, NJ: Prentice-Hall, 2001.

Callahan, Lisa. "The Role of Sensitivity and Ability in the Intellectual Performance of Business Professionals." Master's thesis, North Central College, 2004.

Cameron, Julia. *The Artist's Way*. New York: Jeremy P. Tarcher/Putnam, 1992.

Campo-Flores, Arian, and Evan Thomas. "Rehabbing Rush." *Newsweek*, May 8, 2006.

Chaffee, John. *The Thinker's Way*. New York: Little, Brown, 1998.

Clinchy, B., and C. Zimmerman. "Epistemology and Agency in the Development of Undergraduate Women." In *The Undergraduate Woman: Issues in Educational Equity*, edited by P. Perun, 161–81. Boston: D. C. Heath, 1981.

"Courage to Refuse—Combatant's Letter." http://www.seruv.org.il/defaulteng.asp (accessed April 25, 2006).

Cowley, Geoffrey, and Karen Springen. "The End of the Age of Estrogen." *Newsweek*, July 22, 2002, pp. 38–45.

Dalton, Harlon. *Racial Healing: Confronting the Fear between Blacks and Whites*. New York: Doubleday Anchor Books, 1995.

Damasio, A. R. *Descartes' Error*. New York: Avon, 1994.

Damer, T. Edward. *Attacking Faulty Reasoning*. 3rd ed. Belmont, CA: Wadsworth, 1995.

Darley, John M., and C. Daniel Batson. "'From Jerusalem To Jericho': A Study of Situational and Dispositional Variables in Helping Behavior." *Journal of Personality and Social Psychology* 27 (1973): 100–108.

Davis, Matt, "Aoccdrnig to a rscheearch at Cmabrige." http://www.mrc-cbu.cam.ac.uk/~mattd/Cmabrigde/index.html (accessed May 5, 2006).

Dawkins, Richard. *Unweaving the Rainbow*. Boston: Houghton Mifflin, 1998.

Deming, W. Edwards. *Out of the Crisis*. Cambridge, MA: Massachusetts Institute of Technology, 1986.

Dewey, John. *How We Think*. Chicago: Henry Regnery, 1933.

Donaldson, Margaret. *Human Minds*. New York: Penguin, 1993.

———. *Children's Minds*. London: Croom Helm, 1978.

Drucker, Peter F. *Managing in a Time of Great Change*. New York: Truman Talley Books/Dutton, 1995.

Eisler, Riane. *The Chalice and the Blade*. New York: HarperCollins, 1987.

Evans, J. *The Psychology of Deductive Reasoning*. London: Routledge & Kegan Paul, 1982.

Farrar, Steve. "Fatal Steps." *Sunday Times* (UK), August 23, 1998.

Fischer, K. W., and S. L. Pipp. "Processes of Cognitive Development: Optimal Level and Skill Acquisition." In *Mechanisms of Cognitive Development*, edited by R. J. Sternberg, 45–80. New York: Freeman, 1984.

Flavell, John. *Cognitive Development*. Englewood Cliffs, NJ: Prentice-Hall, 1985.

Flavell, John H., Frances L. Green, and Eleanor R. Flavell. "Young Children's Knowledge about Thinking." *Monographs of the Society for Research in Child Development* 60 (1995): 1–96.

Frank, Thomas. *What's the Matter with Kansas?* New York: Metropolitan Books, 2004.

Frey, Richard. *How to Write a Damn Good Novel.* New York: St. Martin's Press, 1994.

Friel, Brian. *Molly Sweeney*. Old Castle, CO: Gallery Books, 1995.

Gardner, Howard. *Intelligence Reframed: Multiple Intelligences for the 21st Century*. New York: Basic Books, 1999.

Geis, M., and A. M. Zwicky. "On Invited Inferences." *Linguistic Inquiry* 2 (1971): 561–66.

Gladwell, Malcolm. *Blink: The Power of Thinking without Thinking*. New York: Little, Brown, 2005.

Goleman, Daniel. *Emotional Intelligence*. New York: Bantam Books, 1995.

Goodfield, June. *The Quest for the Killers*. Boston: Birkhauser Press, 1985.

Gopnik, Alison, Andrew Meltzoff, and Patricia Kuhl. *The Scientist in the Crib*. New York: HarperCollins, 2001.

Hawkins, J., R. D. Pea, J. Glick, and S. Scribner. "Merds That Laugh Don't Like Mushrooms: Evidence for Deductive Reasoning by Preschoolers." *Developmental Psychology* 20 (1984): 584–94.

Henig, Robin Marantz. *The Monk in the Garden*. New York: Houghton Mifflin, 2000.

Hillerman, Tony. *Coyote Waits*. New York: FirstHarperPaperbacks, 1992.

Hoffman, Martin L. "Developmental Synthesis of Affect and Cognition and Its Implications for Altruistic Motivation." In *Social and Personality Development: Essays on the Growth of the Child*, edited by William Damon, 258–77. New York: Norton, 1983.

Holeywell, Ryan. "Don't Judge Him Yet." *USA Today*, July 28, 2003, 12A.

"How Can 59,054,087 People Be So Dumb?" *Daily Mirror* (London), November 4, 2004, front-page headline.

Jablonski, Joseph R. *Implementing TQM*. Hoboken, NJ: Pfeiffer Wiley, 1993.

John-Steiner, Vera. *Notebooks of the Mind*. New York: Oxford University Press, 1997.

Kafka, Franz. *The Metamorphosis and Other Stories*. New York: Penguin, 1992.

Kass, John. "Moral of This Election: Don't Dismiss Values." *Chicago Tribune*, November 7, 2004.

Keen, Sam. "What You Ask Is Who You Are." *Spirituality and Health* 3, no. 2 (2000): 30.

Kegan, Robert. *The Evolving Self: Problem and Process in Human Development*. Cambridge, MA: Harvard University Press, 1982.

———. *In over Our Heads: The Mental Demands of Modern Life*. Cambridge, MA: Harvard University Press, 1996.

Kegan, Robert, and Lahey, Lisa. *How the Way We Talk Can Change the Way We Work*. San Francisco: Jossey-Bass, 2001.

Kenney, Jim. "The Coming Giant Wave of Change." *Conscious Choice*, August 2003.

King, Patricia, and Karen Strohm Kitchener. *Developing Reflective Judgment*. San Francisco: Jossey-Bass, 1995.

Klitzman, Robert. *The Trembling Mountain: A Personal Account of Kuru, Cannibals, and Mad Cow Disease*. New York: Plenum Trade, 1998.

Lakoff, George. *Moral Politics: How Liberals and Conservatives Think*. Chicago: University of Chicago Press, 2002.

Langer, Ellen. *Mindfulness*. Reading, MA: Addison-Wesley, 1989.

Levitt, Theodore. "Marketing Myopia." *Harvard Business Review* 38 (1960): 45–56.

Levy, David. *Tools of Critical Thinking: Metathoughts for Psychologists*. Boston: Allyn and Bacon, 1997.

Luria, A. R. *The Making of Mind*. Cambridge, MA: Harvard University Press, 1979.

Maalouf, Amin. *In the Name of Identity*. New York: Arcade, 2001.

Maisel, Eric. *Fearless Creating*. New York: Jeremy P. Tarcher/Putnam, 1995.

Mansfield, Annick, and Blythe Clinchy. "The Early Growth of Multiplism in the Child." Paper presented at the Fifteenth Annual Symposium of the Jean Piaget Society, Philadelphia, PA, June 1985.

Minuchin, Salvador. *Families and Family Therapy*. Cambridge, MA: Harvard University Press, 1974.

Moses, Kenneth, and Madeleine Van Hecke-Wulatin. "A Counseling Model re: The Socio-emotional Impact of Infant Deafness." In *Early Management of Hearing Loss*, edited by G. T. Mencher and S. E. Gerber, 243–78. New York: Grune and Stratton, 1981.

Moshman, David. "The Development of Metalogical Understanding." In *Reasoning, Necessity, and Logic: Developmental Perspectives*, edited by Willis E. Overton, 205–25. Hillside, NJ: Erlbaum Associates, 1990.

Murray, Frank B. "The Conversion of Truth into Necessity." In *Reasoning, Necessity, and Logic: Developmental Perspectives*, edited by Willis E. Overton, 183–203. Hillside, NJ: Erlbaum Associates, 1990.

Newman, Katherine S. *No Shame in My Game: The Working Poor in the Inner City*. New York: Knopf, 1999.

Noddings, Nel. *Caring: A Feminine Approach to Ethics and Moral Education*. Berkeley: University of California Press, 1984.

Northcutt, Wendy. *The Darwin Awards*. New York: Dutton, 2000.

Nussbaum, Martha. *Upheavals of Thought: The Intelligence of Emotions*. Cambridge: Cambridge University Press, 2001.

Pachter, Barbara. *The Power of Positive Confrontation*. New York: Marlowe, 2000.

Panati, Charles. *Panati's Extraordinary Origins of Everyday Things*. New York: Harper and Row, 1987.

Park, Robert. *Voodoo Science*. New York: Oxford University Press, 2000.

Pask, Gordon. "Styles and Strategies of Learning." *British Journal of Educational Psychology* 46 (1976): 128–48.

Perkins, D., N. E. Jay, and S. Tishman. "Beyond Abilities: A Dispositional Theory of Thinking." *Merrill-Palmer Quarterly* 39 (1993): 1–21.

Perkins, D., and S. Tishman. "Dispositional Aspects of Intelligence." Unpublished paper, 1998, 1–45.

Perkins, D. N., R. Allen, and J. Hafner, "Difficulties in Everyday Reasoning." In *Thinking: The Frontier Expands*, edited by W. Maxwell, 177–89. Hillsdale, NJ: Erlbaum Associates, 1983.

Perry, William G. *Forms of Intellectual and Ethical Development in the College Years: A Scheme*. New York: Holt, Rinehart, and Winston, 1970.

Root-Bernstein, Robert, and Michele Root-Bernstein. *Sparks of Genius*. New York: Houghton Mifflin, 1999.

Rumain, B., J. Connell, and M. D. Braine. "Conversational Comprehension Processes Are Responsible for Reasoning Fallacies in Children as Well as Adults: If Is Not the Biconditional." *Developmental Psychology* 19 (1983): 471–81.

Sachar, Louis. *Holes*. New York: Farrar, Straus and Giroux, 1998.

Salsburg, David. *The Lady Tasting Tea: How Statistics Revolutionized Science in the Twentieth Century*. New York: Freeman, 2001.

Seligman, Martin. *Learned Optimism: How to Change Your Mind and Your Life*. New York: Simon and Schuster, 1998.

Shermer, Michael. *Why People Believe Weird Things*. New York: Freeman/Owl Books, 2002.

Smith, Huston. *Why Religion Matters*. San Francisco: HarperSanFrancisco, 2001.

Solzhenitsyn, Alexander. *Cancer Ward*. New York: Modern Library, 1983.

Somerville, S. C., B. A. Hadkinson, and C. Greenberg. "Two Levels of Inferential Behavior in Young Children." *Child Development* 50 (1979): 119–31.

Sternberg, Robert J., ed. *Why Smart People Can Be So Stupid*. New Haven, CT: Yale University Press, 2002.

Tannen, Deborah. *You Just Don't Understand!* New York: Harper, 2001.

Thomas, L. *The Medusa and the Snail*. Harmondsworth, Middlesex: Penguin, 1981.

von Oech, Roger. *A Whack on the Side of the Head: How You Can Be More Creative*. New York: Warner, 1990.

vos Savant, Marilyn. *The Power of Logical Thinking*. New York: St. Martin's Press, 1996.

Wallis, Jim. *God's Politics: Why the Right Gets It Wrong and the Left Doesn't Get It*. HarperSanFrancisco, 2005.

Wolpert, Lewis, and Alison Richards. *A Passion for Science*. New York: Oxford University Press, 1988.

Wycliff, Don. "2004 Campaign May Qualify As the Most Divisive." *Chicago Tribune*, October 28, 2004.

INDEX

Abagnale, Frank W., 76, 87, 243
abortion, 119–20
abstract thinking, 227–34
accountability and blind spots, 29–30, 102–103, 147–48
ambiguity, 126–27, 191–92
Artist's Way, The (Cameron), 213, 216
Asking the Right Questions (Browne and Keeley), 164, 176
Attacking Faulty Reasoning (Damer), 164, 176
attention
  asset and liability of paying attention to detail, 20–21
  blind spot of not noticing, 73–74
    causes of, 74–76
    cost of failing to notice, 85–86
    not noticing your own thoughts, 76–79
    tactics to overcome, 81–84
  thinking and learning styles, 79–81

Bandler, Richard, 82, 87, 243
Bartholomew, Robert E., 177, 196, 243
Basseches, Michael, 130, 243
Bateson, Mary Catherine, 138–39, 149, 243
Batson, C. Daniel, 108, 244
Bean, J. C., 71, 243
Beautiful Mind, A (film), 173
Belenky, Mary Field, 71, 243
Berry, Michael, 139
Best, Joel, 183, 196, 243
blind spot of
  fuzzy evidence. *See* evidence
  jumping to conclusions. *See* jumping to conclusions
  missing hidden causes. *See* causality
  missing the big picture. *See* missing the big picture
  not knowing what you don't know. *See* ignorance
  not noticing. *See* attention
  not seeing other perspectives. *See* my-side bias
  not seeing yourself. *See* self-awareness

not stopping to think. *See* failing to think
trapped by categories. *See* categorical thinking
Blink (Gladwell), 170–71, 176
Braine, Martin, 34, 156, 175, 243, 247
Browne, M. Neil, 176, 243
Bryant, Kobe, 186–87
Bush, George W., 27, 192

Callahan, Lisa, 37, 50, 243
Cameron, Julia, 213, 216, 244
Campo-Flores, Arian, 109, 244
Cancer Ward (Solzhenitsyn), 116, 130
Catch Me If You Can (Abagnale), 76, 87
categorical thinking
blind spot of being trapped by categories, 133–34
causes of, 134–36
tactics to overcome, 136–40
classification and stereotypes, 140–45
how to offset negative repercussions of classifying people, 145–47
older children and ability to shift perspectives, 136
personal identity and group identifications, 142–45
causality
blind spot of missing hidden causes, 199–200
childhood roots of, 200–201
tactics to overcome, 205–206, 211–13
complex causes, 203–205
probability and randomness, 201–205, 207–11
problem of believing there are no accidents, 213–14
Chaffee, John, 165, 176, 244
challenge and support
difficulty in finding, 104–105, 95–96
importance of blending, 30–31
Clinchy, Blythe, 130, 196, 243, 244, 246
Columbia space shuttle disaster, 214
common sense, 165–66
concrete thinking, 227–33
Connell, J., 34, 175, 247
courage in overcoming blind spots, 104–105, 126–28, 193
Courage to Refuse (letter), 126–27, 130, 244
Cowley, Geoffrey, 216, 244
Coyote Waits (Hillerman), 117, 130
creativity
ability to tolerate ambiguity and, 191–92
everyday problem solving and, 140
getting to the second right answer, 53–54
how to get constructive feedback on creative efforts, 94–97
interviews with artists and scientists, 76–77
thinking in categories and, 134
curses, 178, 182–83

Daily Mirror (London), 27, 34, 245
Dalton, Harlon, 144, 146, 150, 244

Damasio, A. R., 172, 176, 244
Damer, T. Edward, 164, 176, 244
Damned Lies and Statistics (Best), 183, 196
Darley, John M., 108, 244
Darwin, Charles, 209
Darwin Awards, The (Northcutt), 16
Davis, Matt, 21, 34, 244
Dawkins, Richard, 48, 50, 244
decision making and emotions, 172
deductive reasoning, 149
Deming, W. Edwards, 223–24, 237, 244
Dewey, John, 6, 244
Dilbert quotes contest, 17
diversity as a way of discovering blind spots, 239–40
Donaldson, Margaret, 156, 175, 232–33, 238, 244
Drucker, Peter, 229, 237, 244

Einstein, Albert, 195
Eisler, Riane, 185–86, 196, 244
emotional intelligence, 65–66
ethnocentrism, 240
Evans, J., 34, 244
Evans-Pritchard, E. E., 153–54
evidence, 177–78
  fuzzy evidence as a blind spot, 177–78
    childhood roots of misjudging evidence, 178–82
    counterexamples and tendency to seek confirming data, 189–90
    influence of our worldviews, 183–86
    tactics to overcome, 186–91
  intentional deception, 184–85
  relying on authority, 179–82
experiential knowledge, 116–17

failing to think
  as blind spot, 35–38
    causes of, 38–40
    tactics to overcome, 41–46
  objections to being more reflective, 47–49
  impatience with reflective leaders, 46–47
family therapy, 224
Farrar, Steve, 196, 244
Fearless Creating (Maisel), 94
feedback from others, 94–97
Feldman, Michael, 111
Fischer, K. W., 220, 233, 237, 244
Flavell, Eleanor R., 87, 245
Flavell, John, 77, 87, 113, 130, 244–45
Frampton, Peter, 70
Frank, Thomas, 26, 34, 245
Frey, Richard, 231, 237, 245
Friel, Brian, 118, 130, 245

Gajdusek, D. Carleton, 53
Gardner, Howard, 65–66, 71, 245
Gardner, Martin, 202
Gauss, Carl Friedrich, 171
Geis, M., 175, 245
gender differences
  in communication, 121–22
  stereotyping and, 141–42
Gladwell, Malcolm, 170–71, 176, 245
Glasse, Robert, 135

Glick, J., 34, 175, 245
God's Politics (Wallis), 119, 130
Goleman, Daniel, 65–66, 71, 245
Goodfield, June, 53, 71, 149, 245
Good Samaritan study, 89–90
Gopnik, Alison, 149, 245
Green, Frances L., 87, 245
Greenberg, C., 248
Grinder, John, 82, 87, 243

Hadkinson, B. A., 248
Hafner, J., 50, 247
Hagelin, John, 199–200
Haring-Smith, Tori, 170
Hawkins, J., 34, 175, 245
Henig, Robin Marantz, 209, 216, 245
Hillerman, Tony, 117, 130, 245
Hitler, Adolf, 124–25
Hoffman, Martin L., 130, 245
Holes (Sachar), 121, 130
Holeywell, Ryan, 186–87, 197, 245
hope, 239–42
Hornabrooke, R. W., 135
Hussein, Saddam, 192

identity and group membership, 142–45
ignorance
- acceptance of, 60–61, 64
- blind spot of not knowing what you don't know, 23, 51–52
  - causes of, 52–54
  - tactics to overcome, 54–58
- humiliation and, coping with, 58–64

implicit knowledge, 170–71
information overload, 38–39
invited inferences, 155
intuition, 170–71
Israeli-Palestinian conflict, 126–27

Jablonski, Joseph R., 223, 237, 245
John-Steiner, Vera, 76–77, 87, 245
judging others as stupid or bad
- fear of losing our moral compass and, 124–26
- how quickly "stupid" turns to "bad," 61–62
- judging medical researchers, 204–205
- regarding differences in intelligence, 69
- role of our own blind spots, 27
- when others misunderstand us, 120–22
- why we should be slow to judge, 29–30

jumping to conclusions
- as blind spot, 160
  - tactics to overcome, 161–67
- distinguishing meaningful patterns from flukes, 201–205, 207–11
- logical necessity, 152–57
- logical puzzles, methods for solving, 157–59
- politics and argument by fallacy, 167–69
- problem of believing in no accidents and, 213–14

Kafka, Franz, 119, 130, 245
Kass, John, 26, 34, 245
Keeley, Stuart, 176, 243
Keen, Sam, 78, 87, 246

Kegan, Robert, 40, 50, 99, 105, 109, 246
Kenney, Jim, 240–41, 242, 246
King, Patricia, 113, 130, 246
King Tut, 178–79
Kitchener, Karen, 113, 130, 246
Klitzman, Robert, 71, 246
Koppel, Ted, 46
Kuhl, Patricia, 149, 245
kuru, 53, 55, 57, 135, 205

Lady Tasting Tea, The (Salsburg), 208, 216
Lahey, Lisa, 99, 109, 246
Lakoff, George, 165–66, 176, 246
Langer, Ellen, 133, 149, 246
language and invited inferences, 155
lateral moves in self-awareness, 105–107
law of unintended consequences, 226–27
learned helplessness, 98
learning styles, 79–80
Levitt, Theodore, 230, 237, 246
Levy, David, 130, 246
Limbaugh, Rush, 106–107
Lindebaum, Shirley, 135
listening, role in seeing other perspectives, 117–18
logic
  closed puzzles vs. messy problems and, 173
  criticisms of logical thinking, 169–74
  emotions and, 171–72
  fallacies, 164–65
  invited inferences and, 155–57
  language and, 155–57
  limits of childhood reasoning, 200–201
  logical necessity, 152–54
  methods to solve logical puzzles, 157–59
  natural logic, 156
  psychological resistance to, 187–88
  reasoning in everyday life and, 155–57
Luria, Alexander, 151, 175, 246

Maalouf, Amin, 142, 150, 246
mad cow disease, 53
Maisel, Eric, 94, 108, 246
Managing in a Time of Great Change (Drucker), 229, 237
Mansfield, Annick, 196, 246
Mattuck Tarule, Jill, 243
McClintock, Barbara, 171
meditation and crime in Washington, DC, 199–200
Meltzoff, Andrew, 149, 245
Mendel, Gregor, 129, 209
Metamorphosis, The (Kafka), 119, 130
metaphorical thinking, 165–66
Minuchin, Salvador, 237, 246
missing the big picture
  as blind spot, 217–19
    causes of, 219–22
    tactics to overcome, 222–27
  blaming the system, 234–36
  dot people, 220–21
  dynamic systems, 218–19
  role of abstract vs. concrete thinking, 227–33

Molly Sweeney (Friel), 118, 130
morality
  blind spots and accountability, 30, 102–103, 147–48
  blind spots and evil, 29
  difference between shame and moral guilt, 31–32
  seeing other perspectives and losing one's moral compass, 123–26
Moral Politics (Lakoff), 165, 176
Moses, Kenneth, 187, 197, 246
Moshman, David, 34, 246
multiple intelligences. *See* theory of multiple intelligences
Murray, Frank, B., 175, 247
my-side bias
  blind spot of not seeing other perspectives, 111–12
    causes of, 113–15
    obstacles to overcoming, 123–26
    tactics to overcome, 115–20
  juggling different perspectives, 127–28
  resistance to seeing different perspectives, 114–15
  role of listening, 117–18
  role of the arts, 118

Nash, John, 173
national blind spots, 103–105
natural logic, 156
need-to-know lists, 54–55, 57–58
Newman, Katherine, 227, 237, 247
Noddings, Nel, 117, 123, 130, 247
Northcutt, Wendy, 34, 247
No Shame in My Game (Newman), 227, 237
Nostradamus, 202
numerology, 202
Nussbaum, Martha, 31–32, 34, 125–26, 130, 247

Pachter, Barbara, 27, 34, 247
Palestine, 126–27
Panati, Charles, 134, 149, 247
Panati's Extraordinary Origins of Everyday Things, 134, 149
Park, Robert, 184–85, 196, 199, 216, 247
Pask, Gordon, 87, 247
pattern finding
  both as asset and as liability, 21–22, 135–36
  discovering of dominant and recessive genes, 129
  drawbacks to, 201–203
  tendency to label and, 134–36
Pea, R. D., 34, 175, 245
Perkins, D., 37, 50, 113, 130, 247
Perry, William G., 125, 130, 247
Piaget, Jean, 60
Pipp, S. L., 220, 233, 237, 244
poles-apart assignment, 123–24
politics
  calling opponents corrupt, 27–29
  calling opponents stupid, 26–27
  demand for decisive leaders in, 46–47
  illogical campaign arguments and, 167–69
  metaphorical thinking in, 165–66
  reactions when we are wrong and, 192–94
probability theory, 209

randomness and, 201–205, 207–11
problem-based learning, 54

question maps, 54

Racial Healing (Dalton), 146, 150
Radford, Benjamin, 177, 196, 243
Ramage, J. D., 71, 243
reading test, 20–21
Redding, Stan, 87, 243
Reeves, Martin, 77
religion and criticism of scientism, 194–95
research
Azande tribe and logic, 153–54
BBC interviews with scientists, 139
cat in the box study, 18, 157
classification, babies sort objects, 134–35
empathy in preschoolers, 121
genetic experiment, McClintock's, 171
Good Samaritan study, 89–90
Hitler question in college-student interviews, 124–25
law students and seeing both sides of an argument, 37
learned helplessness in dogs, 98
levels of statistical significance and, 209
Mendel's pea plant, 129
menopausal women, 204
Merds study, 18, 154
preschoolers and toothbrush study, 77–78
red hat, white hat study, 154
Russian peasant logic, 151–52
will it float? preschooler study, 179
rhetoric of the merely, 138–39
Richards, Alison, 87, 150, 248
Root-Bernstein, Robert and Michele, 171, 176, 247
Rule Goldberger, Nancy, 243
Rumain, B., 34, 175, 247
Rumsfeld, Donald, 192

Sachar, Louis, 120–21, 130, 247
Salsburg, David, 208, 216, 247
Satir, Virginia, 82
Schau, Leanne, 237
scrambled letters reading test, 21
Scribner, S., 34, 175, 245
self-awareness
blind spot of not seeing yourself, 89–90
causes of, 90–92
difficulties in overcoming, 105–107
national blindness, 103–105
tactics to overcome, 92–101
personal responsibility and, 102–103
power to change and, 97–102
self-image, 100–101
Seligman, Martin, 98, 109, 247
shame vs. guilt, 31–32
Shermer, Michael, 178, 196, 202, 216, 248
Slinky (toy), 134
Smith, Huston, 194, 197, 248
Solzhenitsyn, Alexander, 116, 130, 248
Somerville, S. C., 248
Sparks of Genius (Root-Bernsteins), 171, 176

Springen, Karen, 216, 244
Star Trek and Mr. Spock's logic, 171–72
statistics, erroneous child murder statistics, 183–84
Sternberg, Robert J., 14, 248
stupidity
  children at risk for feeling stupid, 66–67
  clue for finding blind spots, 25
  as mental blind spot, 19
  missing the obvious and, 16
  as puzzle to be solved, 17–19
swimming pools and light refraction, 139
syllogisms
  adults' difficulty with, 18
  children's competency in solving, 18–19
  interference of language and practical knowledge in solving, 155–56
  Russian peasants' difficulty with, 151–52

Tannen, Deborah, 121–22, 130, 248
Texas A&M bonfire tragedy, 75
theory of multiple intelligences, 65–66
  objections to accepting different intelligences, 68–69
There's a Boy in the Girl's Bathroom!! (Sachar), 121
Thinker's Way, The (Chaffee), 165
thinking opportunities, 37–38
Thomas, Evan, 109, 244
Thomas, L., 50, 248
Tishman, S., 50, 130, 247
troubles talk, 121–22

Unweaving the Rainbow (Dawkins), 48, 50
Upheavals of Thought (Nussbaum), 125, 130

Van Hecke-Wulatin, Madeleine, 197, 246
von Oech, Roger, 53–54, 71, 248
Voodoo Science (Park), 200, 216
vos Savant, Marilyn, 209–11, 216, 248

Wallis, Jim, 119–20, 130, 248
Whad'Ya Know? (radio program), 111
What's the Matter with Kansas? (Frank), 26, 34
Who Wants to Be a Millionaire? (TV program), 50
Why People Believe Weird Things (Shermer), 202, 216
Why Religion Matters (Smith), 194, 197
Wolpert, Lewis, 87, 150, 248
Women's Ways of Knowing (Belenky et al.), 62
Wycliff, Don, 27, 34, 248

Zimmerman, C., 130, 244
Zwicky, A. M., 175, 245